Women of the Portuguese Guinea Liberation War

Women of the Portuguese Guinea Liberation War

De-gendering the History of Anticolonial Struggle

Aliou Ly

ZED

LONDON • NEW YORK • OXFORD • NEW DELHI • SYDNEY

Zed Books
Bloomsbury Publishing Plc, 50 Bedford Square, London, WC1B 3DP, UK
Bloomsbury Publishing Inc, 1359 Broadway, 12th Floor, New York, NY 10018, USA
Bloomsbury Publishing Ireland, 29 Earlsfort Terrace, Dublin 2, D02 AY28, Ireland

BLOOMSBURY, Zed Books and the Zed Books logo are trademarks of
Bloomsbury Publishing Plc

First published in Great Britain 2024
Paperback edition published 2026

Copyright © Aliou Ly, 2024

Aliou Ly has asserted his right under the Copyright, Designs and Patents Act, 1988,
to be identified as Author of this work.

For legal purposes the Acknowledgments on pp. xii–xiii constitute
an extension of this copyright page.

Series design by Adriana Brioso
Cover image © Reg Lancaster/Daily Express/Hulton Archive/Getty Images

This work is published open access subject to a Creative Commons Attribution-NonCommercial-NoDerivatives 4.0 International licence (CC BY-NC-ND 4.0, https://creativecommons.org/licenses/by-nc-nd/4.0/). You may re-use, distribute, and reproduce this work in any medium for non-commercial purposes, provided you give attribution to the copyright holder and the publisher and provide a link to the Creative Commons licence.

Bloomsbury Publishing Plc does not have any control over, or responsibility for,
any third-party websites referred to or in this book. All internet addresses given
in this book were correct at the time of going to press. The author and publisher regret any
inconvenience caused if addresses have changed or sites have ceased to exist, but can accept no
responsibility for any such changes.

A catalogue record for this book is available from the British Library.

Library of Congress Cataloging-in-Publication Data
Names: Ly, Aliou, author.
Title: Women of the Portuguese Guinea liberation war: de-gendering the
history of anticolonial struggle / Aliou Ly.
Description: London; New York: Zed, 2024. | Includes bibliographical
references and index.
Identifiers: LCCN 2023019837 (print) | LCCN 2023019838 (ebook) | ISBN
9781350383043 (hb) | ISBN 9781350383050 (epub) | ISBN 9781350383067
(epdf) | ISBN 9781350383074
Subjects: LCSH: Women revolutionaries—Guinea-Bissau. | Women in war—
Guinea-Bissau. | Women—Guinea-Bissau—Social conditions—twentieth
century. | Guinea-Bissau—History—Revolution, 1963–1974—Women.
Classification: LCC DT613.78.L9 2024 (print) | LCC DT613.78 (ebook) |
DDC 966.5702–dc23/eng/20230424
LC record available at https://lccn.loc.gov/2023019837
LC ebook record available at https://lccn.loc.gov/2023019838

ISBN:	HB:	978-1-3503-8304-3
	PB:	978-1-3503-8308-1
	ePDF:	978-1-3503-8306-7
	eBook:	978-1-3503-8305-0

Typeset by Integra Software Services Pvt. Ltd.

To find out more about our authors and books visit www.bloomsbury.com
and sign up for our newsletters.

BLOOMSBURY OPEN ACCESS

An ebook edition of this book is available open access on bloomsburycollections.com. Open access was funded by the Bloomsbury Open Collections Library Collective.

Bloomsbury Open Collections is a collective-action approach to funding open access books that allows select authors to publish their books open access at no cost to them. Through this model, we make open access publication available to a wider range of authors by spreading the cost across multiple organizations, while providing additional benefits to participating libraries. The aim is to engage a more diverse set of authors and bring their work to a wider global audience.

More details, including how to participate and a list of contributing libraries, are available from bloomsbury.com/bloomsbury-open-collections.

Contents

List of Figures	ix
Bibliographical Abbreviations	x
Acknowledgments	xii

Introduction		1
	My New Focus or Reasons for a Changing Focus on the Guinea Bissau Liberation War	1
	Scholarly Approach, Liberation Wars, and Female Participation	2
	Marxism and Charismatic Leadership	3
	Female Participants Voices and Narratives	10
	Academia and Gender Biases	15
	Biases Implications	19
	The New Approach and Methodology	21
	Structure of the Book	26
1	Colonial Policies and Women in Portuguese Guinea, 1938–62	29
	Women in Pre-Colonial Guinea Bissau	30
	Colonial Administration and Gendered Roles	34
	Women and Anti-Colonial Organizations, 1938–62	38
	Women and Anti-Colonial Organizations, 1938–59	39
	Women and the PAIGC, 1959–62	43
	Conclusion	48
2	Female Work and Participation in the Armed Struggle in Portuguese Guinea	51
	Reasons for Female Participation and Mobilization	51
	Women's Roles	55
	Fighters, Logistics Transporters, and Medics	59
	Women as Socio-economic Agents	61
	Warfare and Female Sufferings	63
	Conclusion	64

3	Female Combatants and Portuguese Guinea National Liberation War Narratives: Do They Tell the Whole Story?	67
	Downplaying Their Roles in the War	68
	Why Women Were Downplaying Their Roles	69
	How Women Viewed Their Roles	70
	The Self-Paradox Discourses	73
	Bringing Women's Roles and Voices Back into the Official Discourses	78
	Conclusion	80
4	Gendering War Space and Heroinization of Female Fighters	81
	The Gendering of War Zone Space	81
	War and Manhood from Female Fighters' Perspectives	84
	Societal Structure in War Narratives	85
	Gendered Liberated Zones	88
	Women Defining Their Roles and Participation in the War	89
	Conclusion	93
5	Gender Roles and the First Republic	95
	Old Societal Structure: Back to Normal	95
	Female Participants in the First Republic	100
	Why No Changes and Continuation of the "Old Behavior"	104
	PAIGC and the Failure to Respect the Gender Equality Promises in Postwar Guinea Bissau	111
	Conclusion	113

Conclusion	115
Selected Interviews in Guinea Bissau	127
Notes	129
Selected Bibliography	161
Index	195

Figures

1	PAIGC Headquarters in Bissau (Photo Aliou Ly 2008)	121
2	Joanita Da Silva Rosa. During a direct combat operation in the southern front she lost her right eye and was sent to La Havana for medical treatment (Photo Aliou Ly 2010)	121
3	Joanita Da Silva Rosa, ID card as veteran of the liberation war (Photo Aliou Ly 2010)	122
4	NDo Mane, Na Ndjati and Udé Camara, veterans of the liberation war, waiting to get their veteran pension in Bissau (Photo Aliou Ly 2010)	122
5	Quinta Da Costa and Segunda Sambu, both veterans of the liberation war, waiting to get their pension in Bissau (Photo Aliou Ly 2010)	123
6	Quinta Da Costa, veteran who was shot in her left leg during the liberation war. After the war she was nominated Captain in the Bissau Guinean Army (Photo Aliou Ly 2010)	123
7	Barnaté Shana was under the commandment of Osvaldo Vieira in the eastern front. He lost his eye during combat. He was one of the fierce opponents of female participation in combat operations (Photo Aliou Ly 2010)	124
8	Remembering the 1959 Pijiguiti Massacre in Bissau, August 3, 2010 (Photo Aliou Ly 2010)	125
9	Remembering the 1959 Pijiguiti Massacre in Bissau, August 3, 2010 (Photo Aliou Ly 2010)	125
10	Remembering the 1959 Pijiguiti Massacre in Bissau, August 3, 2010 (Photo Aliou Ly 2010)	126

Bibliographical Abbreviations

ANP	National Popular Assembly
CP	Permanent Commission
CSL	*Conselho Superior de Luta* / Superior Council for the Fight/Executive Committee of the Struggle/Highest Council of the Struggle
FAL	*Forças Armadas Locais* / Local Armed Force
FARP	*Forças Armadas Revolucionárias do Povo* / People's Revolutionary Army
FRELIMO	Front for the Liberation of Mozambique
INCIDI	International Institute of Differing Civilizations
JAAC	*Juventude Africana Amílcar Cabral* / Amílcar Cabral's African Youth
MLCP	*Movimento pela Libertação das Colónias Portuguesas* / Movement for the Liberation of the Portuguese Colonies
PAIGC	*Partido Africano da Independencia da Guine e Cabo Verde* / African Party for the Independence of Guinea and Cape Verde
PDCI/RDA	*Parti Démocratique de Côte D'Ivoire-Rassemblement Démocratique Africain* / Ivory Coast Democratic Party section of the African Democratic Rassemblement
PIDE	*Polícia Internacional e de Defesa Do Estado* / Portuguese Colonial Police
SFIO	*Section Française de l'Internationale Ouvriére* / French Section of the International Workers Organization

UDEMU	*União Democrática das Mulheres da Guiné e Cabo Verde* / Democratic Union of the Women of Guinea and Cabo Verde
UNTG	*União Nacional dos Trabalhadores de Guiné* / National Union of Workers of Guinea Bissau
ZANU	Zimbabwe African National Union

Acknowledgments

This book would not be possible without the unconditional support of my late parents: my father; Abdoulaye Bocar Ly and my mother Oureye Hamath Thiam. When they migrated from the Peulh/Fulani region along the Senegal River to Dakar in the late 1940s, my father saw that without a Francophone education, he missed opportunities for good jobs in Dakar and to be more involved in the future of his country and the anti-colonial movement. He therefore decided that at all costs his children, boys and girls, would complete their Francophone education and be fully committed to that journey. He and my mother never shied away from that decision. Today, every family gathering is a cause for my siblings and I to recognize how lucky we were to have those parents and their educational commitment to us. In fact, all our neighbors in the Quartier Champs de Courses I, Pikine, Dakar recognized this, and played their part in our education. Yes, it takes a village to raise a child. Through my parents Abdoulaye Bocar Ly and Oureye Hamath Thiam, I thank all my siblings and the neighbors in Pikine for supporting and loving me throughout my journey. My family and the Pikine neighborhood represent everything for me and made me who I am today.

The Senegalese educational system included great teachers, administrators, and staff people who made this journey possible. Special thanks to my primary schoolteachers Mr. Diéye and Mr. Mbaye. Thanks to secondary school teachers Mr. Bangoura, who awoke my interest in history and geography, and Mr. Teixeira, who helped me develop responsibility, organization, and method. My experience with the US education system has proven to me how good and how undervalued Senegal's educational system is.

My journey in the United States would not have happened without Leslie and Merle Rabine, Joan and Thomas Klammer, Lydia Chavez, and Mark Rabine. Dr. Leslie Rabine and I met in Dakar. Since that meeting, she, Merle Rabine, Joan, and Dr. Thomas Klammer have been valuable mentors and advisors—and my American family. They have been my rock through this US journey. They are always there when I need them and have provided advice and comfort.

A tiny fraction of immigrants in the United States receives the support and extraordinary life experience that I have had with this group of exceptional persons, who embrace me as their own son. I cannot thank them enough, especially my spiritual "Badien" [my spiritual father's sister] Leslie Rabine. My experience as a master's student at California State University, Fullerton was fulfilling because Dr. Klammer, then Dean of the College of Humanities, took me under his wing, while Christine Pirsche-Barnes, CSU Fullerton American Language Program Advisor, adopted me as her brother.

From my doctoral education at the University of California, Davis, History Department, I give special thanks to Dr. Benjamin Lawrance, the late Dr. Cynthia Brantley, and Dr. Moradewun Adejunmobi, for their constant support. Thanks also for their support to my UC Davis African History graduate student group: Baba G. Jallow, Nathan Carpenter, Marcus Filippello, Joanna Tague, and Chau Kelly, as well as fellow grad student Michael Collins.

My deepest thanks to my eldest brother Bocar Ly who facilitated my stay in Bissau during all my years of fieldwork in that lovely and warm country. Big thanks to Armando and Felicidade Brito Abelha, Mr. Sy, his nephew Adama Sy, and Joao Fadia's (El Hadji) families. They graciously and warmly housed me. They gave support, advice, and incommensurable help in introducing me to Bissau Guineans, which furthered my research projects. Unforgettable are the discussions I had with the two Brunos, Da Costa and Abelha, on the front porch of Abelha's house at Bissau's Barrio Luanda. Thanks to Juliao Lopes Mané, whom I met at the PAIGC headquarters on my first visit there, and who gave me meaningful guidance through my research project. He has become a good brother and friend.

For the completion of this manuscript, big thanks to Drs. Benjamin Lawrance, Toby Green, Philipp Havik, William Waters, Thomas Klammer, Leslie Rabine, Joanna Tague, Marcus Filippello, Nathan Carpenters, and Moses Klevor. Some were testing grounds for new ideas, concepts, and theories. Some read, edited, and commented on the many versions. Dr. Benjamin Lawrance, my PhD Chair, continues to provide constant support.

For the editing of this book, I would like to thank Meredith Murray and the staff at Bloomsbury, especially Nick Wolterman and Olivia Dellow.

My biggest, warmest, and deepest thanks to my wife Khadijetou Ly, my son Ousmane, and daughter Oureye for their incommensurable love, joy, and support. I love you all.

Introduction

My New Focus or Reasons for a Changing Focus on the Guinea Bissau Liberation War

In June of 2008, I visited Bissau, the capital city of the Republic of Guinea Bissau (formerly Portuguese Guinea in West Africa), for the first time, for a three-month fieldwork project; my goal was to collect hard facts and oral data on Amilcar Cabral and the Guinea Bissau (or Portuguese Guinea) independence war.[1] On my second day in Bissau, I visited the Partido Africano da Independencia da Guine e Cabo Verde (PAIGC) headquarters to "officially" introduce myself to the leaders of the political organization created by Amilcar Cabral in 1956 and to find out how the party might be able to assist my endeavor.[2] It was during this visit that I was introduced to Carlos Gomes "Junior," the current Party president, by one of his protocol cabinet members, Juliao Lopes Mané.

During my daily visits to the PAIGC headquarters, I was pleased to see so many women actively involved, but I did not attach much importance to their presence. Then one day in the third week, I was in the large second-floor PAIGC meeting room with Juliao Lopez Mané, who had by this time become my research assistant, and Mario Ramalho Cissokho, the former director of Instituto Nacional de Estudos e Pesquisa/Guinea Bissau National Research Institute (INEP), when a light-skinned woman in her seventies entered the meeting room and headed for "Junior" Gomes's office. The room became immediately quiet, and everyone, men, and women alike, approached her respectfully. I decided to follow the group and lined up like everyone else to shake her hand. Mr. Cissokho introduced her to me as Tia Carmen Pereira, a valuable freedom fighter during the independence war.[3] For the rest of the day

I thought about that encounter, about how the dynamics in the meeting room had instantly changed when Carmen entered, and I wanted to find out more.

The next day, in the same place, I started asking questions. Seeking to know more about Carmen and her role in the war led me to a greater interest in women participants in general, and I discovered that both, the historiography, and the narratives of the war were biased. Except for Stéphanie Urdang's work, most of other writings on the Guinea Bissau liberation war mentioned the women combatants only indirectly and very briefly. Could it be that her work was viewed so definitive that many historians or social scientists felt there was nothing further that needed to be added? It was apparent to me that something needed to be done to present a complete picture of the liberation war, and I concluded that another methodological approach was needed to account for all of the female participants who had been excluded from narratives of the revolutionary movement.

The gendered dimensions of the Guinea Portuguese liberation, including female roles and participation, have never been given adequate coverage. Stéphanie Urdang's pioneering work focused on the roles, participation, and hopes of the female liberation war participants. However, she omitted discussions of how the male participants responded to female participation on the battlefield, and of the gendered nature of the roles in general. Overall, Urdang's conclusions regarding women's participation in the liberation war were very far removed from the way most female war participants described gender relations in Guinea Bissau in the post-independence period. Female participants who aided their male counterparties in the liberation war were promised an equal share of the pie, but after the war, the female fighters believed they received only a small part of what they had been promised.

Scholarly Approach, Liberation Wars, and Female Participation

Historians of national liberations have tended to follow a methodology based on state-centered analysis, where ideology and leadership are fundamental keys to understanding the historical significance of the struggles. The abstract realms of "state," "nationalism," and "leadership" develop gender-based narratives and omit important social, economic, and familial factors, ignoring critical aspects of societal participation and structure.[4] Consequently, other key factors are neglected, and many participants became "subalterns" to the historical process. Political ideology and charismatic leadership may be important in analyzing liberation wars, but the reasons for participation and mobilization given by most women combatants and combatants rarely include these issues. As already said by some, scholars need to focus instead on the points of view of the participants and the actual accounts of their experiences, and then build historical theory. The historical approach needs to be inductive rather than deductive.

Marxism and Charismatic Leadership

The historiography of the Portuguese Guinea/Guinea Bissau liberation war is focused on the concepts of nationalism and Marxism and on Amilcar Cabral's persona and political mobilization in the liberated zones.[5] Prominent social scientists such as Lars Rudebeck, Basil Davidson, Patrick Chabal, and Judson M. Lyon have expounded on these aspects of the struggle. The most accepted and common conclusion among these individuals is the importance of the leadership role of Amilcar Cabral and the PAIGC during the independence war. Cabral has been compared to other great African leaders such as Patrice Lumumba and Kwame Nkrumah.[6] "Amilcar Cabral stands almost alone among African nationalists," according to Pablo Luke Idahosa.[7]

Cabral's early experience did not prepare him for a political role. As a student, he was a promising agronomist engineer. He became familiar with African literature while furthering his education in Portugal with other future African leaders such as Agostino Neto, Marcelino dos Santos, and Mario de Andrade.[8] Cabral, Neto, and de Andrade formed the Center for African Studies while they were in Lisbon.[9] What set Amilcar Cabral apart from other African nationalist leaders was that, as an agronomist, he had traveled to all parts of Guinea Bissau and Cabo Verde to analyze the economic aspects of agricultural productions and ethnic groups.[10] This allowed him to initiate contacts and discussions with villagers on issues related to colonialism and their social conditions.[11]

Between 1960 and 1963, when the party was preparing for armed struggle, the party cadres first underwent military training in China, then in Morocco, Algeria, the Soviet Union and Eastern European countries, and Cuba.[12] Finally returning home, they received further training in Conakry and were sent to the countryside to carry out political mobilization and learn about the villagers.[13] Algiers was an entrepot of subversion, where rebels and revolutionaries from other places such as Palestine, Angola, Argentina, and Vietnam lived together and vowed to die together. It was this policy of training with revolutionaries from other countries that inspired the nationalist rebel from Portuguese Guinea-Bissau, Amilcar Cabral, to approvingly dub the Algerian capital the "Mecca of revolutions."[14] This policy also helped the PAIGC to avoid mistakes made by many other African nationalist groups by "invoking the nation ahead of the perceived dangers of tribalism and clan or national integration over local or regional identity, of secular nationalism over religious affiliation."[15]

Amilcar Cabral's leadership could be seen in the quality and nature of the party's cadres or mobilizers and the adaptability and flexibility of the party over the years.[16]

> Both of these directly reflected Cabral's leadership. He believed that *men*, not party *cadres*, were the key to the development and organization of a party capable of evolving and adapting new policies. It was undoubtedly on the human aspect of his political training that he placed greatest emphasis. In fact, he took personal charge of the training of all the cadres during the early years of the struggle. Most of them were dedicated but illiterate young villagers or city dwellers with no political knowledge or even consciousness, little experience of political agitation and even less understanding of war.[17]

Another important aspect of Cabral's leadership was his ability to understand that national liberation becomes more than "the right to self-rule; it means revolution; that is a profound change in the colonized (or neo-colonized) mode of production is required." This meant that Cabral understood the difference between simple national independence and true national independence.[18] According to Patrick Chabal,

> Though, in Mozambique and Angola (and later in Zimbabwe) the nationalists also emerged victorious from a war of independence, it was Guinea-Bissau which captured the imagination the most, both because of its achievements (political, military and moral) and because of the stature of Amilcar Cabral

(founder and leader of the PAIGC), without doubt one of the most able and creative political leaders of modern Africa.[19]

Regarding Cabral's leadership:

> It is always dangerous to attribute the success of a revolution to a particular battle, to a particular action or philosophy or even to a particular individual. But the history, character, and even success of the revolution in Guinea [Bissau], it is safe to say, are very largely due to the force and the personality of one man—Amilcar Cabral. It is this man's concern for his people which has made them such determined guerilla fighters, and his vision of a new nation which has made large members of his followers' literate and fed and clothed many made homeless by Portuguese repression.[20]

On Cabral's evolution, it has been suggested that Cabral was a peasant by empathy in his early years, later becoming a petty bourgeoisie by education and training, and finally a revolutionary leader, ready to lead a guerilla movement against Portugal.[21]

After the importance of the leadership roles of Cabral and the PAIGC, the second most commonly accepted idea among social scientists was the shared nationalism of the revolutionary movement at large, even though the movement in Guinea-Bissau has many characteristics that are unique.[22] The Portuguese Guinea revolution must be analyzed in light of what is known about other twentieth-century revolutions and wars of national liberation, such as those in China, Vietnam, Yugoslavia, Algeria, and Cuba. Cabral's liberation war was not based on purely African perspectives, "because there are numbers of historical and conceptual issues raised by the Guinea case," such as the dynamism whereby a movement of national liberation was transformed into a party that launched an armed struggle in Africa, factors that ultimately account for its success.[23] "Another important aspect of the party [PAIGC] was its lack of ideological dogmatism or rigidity while its general social and political orientation might broadly be defined as socialist."[24] Another important point that sets the Guinea Bissau nationalist movement apart from the other African nationalist movements is the ability of Cabral's organization to avoid the lack of cohesion seen among other nationalist movements in Africa. The PAIGC achieved unity due to the efforts of the political mobilizers during the prewar period, and the armed struggle kept the party united during the war period.

It is after that all clear that the structure and ideology of the party made it relatively immune to internal splits while its political strategy in the countryside made the task of political competitors a difficult one. The PAIGC was *visibly* the only party to carry out the nationalist struggle.[25]

Cabral is one of Africa's most "prescient and principled meaning-giving nationalists."[26] For Russian Oleg Ignatiev and Angolan Mario Pinto De Andrade, Cabral was an over-conscious nationalist able to anticipate the course and configuration of historical events well in advance."[27] The armed struggle in Guinea-Bissau was based on the historical experience of the people, and this served as a framework for Cabral's theory of nationalism. The Guinea-Bissau nationalist movement could be understood as a developmental nationalism, which offered modernizing actions, or in other words, criticized the old political, economic, social, and cultural order.[28]

Amilcar Cabral and the PAIGC nationalist organization took steps to create a truly "new democratic" state for their people, as opposed to an elaborate ceremonial transfer of colonial powers from the Portuguese. In this manner, they were able to eliminate old inequalities from the pre-colonial heritage and new inequalities from the colonial heritage.[29]

The most contested and controversial point is the linkage of the Guinea Bissau national struggle to Marxism. The PAIGC revolution is considered by some to have operated from a Marxist framework, while others believe that, although the anti-Portuguese revolution in Guinea Bissau did indeed operate from a Marxist framework, it avoided being tied to Marxist dogma.[30] The PAIGC approach is close to the Marxist philosophy of dialectical materialism, which is based on two main tenets: class divisions and practical relationships between theory and practice.[31] Assuming Amilcar Cabral to be influenced by Marxist theory is a pointless discussion, but some social scientists such as Hudson Lyon, Jock McCulloch, Timothy W. Luke, Bernard Magubane, and Alain Bockel believe that Cabral was in fact influenced by Marxist theories.[32] One of the most interesting aspects of liberation movements is the growing role of Marxism in their ideologies; in Guinea Bissau, the leadership developed an ideology based in part on Marxism but also greatly influenced by its own economic and social reality.[33] Cabral used the Marxist dialectical method to redefine the situation in Guinea.[34]

Knowing this deficiency of some of the African leaders, Cabral has arrived at socialist solutions to the problems of Guiné Bissau through ideological convictions. The party he leads, PAIGC, is a revolution party based on Marxist analysis of social reality.[35]

According to Maryinez L. Hubbard,

> Gerard Chaliand and Regis Debray, both Marxist commentators, have remarked that the principal difference between Castro and Cabral was the latter's decision to embark on a long program of preparing the peasants for revolution before, rather than after, launching guerrilla action.[36]

Although it is not universally accepted that Cabral was a Marxist, Cabral's work and ideas do prove his Marxist tendencies. Alain Bockel claims that Cabral was introduced to Marxism when he was a student in Lisbon, and his methodological analysis of the Guinea Bissau society is Marxist.[37] Nigel C. Gibson defines Cabral as an African nationalist, African Marxist, and leader of the Marxist-Leninist (democratic centralist) party. Cabral used "Marxian" categories in an analysis of the social structure and made an important contribution to social theory, insisting on the existence of history before class struggle.[38] According to Timothy W. Luke, "Cabral saw himself and his theory as Marxist; yet for the most part, he did not let the historical traditions of Marxism overburden his analysis of colonial Africa's unique revolutionary situation."[39] Luke believes Cabral's Marxism "might provide the ideological tools for changing traditional ways of thinking as the members of African societies confront the challenges of building their economies, nations and states both during and after their struggle for national liberation."[40] Luke continues to affirm that Cabral used Marxism as *method* rather than as an ideology:

> Cabral frees himself from doctrinal necessity of finding a revolutionary proletariat according to the orthodox Marxist-Leninist canon, or a revolutionary peasantry by the classic Maoist formula, in an environment where the forms of colonialism prevented the development of such radicalized classes.[41]

However, Cabral did not let the historical traditions of Marxism overburden his analysis of colonial Africa's unique revolutionary situation.[42]

Amilcar Cabral's Marxism may remain the most up to date in "modernizing and revolutionary ideology, one which, while exalting the sense of national identity, can also prune the socially and culturally conservative elements out of the national tradition and free the energies of the greatest number of people."[43] If Cabral was not a Marxist, he supported the traditional Marxist view of imperialism as the monopolistic stage of capitalism in all his political writings.[44] "Cabral was able to formulate a class analysis of the indigenous population of Guinea that did not rely on irrelevant Marxist categories but was an original reflection on Portuguese Guinea's class structure."[45] Two different modes of thinking were battling in Amilcar Cabral's mind: one marked by a pragmatic "Leninist party theory combined with conventional modernization thinking on socio-economic progress," and the other marked by revolutionary and democratic modes of thinking.[46]

For Pablo Luke Idahosa and others, the depiction of African revolutionary movements as Marxist means little, because all revolutionary movements could be variously qualified as Marxist.[47] But, for Idahosa, Amilcar Cabral reflected his concern for his firsthand view of what he believed was the existing experiences of the colonized. Amilcar Cabral found his force in the folk traditions of Portuguese Guinea and the Cabo Verde islands, as well as in their agricultural and ecological problems.[48]

Yet Cabral refused to define himself as Marxist and was never a member of a Communist party.[49] He never viewed himself as a theorist, nor was he committed to any one theory or ideology.[50] Speaking at the Rome International Conference in support of the people of the Portuguese colonies in Italy, Cabral said,

> The basic principle of our struggle is that those who are struggling for freedom and independence must first be free in thought and action ... We are absolutely convinced our struggle is an act of solidarity towards all people in the struggle for national freedom, but also for all people struggling in Europe, Asia, Africa, Latin America in the general framework of anti-imperialism. We hope that all opinions, all tendencies, which meet here in Rome for solidarity with us, will find here a basis for the unity of the anti-colonialist and anti-imperialist struggle.[51]

The PAIGC was a revolutionary movement with an original approach. Its guidelines were primarily drawn from indigenous circumstances and post-Second World War West African sociopolitical circumstances.[52] Cabral's approach to building theory was from the particular to the general.[53] He was interested not only in challenging the colonial system, but also in changing the sociocultural realities that excluded several facets of Bissau Guinean society from the ability to participate in the decision-making process.[54]

Between 1959 and 1962, Cabral focused on gaining the support of farmers by concentrating his efforts on political orientation in the countryside; he wanted personally to launch a grassroots struggle being physically present, rather than from a foreign country or from exile.[55] This was strategic and extremely important to the success of the movement for Cabral.[56]

Cabral believed that by having party leaders and cadres live in the countryside with the villagers, they would discover at the grassroots the richness of their cultural values and acquire a clearer understanding of the economic realities, the problems, sufferings, and hopes of the popular masses.[57] The groundwork for the revolution was laid "with this equal open, democratic exchange between the party cadres and the villagers, or 'this tireless work of listening and talking, explaining, watching, correcting, suggesting, guiding and generally *representing* the party to the peasant and the peasants to the party.'"[58]

Cabral placed great importance on the training of the political mobilizers, mostly young Guineans from middle class backgrounds who joined them in Conakry, and other young Guineans such as João Bernardo Vieira, Pascoal Alves, and Antonio Bana.[59] Initially, Amilcar Cabral's house in Conakry was the "school," which Amilcar Cabral largely responsible for program content.[60]

> Most of the students, mostly poor, illiterate young men and women from the countryside, went through an intense literacy program, while the literate urban recruits were trained in persuasive techniques informed by lectures on geography, nationalist history and politics, the principles of the PAIGC, and the aims and objectives of the upcoming armed struggle.[61]

Later, the training center will be moved to the "*Lar dos Combatentes*" or "Home of the Fighters" in Bonfi, Conakry, before relocating again at the *Escola Piloto* or Pilot School in 1965.[62] Among the first group of students enrolled in the Pilot School was Florentino "Flora" Gomes; the most well-known Bissau-Guinean filmmaker.

The political mobilization campaigns were well planned. It was well planned because Cabral as a former colonial agronomist who carried out a census in Guinea-Bissau, he acquired knowledge about the countryside that was later useful in mobilizing. Profiting from the harsh lived experiences of the rural population, the trained mobilizers initially descended on the southern and northern regions of Portuguese Guinea, asking questions that aimed to develop awareness of the paysan conditions. Some of the mobilizer's questions were:

> "What is the situation? Did you pay taxes? Did your father pay taxes? What have you seeing from those taxes? How much you get from your groundnuts? How much sweat has it cost your family? Which of you have been imprisoned? You are going to work on road construction: who gives you the tools? You bring the tools/ Who provides you meals? You provide your meals? But who walks on the road? Who has car? And your daughter who raped her?—are you happy about that?[63]

"This was Cabral's greatest achievement," according to Francisco Mendes, one of the young recruits who later became a top PAIGC commander and the first prime minister of independent Guinea.[64] Antonio Bana, or Yamte N'aga, gave a very good summation of how the hundreds of mobilizers or cadres dealt with or mobilized peasants in Basil Davidson's book *The Liberation of Guiné: Aspects of an African Revolution*.[65]

> It is not altogether surprising that it is among those who had been trained in Conakry during the first years of the armed struggle, today's party leadership, that Cabral 's influence was greatest and loyalty to his ideas strongest.[66]

The debate regarding the Marxist affiliation of the PAIGC and Amilcar Cabral obscures individual reasons for participating in the liberation. The roles of participants often became "invisible" because certain historians generally define all liberation wars as representative of worldwide patterns into which all revolutionary armed struggles fit. The consequence of this methodology is bias and exclusion, in which the subjective aspect of human relationships in these revolutionary struggles is missing.

Female Participants Voices and Narratives

These various complementary accounts from early literature touch on important aspects of the liberation war, yet they fail to take account of Guinea Bissau's women combatants, with few exceptions. Most scholars, in their analysis of

Portuguese Guinea, Amilcar Cabral, and the armed struggle in Portuguese Guinea did not mention women or gender issues in Guinea Bissau during the liberation war period.[67] Some do mention gender and women's issues, but only indirectly or obliquely. Women were accepted into the PAIGC, but, with a few exceptions, they were not allowed to bear arms during the liberation war, even though they were trained and armed within the village committees.[68] Amilcar understood that the struggle would not just end with the reconquest of their land, flag, and national anthem, as had happened in many parts of Africa. He pointed out that the exploitation that women had suffered was twice as bad as the exploitation resulting from colonial rule. Independence could not be achieved without women being freed. Crispina Gomes recalls how Cabral viewed the women's struggle in Guinea Bissau.[69]

Another scholar who referred to the role of women in the village council is Patrick Chabal, mentioning two women as members of every village council.[70] Gerard Chaliand, during one of his trips in the PAIGC maquis in the northern front with Amilcar Cabral, remarked at least twice on the presence of female nurses or young females, without naming any of them.[71] However, during his several sojourns to Portuguese Guinea, he interviewed several male fighters or political commissioners, such as Antonio Bana, Chico Mendes, Armando Joaquim Soto Amado, and Tombon Seidi.[72] In his book *Armed Struggle in Africa; With the Guerillas in "Portuguese" Guinea*, one of the very few females recognized is Titina Sila who, he said, accompanied them as a nurse, wearing a FARP uniform. In that section of the book, he discussed gender equality. Even though the book's front cover features a picture of three women, one of whom is holding a military weapon, very few female voices were heard.[73]

Basil Davidson, discussing the early PAIGC recruits, affirms the presence of young women nurses in the group of trainees.[74] He interviewed some male trainees and fighters such Pascoal Alves, Ibrahima Camara, and Sala N'tonton, and mentioned one of Gerard Chaliand's interviewees, Antonio Bana.[75] However, it is important to mention Na N'Kanha, the Balanta woman member of the village council of a village not far from Quitafiné, who participated in a village meeting with Amilcar Cabral and spoke out about how violent the Portuguese army was.[76]

Ronald Chilcote, in his book *Amilcar Cabral's Revolutionary Theory and Practice; A Critical Guide*, interviewed twenty-one PAIGC members for the

"Appendix: Perspectives of the Revolutionary vanguard." All of them were men except Carmen Pereira.[77] Carmen recognized that women had initially been considered as persons who should stay home, with little access to educational opportunity. They then found it necessary for women to join the liberation fight to call for changes in gender relations.[78] She continued to discuss the UDEMU and women's involvement and participation in the new government, the National Assembly, and the State Council.

Scholar and journalist Stéphanie Urdang is one of the few authors who viewed gender and women's issues as main issues during the struggle and revolution. Urdang was practically the only writer who focused on the women's participation in the liberation war in Guinea Bissau. She was primarily concerned with women's roles on the village councils, believing that women were fighting two colonialisms in Guinea Bissau. Urdang mentioned a variety of implicit principles and explicit ground rules that both Amilcar Cabral and the PAIGC laid down, such as no polygyny among party members and a commitment to achieve equal status for women, making women the most enthusiastic supporters of the party.[79]

Prior to Urdang, Chantal Sarrazin drew from her experiences in Guinea Bissau to discuss the roles played by Bissau Guinean women in helping the PAIGC recruit members in the countryside at the beginning of the liberation war, and the emancipation agenda.[80] Finally, Ole Gjerstad and Chantal Sarrazin interviewed Carmen Pereira. In the interview, Carmen talked about participation in the liberation war and about women's emancipation, among other topics.[81] Patricia Godinho Gomes and Kathleen Sheldon recognized the important role played by African women during national liberation struggles, leading to some attempts to eliminate customary practices considered harmful to women.[82] Bissau Guinean women joined the struggle during the clandestine years, offering their houses for meetings, and preparing and distributing propaganda materials.

> The narratives of the struggle [Guinea Bissau national liberation] contain several examples of women's determination, not only to join the process, but also to show the decisive influence they exercised over the men/husbands and children, holding them to the ideals of the struggle.[83]

In a similar perspective, Brandon D. Lundy, Raul Mendes Fernandes Jr., and Kezia Lartey, in their analysis of women's roles in the re-making of the

Guinea-Bissau nation, affirm that after the Guinea Bissau declaration of independence in 1974, women were involved at all levels of decision-making.[84]

In Guinea Bissau, the neglect of African female combatants' voices by social scientists and male politicians during the liberation war (1963–74) was part of a larger policy of male dominance, where women in general were viewed as subjects and not agents in politics and in the academic world. African women have a long history of participating in resistance actions against colonial systems using both passive and active resistance means, and during the armed struggles they participated in combat and supported male fighters in other efforts.[85] In the case of Kikuyu women, economic difficulties compounded by constant labor demands from assorted branches of the colonial administration helped them understand the need to fight the colonial system in order to avoid poverty.[86]

Kenyan women are known for practicing *Guturama* in the 1920s. *Guturama* was a traditional practice in which a woman exposed her genitals to the offending party.[87] This was considered an insult and was the ultimate recourse for those who were consumed by anger, frustration, humiliation, and revenge.[88] Another example of women's militancy during the colonial period is the so-called Igbo women's war. In 1929, thousands of Igbo women collectively organized against the "warrant chiefs," a group of men who served as the functionaries of the British indirect rule system. "The women 'sat' on the chiefs, singing, dancing, and following everywhere. In the end British soldiers killed more than 50 women."[89]

In 1953, the British deported the Buganda king because of his opposition to the proposed East Africa federation. A group of women started traveling though the country to rally support for the king. In the end, the governor conceded, leading to Uganda's independence and the king's return from exile.[90] In the 1950s and early 1960s, many African nations achieved independence. Some, such as Algeria, Namibia, Zimbabwe, Eritrea, Mozambique, Angola, and Guinea Bissau had to achieve their independence through armed struggles, in which African women were actively involved, participating in direct combat operations and also playing supportive roles, including transporting weapons.[91]

All these examples of women's militancy came to light only after the 1970s, as that period corresponded with the development of feminist movements that challenged political and academic spheres, forcing scholars to start borrowing gender-based lenses and revisiting the analysis of the past. The scholarship related to the female fighters and members of the Guinea Bissau liberation war resulted from the worldwide context of the time. The 1960s and 1970s corresponded to the periods in which women's emancipation and attainment of basic rights such as freedom of expression and agency and their role in knowledge productions were given much attention. These periods were characterized by the removal of taboos that excluded women from effective participation in public institutions.[92] However, it is important to note that scholars did not automatically jump on the bandwagon of gender relations shifts as soon as they were happening. Because of that, viewing women as agents of sociocultural, political, and economic change was a major challenge for the world, as very few of the large numbers of scholarly works related to the Guinea Bissau liberation war focused on the questions of gender and women's emancipation agendas or women as agents of sociocultural, political, and economic changes.

We need to take women's voices into account in Portuguese Guinea/Guinea Bissau as in the other African liberation and revolutionary wars.[93] This would create a new understanding of the meaning and outcomes of the war as the particularities and specificities of a marginalized group are accounted for. Listening to women's voices and seeing female fighters as a centerpiece of the narrative demonstrates that historians must not use a "single, universal representative for the diverse populations of any society or culture without granting differential importance to one group over another."[94] Such a focus will allow us to view the Guinea Bissau liberation war from a different perspective, which until now was almost untold or unwritten. To do so, we must ask questions such as:

(1) How can we account for the women's roles of the Guinea Bissau national liberation war, 1963–74?
(2) Why did historiographical debates until now not account for female combatants' roles in the national liberation war as an essential component of the war?
(3) What are the difficulties in gathering sources related to the gendered dimensions of the war?
(4) What roles did women combatants play in the liberation war?

(5) After the war, what have been the implications of women's participation in the war?
(6) Did women's participation in the war have any effect on gender dimensions after the war?

Academia and Gender Biases

While these variously conflicting and complementary historical accounts touch on important aspects of the liberation war, they collectively fail to take account of women's roles because they turn theory into national political abstractions, thereby excluding the perspectives of women. This does not mean the question of women's advancement was not yet in the mind of certain political decision-makers or intellectuals. In September of 1958, at the International Conference on Women's Role in the Development of Tropical and Sub-Tropical Countries in Brussels, under the leadership of the International Institute of Differing Civilizations (INCIDI), more than one hundred delegates from eighteen countries gathered to discuss questions related to women's roles in the colonies.[95] During the conference, while the French activist and defender of women's rights Marie-Helene Lefaucheux deplored the general lack of access to education for women in developing countries and the relegation of housekeeping task to women, most of the participants wanted to maintain women under male dominance, even though they recognized that something must be done.[96] Male participants, politicians, and so-called experts decided to not disrupt established gender paradigms and gave their support to furthering women's purposed soft skills in the social realm and the domestic sphere.[97] "When these politicians and experts gathered in Brussels in 1958, the historiography of empire and colonialism was shaped by accounts of those who were themselves practitioners of colonial policies."[98]

But during the following decades, perspectives that integrate gender as a key analytical tool have been increasingly introduced into historical research on empire. Scholars such as Antoinette Burton, Karten Tranberg Hansen, Ann Laura Stoler, Philippa Levine, Susan Martin-Marquez, Hilary Owen, Anna M. Klobuscka, and others have published works that contributed to a better understanding of the "ways in which colonialism restructured gender dynamics of both colonizing and colonized societies."[99] As Andreas Stucki stated, "There is a need to rethink Portuguese and Spanish decolonization in Africa from a gendered perspective, bringing into the discussion newly available (and to date neglected) primary material from archives in Portugal, Spain, and the USA, including accounts from African women themselves."[100] For Stucki, in the 1960s and 1970s a distinctively women-centered way of engaging with empire emerged among male and female "colonial figures, administrative bodies, and the armed force." "The late colonial era synchronized with the emancipation of western women, and feminist demands for equality and women's rights articulated in international forums stimulated concern for the welfare of colonized women," as historian Barbara Bush explains.[101]

These ideas were part of the larger strategy of the colonizers to stabilize their empires, or at least to ensure advantageous conditions for the colonial powers during and after decolonization in the Portuguese and Spanish colonies.[102] In conceiving women as cultural mediators, Portuguese and Spanish colonial officers underscored the argument that African women were passive and must be stimulated and instructed. "In this Iberian version of uplifting African women, we find white women trying to save black and brown women from black and blown men—and from themselves."[103]

> Hence, in the early 1960s the stage was set for the "feminization" of the Iberian empires. In fact, "lifting up" African women and fostering their social advancement and in effect embarking on a path toward a gendered form of welfare colonialism had become a major issue in securing imperial dominance throughout the Portuguese—and Spanish—speaking world, particularly as the colonial powers faced armed resistance in Western Sahar (1957–1958), Angola (1961–1974), Guinea-Bissau (1963–1974), and Mozambique (1964–1974). Since the 1940s, education and socio-economic development together with military force were important schemes for countering anticolonial movements and insurgencies throughout the colonial world. What was termed as development was closely connected to gendered ideas about control and domination.[104]

The early historiography of Guinea Bissau has generally ignored the gendered dimensions of the liberation war for two reasons. First, using nationalism, anti-colonialism, and Marxism as theoretical frameworks has often led historians to omit the perspectives of the colonized subalterns.[105] Ranajit Guha argues that Marxism and nationalism caused such exclusion because leaders prioritize matters of state over other factors.[106] This prioritizing tendency has understandably been very strong in the field of African history because questions of state and national economy have become fundamental in struggling African countries.[107] The consequence of this approach is a focus on abstract notions and dogmas instead of an analysis of the concrete agency of people in actual conflicts.

To develop a historical narrative in which both male and female participants will recognize themselves, historians must focus on the participants' perspectives, as each group or participant has been guided by specific exigencies with which the group or participant must negotiate. Hence, for us to account for women's fighters' roles in the Guinea Bissau liberation war, attention must first be turned to the domestic setting and to local communities, villages, and families. Next, we need to challenge conventional historical methodologies. Most of other works, interviewed often, male fighters while female fighters were rarely interviewed. In many studies, women combatants' presence in the liberation war is mentioned very briefly, and the question of gender relations within the context of war is never assessed. For example, Gérard Chaliand and Basil Davidson conducted fieldwork in Guinea Bissau during the war. They interviewed many male fighters, and they mentioned the presence of woman fighters, but they did not interview the women.[108]

During the war period, Chaliand and Davidson interviewed or had conversation with several PAIGC male fighters or members such as Antonio Bana, Pascoal Alves, Ibrahima Camara, Sala N'tonton, Chico, Armando Joaquim Soto Amado, Tombon Seidi, Ireño do Nascimento Lopes, Yante N'aga, and Jose Augusto Teixeira Mourao, in addition to the PAIGC leaders. They asked such questions as their age, origin, what kind of job they had before the war begin, when they joined the PAIGC, what was their rank and occupation with the PAIGC structure.[109] Both of them mentioned the presence of women obliquely. For example, Basil Davidson acknowledged the presence of women as members at the early stage of the struggle, in 1960. "By 1960 they [PAIGC leaders] were able to begin sending a small stream of young men and women into the shelter of the neighboring Republic of Guinea."[110] He met a woman named Na N'Kanka, who was a member of the village committee of a village he referred as "C—" located not far from Quitafiné. He mentioned she compare the Portuguese to the ants, observing that she is a Balanta woman and nothing else.[111]

Chaliand had a section "With the Maquis" in his book *Armed Struggle in Africa*. "With the Guerillas in 'Portuguese' Guinea" was dedicated to the interviews he held with the PAIGC male members and fighters.[112] In that book, references to women are made vaguely. For example, he recognized the presence of two female nurses in their group when leaving Dakar (Senegal) going to Portuguese Guinea. All persons named in the group were males: Chaliand, Amilcar Cabral, Jose Mendes, Fidelis (a cadre). The four unnamed participants were the two female nurses and the two male drivers.[113]

Later, at the Maké base where he interviewed some of the male fighters or militants, he mentioned their waitresses were "a group of lively student nurses between the ages of twelve and fifteen who appeared quite attractive in their boubous."[114] He recalls in their meeting with schoolchildren that Cabral had introduced Titina to them and emphasized the importance of men and women as the country's resources, stating that they must treat each other as equals. He continued to say, "Look at Titina who's standing here next to me. She is a PAIGC cadre and qualified nurse. Men and women must have the same right and duties."[115]

One of the very few times a female voice was recalled, it is when at the same meeting with the schoolchildren Titina asked if they have someone in charge of public health. After a negative response, she advised them to elect someone to be in charge. Later, Titina's name was mentioned when she was making Nescafe in a small tin can.[116] What a great opportunity to interview a female fighter who has been later presented as one of the greatest PAIGC cadre members.

Another issue that hinders the process of recovering the voices of women combatants and the gendered dimension of the war is the nature of historical memory. The way in which male fighters present the liberation war during interviews, both then and now, makes it very difficult to recover the voices of the women combatants. Men reside at the core of male narratives of the liberation war. Most of the names cited in the histories and other sources are men's names. The story of Malan Sanha, who is also known as Malam Bacai Sanha, became president of Guinea-Bissau in 2009–12, is a good example of how males excluded women combatants in the general narrative of the war. Mario Cissokho recalled how a male Balanta came up with the idea of using women as weapons transporters as the Portuguese army reinforced controls and patrols in the south region. According to Cissokho, Malan Sanha, in his Balanta traditional dress, under which he kept a gun, led a large group of women who carried baskets full of weapons and munitions on their heads. Portuguese soldiers arrested the women weapon transporters at the Gebu military checkpoint in the corridor of Guiledje, and Malan Sanha was forced to intervene.[117] He shot the Portuguese soldiers. This occurred in August 1962, and his action represented the first direct military attack against the Portuguese army.[118] The traditional story emphasizes the role played by Malan Sanha, and most of interviewees remember Malan Sanha's name. But no one remembers even one of the names of the women. Mario Cissokho simply refers to them as "a large group." Another Balanta male, Gaitano Barboza, who was a PAIGC member since 1959, claims there were between thirty and fifty women in this encounter.[119] Further complicating the story, rumors circulate of Nino Vieira; another PAIGC mobilizer, dressing as a woman in villages during mobilization and fighting to avoid and escape detection by the Portuguese.

As in most histories of liberation wars, the official narrative of the Guinea Bissau liberation war has focused on painting the leaders and combatants of the PAIGC as heroes. The party wanted to present the liberation war as the most politically and socially enlightening and positive period of the history of the new country. In this manner, the narrative focused on general aspects of the struggle and on its martyred fighters. The most important aspect of the official narrative is that it has been written by the party and by conservative men. The consequence was that women were left out.

Biases Implications

"Where are the missing women?"[120] Lerner argued that women were underrepresented or forgotten in the reconstruction of social history.[121] This remains the case. Male authors produce most studies, and they often use the term "people" as a metonym for both women and men.[122]

"The view of women's roles in war vis à vis their perceived natural roles in the domestic sphere has dominated the perception, assumptions and stereotypes of women in war."[123] The war discourses have failed to mention women's wartime roles because of the sociocultural structures that isolated women.[124] Even though the reality of the terrain has shown that war was less gendered, popular beliefs and the academic world would have us believe the contrary.[125] Since the 1970s and 1980s, the previous analytical distances between gender and war have become of increasing interest to academia through the usage of gender-sensitive lenses. Most of the interest focused on Western women and Eurocentric points of view.[126]

It was later, during the late 1970s and 1980s that more and more books on African women and war started to come out.[127] Studies of the Namibian war by Tessa Cleaver and Marion Wallace, of the Mozambican war by Stephanie Urdang, and Frantz Fanon's essay on Algerian women are early analyses of gendered war and anti-colonial struggle.[128] Since then, many books have come out on African wars and the roles of women in them.[129] The women of Mozambique played an active role in the anti-colonial struggle against Portugal as early as 1964 by joining the Front for the Liberation of Mozambique (FRELIMO). At first, they were barred from guerilla training, but they fought for the right to participate in combat operations.

By 1973, the FRELIMO had a women's detachment, allowing women to participate actively in the struggle and allowed the creation of the women's organization.[130] In Algeria, the contribution made by women to Algerian independence has been praised by the men who assumed power since 1962.[131] In 1981, the new Zimbabwe African national Union (ZANU) government of Zimbabwe nominated Mrs. Teurai Ropa Nhongo, a former key guerilla leader, as Minister of Women's Affairs.[132]

Stéphanie Urdang, the sole author who has focused directly or in depth on the women of Guinea Bissau, studied the mobilization of women in Guinea Bissau's liberation war, but narrowed her examination. She argued that the issue of women's emancipation was an integral component of the PAIGC's creation of a new society during and after liberation from the Portuguese. She argues since 1959/60 the PAIGC's political education program included raising the consciousness of both women and men about the oppression of women and the need to fight against it.[133] In 1961, the PAIGC created the

UDEMU and decreed in 1964 that two members of the village councils in liberated zones must be women. In this way, women were included in the political leadership at a grassroots level.[134] Each member of the village council was charged with specific tasks, and women members dealt directly with guerilla forces' food supply and collecting rice. The PAIGC paved the way for increased social freedom for women by singling out traditional customs felt to be most detrimental and oppressive to women such as polygyny and imposing the civil recognition of children born outside of traditional or civil marriages. To Urdang, the party decided also to eradicate forced marriage and polygyny, and it allowed women to divorce their husbands in the liberated zones. What the party did not anticipate was the way Balanta women could refuse, and deny their husbands.[135] In Urdang's view, women took over the female emancipation agenda as their own from the very beginning of their mobilization. One of the measures of the success of such a struggle is whether women were able to engage in what was traditionally "men's work." Her response was that the opposition to ideas of female emancipation was still strong, but important gains had been made.

However, Urdang left out important points of the story. First, she did not consider the PAIGC's refusal to allow women as members during the period from 1956 to 1959. Urdang argues that the PAIGC had the women's emancipation in mind from its earliest stages. But in fact, the party only adopted the women's agenda after 1959. Third, Urdang did not critique the collective memory and official narrative of liberation for gendered aspects of ideology and social discrimination. These issues need closer examination.

The New Approach and Methodology

The research methods I employed include conducting oral interviews with liberation war participants in Guinea Bissau and collecting archival data (war notes, correspondence, pictures, and official documents in the hands of private citizens). There are several reasons for the use of interviews as the primary means of gathering information. First, since the liberation war lasted from 1963 to 1974, many war participants are still alive in Guinea Bissau. The war participants and combatants represent important sources of primary data, and interviews provide a way to record and save these personal and collective wartime memories. A second reason for conducting interviews was that the Portuguese colonial administration and later the Guinea Bissau post-independence administration did not efficiently collect prewar documentation or colonial administration data. Most of the few archival documents related to the Guinea Bissau colonial period have been moved to Cabo Verde or Portugal by the colonial administration or are in the personal collections of Bissau Guineans. The few places where it was possible to find archival evidence included the PAIGC headquarters and the University of Bissau; now called Amilcar Cabral University. However, both locations were destroyed or heavily damaged during the 1998–9 civil wars. In the process of conducting interviews with the ninety-six combatants (men and women) and persons who witnessed the war, I occasionally came across 1,032 written/photograph evidence pages such as correspondence, notes, pictures, and official documents.

My first interviewees were female former combatants and political activists, followed by male former combatants and political activists, and finally witnesses of military-socio-political activities from the 1950s to the 1980s. I chose the female former fighters as primary interviewees, first of all because they were the missing link of the official narrative of the war, and second, because I wanted to avoid falling into the general historiographical pattern in which, in my view, nationalism, charismatic leadership, and Marxism were exclusively placed at the center of the analysis.[136]

The female interviewees responded to questions related to their interactions with their male counterparts during and after the war, how they viewed their relationships in the social, political, and economic context of the war and in the construction of the new Bissau Guinean societies, how they saw themselves in the war space, and what their specific roles were from their own point of view. Another point of interest was how they viewed their roles in the success of the war.

The second group of interviewees were male combatants. The types of questions I asked them were mostly driven by my interviews with female combatants, but I also sought to learn how they viewed female combatants' participation in the war, including how women's participation contributed to the success of the war.

The third group of interviewees consisted of participants in and witnesses of the war and the period prior to the war. These individuals had interesting information that helped shape my questions or guide my follow-up questions to the liberation war participants. They were also a major asset with regard to identifying whom I should talk to, based on their points of view and their understanding of the struggle.

To complete this work, I visited Guinea Bissau several times for periods lasting for months between 2008 and 2017. These trips allowed me to gather valuable information. During the research trips, Bissau, as the capital city, was my port of entry. Bissau is also where the PAIGC headquarters is located and where most government officials, administration workers, union labor representatives, and parliamentarians live. Another reason for visiting Bissau first was related to the fact that on August 3, 1959, a massacre of between fifty and fifty-nine dockworkers there during a union protest played a pivotal role in the PAIGC's decision to launch an armed struggle for independence.[137] Joao Emilio, a dock worker since 1949, recalls how on August 3, 1959, he and 500 other men gathered at Pijiguiti for a strike. He affirms that at 4:30 pm, several trucks of armed police arrived. "Then hell broke ... I don't know how long this had lasted when a PIDE inspector named Emmanuel Correia arrived and ordered the firing to stop."[138] Under the Portuguese, violence and arrests had been part of life Bissau Guineans and the Cabo Verde islanders since the early 1950s. The Portuguese colonial police (PIDE or Policia Internacional e de Defesa Do Estado) killed and arrested many political activists during the months following the Pijiguiti massacre.[139] Several hundred were deported to concentration camps on the island of Galinhas for people from Guinea Bissau and Tarrafal for Cabo Verdeans.[140] For example, the police arrested and transferred several pro-Portuguese activists to the prison of Caxias, near Lisbon, including Augusto Silva, a lawyer and anti-nationalist, and Severino de Pina, an important businessperson and general secretary of the Municipality of Bissau.[141]

The border regions (south with Guinea and north with Senegal) were the next most important places to gather information. In the southern region, I visited Boé, where the first military attacks took place and where the first village councils were established, and the Nucleo Museologico in Guiledje and Cassacá, the site of the first party Congress in 1964. In the northern border of Guinea Bissau (the frontier with Senegal), I visited Cacheu, the former

Portuguese capital of Guinea Bissau. In this region, Guinea Bissau nationalists, with the Senegalese government's permission, from 1967 onwards conducted military attacks against the Portuguese army stationed in Farim and Cacheu.[142]

For a deeper understanding of the continued exclusion of women or as often, their presentation as victims in the historiography of the Bissau Guinean liberation war, and by Bissau Guinean male fighters, it is important for us to reassess the impact of the women in the national liberation movement. A gender-sensitive lens and the concept of "exclusion" are useful theoretical tools for highlighting the roles of women in contemporary discourses about the war.[143] These two theoretical conceptualizations will allow us to move away from the general historical narratives based on abstract theorization and charismatic leadership. This will provide a discourse that goes beyond one-sided oppositional thinking and will contribute five major changes to the historiography of the war in Guinea Bissau.

The first result of this approach is the recognition that women participated because they needed to take care of their families and communities rather than simply for national reasons. Hence, participation in war need not be ideological. The needs of households became more and more difficult to satisfy because of Portuguese taxation and exploitation. For Francisca Pereira, one of the only female members of the PAIGC between 1959 and 1961, women were more concerned with concrete Portuguese exactions and forced labor than with abstract ideologies.[144] The first women to join the organization were members of the anti-Portuguese colonial resistance, immigrants living in Conakry, and the wives of the early PAIGC members who moved to Conakry after being forced to leave Bissau. They joined their husbands in Conakry or moved to Ziguinchor (Sénégal) because of police persecution.[145] One of these early women members was Francisca Pereira. She was a seventeen-year-old Bissau Guinean student living in Conakry without any political affiliation or awareness, but she later became a major figure in the PAIGC diplomatic strategy during the war and one of the leaders of the party and the postwar government. Francisca told me, "The first women to join the party were the daughters of exile."[146] The daughters of the exiled joined the organization with the primary goal of returning home and resuming a peaceful life.

Second, this approach will demonstrate that women participated in every aspect of the war, even though they faced some restrictions and challenges. Women went far beyond the social roles assigned to them by men. They not only participated in combat operations, they also participated in placing land and maritime mines, as well as in espionage activities such as Teresa NQuamé, a Balanta woman who joined the PAIGC in 1963. The PAIGC trained her as a "*sapadura*," someone who set mines in water and on land to destroy Portuguese naval embarkations, bridges, and roads. After training in PAIGC's facilities around Boé, the PAIGC military commanders sent her to the northern front. NQuamé affirmed that she was not the only woman who specialized in mine setting in the north region. Two other women in the groups of men specialized in those tasks.[147]

Joanita Da Silva Rosa, a Cabo Verdean woman, was born in 1934 in Bissau and married Eusebio da Costa Ribero, an early PAIGC member. She joined the PAIGC in 1961, after the arrest of her husband for political activism. Joanita was arrested the same year she became a PAIGC member, while she was pregnant. She spent eighteen days in prison, four of them without eating because of harsh questioning tactics. After her release, she decided to join her husband in Conakry. After military and political training, she was sent to the southern front. In 1966, she participated with her friend Kanhinan NTunqué in combat operations under the command of Malan Sanha. She was shot and as a result lost her right eye; her friend was killed in the same battle. Her husband also died during the war as a guerilla fighter.[148]

Third, the PAIGC's inconsistency about women's roles in the war is one of several reasons why women's roles and participation have been undermined or overlooked. Instead of viewing women who participated in direct combat operations as freedom fighters who were doing their share of the struggle, male fighters and party-political mobilizers tended to picture these women as exceptional, as heroines. By contrast, male fighters were pictured as regular people who were doing their jobs by contributing to the country's liberation. The women combatants who were in the bases and militias worked as guards, cooks, logistic transporters, and nurses, but were simply regarded as subaltern participants because their tasks were mostly related to housework. The best example is the heroization of Titina Silla or her portrayal as super woman in the general Bissau Guinean culture.

Fourth, women's social and political emancipation, as Stephanie Urdang presents it, did not succeed for two central reasons. The idea of emancipating women arrived from outside of the female group of revolutionaries, because it was the PAIGC leadership who initiated it.[149] However, within the party leadership, the discourses about the issues were hesitant and inconsistent, and various factions were not working at the same speed to tackle the matter. Additionally, the women in the party and in exile in Conakry accepted the idea of female social and political emancipation but were not able to translate the concept in a theoretical manner with a mobilizing discourse. They were more interested in liberating the country and having a better life than challenging the sociocultural organization of Bissau Guinean society.

Structure of the Book

Women of the Portuguese Guinea Liberation War consists of several chapters.

Chapter 1, entitled "Colonial Policy and Women in Portuguese Guinea, 1938–1962," explores the implications of colonialism in the shaping and reshaping of gender roles. First, I describe gender roles in the pre-colonial period (in the Fula, Balanta, Biafada, Bijagós, Felupe, Mankañe, Majaku, Mandinga, Nalu, Papel, and Creole communities) and then explores the colonial state's capacity to reshape gender roles. Some scholars view the Fula as a semi-feudal or feudal community (Havik, 2004). On the other hand, the Balanta are often identified as "stateless" (Havik, 2004; Handem, 1986; Nafafe, 2007). Between these two extremes, there are other intermediary ethnic group formation dynamics. Colonial policies and practices focused on only one segment of colonized society while colonial structures constructed men as interlocutors. Then, I examine the reasons behind this colonial choice. Was the choice made consciously because most colonial officers were men? Or was the choice made unconsciously? Could it also be that the structure of Portuguese society at home treated women as subalterns? Isn't it possible that the colonizers, intentionally or blindly, were trying to recreate in the colonial society the same male-dominant social structures that they lived with at home? By empowering men as heads of households and as direct interlocutors of the colonial administration, the colonial system presented women as subalterns or second-class citizens, with major implications for colonial social and political organization. For example, in Guinea Bissau, women had to wait until 1959 before being accepted as members of political parties, even though they were already accepted in sociocultural organizations (Urdang, 1979).

Chapter 2, entitled "Female Combatants and Portuguese Guinea National liberation war narratives: Do they tell the whole story?," examines participation and mobilization in the liberation wars. Using Fulani, Ouolof, French, Bissau Guinean Creole, Portuguese, and French as it depended on who I was interviewing, I ask what constitutes participation and mobilization. In what ways and for what reasons were both sexes mobilized? Listening to women's voices reveals that women participated for reasons of choice and survival. I argue that in Guinea Bissau's women mobilized and participated primarily for reasons that can best be understood in the context of micro historical processes linked directly to their daily social and economic lives. While men are often portrayed as participating for political reasons, women participated and mobilized for reasons linked to their daily lives (Seydi, 2008). Most of the women combatants' narratives have common themes: displacement, family hardship, sexual violence, hunger, and pain. "Official" narratives obscure these personal complexities by highlighting the romance of liberation. Many of these elements resonate in the representation of contemporary African conflicts. Contemporary reporting on today's African wars often highlights these same themes: sexual harassment and violence, displacement, family dislocation, hunger, and pain.

Chapter 3, entitled "Female Combatants and Portuguese Guinea National Liberation War Narratives," explores the creation of narratives of liberation. I describe how "official" narratives of liberation wars are invested in sustaining the prevailing view of a correlation between war and manhood and the charismatic leadership of male political agents as warriors. I argue that these views contribute to the misrepresentation of women fighters and their roles. A further consequence of these views is what I call the women's self-paradox agenda. I demonstrate, that in their own narratives, female fighters tended to minimize their roles in the liberation wars and refuse to view or highlight the importance of their participation. I subsequently examine the ways in which women combatants or freedom fighters portray themselves and their roles in the liberation wars. I interpret elements of these narratives as a self-paradox agenda, insofar as the women fighters acknowledge their roles (as freedom fighters, weapon transporters, spies, militia members, and more) but frequently downplay the importance of their participation and highlight the contribution of male leaders and male combatants. Finally, I demonstrate that the downplaying of Guinea-Bissau women's roles has its origins in perceptions of the gendered nature of the household and the belief that war zones are male spaces. Another important argument in this chapter is that women's narratives reveal war zones and military tasks to be highly gendered. Female combatants frequently recount how they were often advised to remain behind the frontlines, focus on "domestic tasks," and leave the direct fighting to male combatants.

Chapter 4, entitled "Gendering War Space and Heroization of Female Fighters," argues that participation, mobilization, war zones, tasks, and narratives are gendered. Even though women underwent military training, they were generally discouraged from participating in military direct combat operations. For example, exceptional women who participated in military operations, such as Titina Silla, are presented as heroines. But in the diplomatic sphere, individuals such as Francisca Pereira are portrayed as having a more figurative than effective role. While the official records of the war portray women as medics, as political organizers in liberated zones, and as weapons transporters, cooks, and teachers in war zones the micro-history of the liberation war situates them not as subaltern actors but offers a very different explanation. Finally, I explain that although gender equality was never a major objective of women combatants in Guinea Bissau, women combatants played major roles in the success of the liberation war. The micro-narratives of women combatants reveal the similarity between historical liberation wars and contemporary African conflicts.

Chapter 5, entitled "Gender Roles and the First Republic," argues that while the Guinea Bissau revolution was motivated by a desire to change the political structure imposed by the Portuguese, the freedom fighters were never able to change the structures of inequality and marginalization of certain groups. Amilcar Cabral, like most revolutionary leaders, understood that changes must be both political and social, but most of his followers were not interested in changing the social dynamics of the country. What Amilcar Cabral's followers did instead was to develop new economic and social classes within the Bissau Guinean society, in which Cabo Verdean background and education were prioritized. This ultimately led to the 1980 military coup under the leadership of a Balanta and former south front commander during the liberation war, Nino Vieira.

1

Colonial Policies and Women in Portuguese Guinea, 1938–62

Throughout the pre-colonial and colonial periods, Bissau Guinean communities experienced gender bias, which had its origin in the Bissau Guinean patriarchy and colonial systems, in which male dominant groups relegated women to second-class participation in decision-making.[1] Philip Havik mentions women being viewed mainly as mothers and wives in early Portuguese Guinea.[2] These pre-colonial and colonial behaviors were reproduced by most of the Bissau Guinean nationalists during the twentieth-century struggle for independence. For example, according to Idahosa, "Among the Balantas [in comparison to Fula and Muslim women], the oppression of women was less, despite relatively earlier marriages, polygyny and patrilineal descent, because women were allowed to keep what they produced [agriculturally or economically]."[3]

During the struggle for independence, in most cases, African men reproduced masculine dominance. From 1938 to 1959, all the Guinea Bissau nationalist movements eliminated women from their political structures and focused on issues related to nationalism and ethnicity, until the political realities proved to them the importance women have in a national liberation movement. From that period onward, the acceptance of women as political members and fighters became an object of discussion between pro-women individuals, such as Amilcar Cabral, and those in favor of maintaining the traditional gender-biased structure, such as Luis Cabral and Umaro Djalo, based on Carmen Pereira's statement during one of our conversations.[4]

Amilcar Cabral, like most of the revolutionary leaders of the twentieth century, believed that political and social emancipation must proceed together in order to really liberate colonized societies, but he faced strong opposition from male fighters and other political leaders within his organization when the time came to actually implement women's emancipation. The fundamental point of this chapter is that in colonial times, Bissau Guinean men relegated women to second-class status in the social and cultural sphere.

The state that is today Guinea-Bissau was preceded by a complex history of indigenous empires and more broadly based political kinship and gender-based societal structures.[5] Before the European arrival on the West African coast, most of the political structures of the local societies remained under the control of African chiefs.[6] It is clear that many pre-colonial societies manifested both strong centralized and decentralized political organizations and a powerful commitment to local and territorial autonomy.[7]

Women in Pre-Colonial Guinea Bissau

There were many diverse ethnic and sociopolitical groups during the pre-colonial period; the largest among them were the Fula (or Fulani); 28.5 percent, the Balanta; 22.5 percent, the Mandinka; 14.7 percent, the Papel; 9.1 percent, the Manjaca; 8.3 percent, the Beafada; 3.5 percent, Mancanha; 3.1 percent, the Bijagos; 2.1 percent, the Felupe; 1.7 percent, the Mansoanca; 1.4 percent; the Balanta Mané; 1 percent, the Nalu; 0.9 percent, the Saracule; 0.5 percent, the Sosso; 0.4 percent to name few.[8] The Balanta were among the earliest settlers of the lands of Guinea Bissau.[9] They were among groups of settlers who moved into what is called now Guinea-Bissau during the thirteenth century.[10] The Balantas are composed of a number of subgroups that nowadays populate the Guinea-Bissau littoral from the Casamance to the Tombali region in South Guinea-Bissau. They are "credited with being among the original inhabitants of the region, oral sources refer to the Balanta, Djola, the Bañun, Biafada and Nalñu as being present in the region before the time of the Mandé invasions in the thirteenth century."[11]

Early Balanta communities were decentralized and "male elders held power, but regionally and within communities this power was not concentrated in a single household or ruling class."[12] They were known or described as a "stateless society," living in villages based upon egalitarian structure. Among them, rice cultivation labor was "genderly divided."[13] Balantas did not isolate themselves but maintained gendered commercial relations with surrounding groups and settlements. Later, they became voluntarily involved with or were employed by Atlantic trader-settlers before being forced in large numbers to migrate throughout the Lower Casamance region during the nineteenth century. Their roles in the growing export crop economy did not go unnoticed by Portuguese governors. By the late 1770s and early 1880s, the Balantas had transitioned to latex production and become major sources of labor for the Portuguese administration.[14]

In hierarchical and Islamized communities, such as the Fula or Fulani, during the colonial period, the roles and positions of women could shift but within community rules.[15] Elderly men, as household decision-makers before the seventeenth century, shifted strategies in order to maintain power over women and to withstand the effects of Atlantic trade in the region. Because of the Atlantic slave trade, Balanta women were assigned the task of rice trading in the Guinea-Bissau area, while youths had to stay in their villages.[16] They transformed the institution of marriage and created a council of elders to serve as local decision-making bodies for the survival of their communities. The goal of this new institution of marriage was to link or unite people within *tabanças* (villages) and link *tabanças* at a regional level.[17] In the period of the Atlantic slave trade, "marriage served to cement bonds of trust between neighboring *tabanças*. Those that were tied together through marriage aided one another in conflicts with people from outside the immediate area."[18] The restructuring of the age grades was a way to organize youth and women for labor-intensive projects.[19] To keep control over young men, *b'alante b'ndang* (elders) worked with outsiders through women. They relied on women to carry out exchanges with outsiders.[20] These women played different functions such as rice traders, intermediaries, communicators, facilitators, adjudicators, and other roles.

Women were thereby able to exploit opportunities made available through contacts with Cabo Verdean, Portuguese, and Luso-African merchants to develop familial and personal wealth. Women's mobility and ability to accumulate capital increased, but women also found themselves in the unique position of acting as intermediaries between African and European traders.[21] The result of this new situation was personal economic and social advancement for women.[22] As Balanta women were in the best position to establish contacts with merchants, they sometimes married regional merchants. In this way, they provided lasting ties to merchants who could provide imports and might strengthen the position of *b'alante b'ndang*. *B'alante b'ndang* subsequently lost some control over women because "whatever wealth Balanta women accumulated was their own, not controlled by their husbands, but held separately, so much so that nephews and other relatives inherited it."[23]

Recognizing the importance of Balanta women in the economic system, the Portuguese governor enacted legislation aimed to protect those traders beyond the fortified towns in the 1840s.[24] In this process, Balanta women moved from a household mode of production to participating as traders in their own right in mercantile networks, as they had since the fifteenth and sixteenth centuries. They simultaneously transcended the traditional bonds of ethnicity, kinship, and age by creating mercantile networks through new forms of conjugal relationships in marriage outside of their own kin.[25] The Bijagos, also, have gotten a lot of attention for having queen mothers and have been described as matriarchal society.

During the seventeenth century, communities in Guinea Bissau and Cabo Verde served as connectors between African interiors and the Atlantic coastal areas. These Bissau Guinean and Cabo Verdean communities, composed of Christianized Africans, also operated entrepots that were frequented by trans-Atlantic shipping equipages. The development of these settlements created new opportunities for African women by allowing them to engage in cross-cultural trade and providing them a broad range of services associated with navigation, trade and crafts, health care, and subsistence networks.[26] "By the 17th Century they were well established brokers and traders in their own right."[27] These women traders were present in Guinea Bissau during the seventeenth century, as attested in Portuguese documents, and they were aware of their political, economic and cultural influence.[28]

> [Women were] viewed with increasing suspicion by authorities in Lisbon and Cabo Verde, some women well connected with surrounding societies were singled out as culprits of Portugal's loss of influence in the region. These so-called *tungumá* controlled and brokered trade and care networks skillfully exploring the various ties that existed between settlement and rural communities .... The persecution by church and state of these women in the Guinea Bissau region, albeit unintentionally, served to highlight their dynamic agency in a region of great commercial importance. These case

study also document the emergence of mercantile clans or *gan* as core elements in trade settlement, their influence over cultural political and economic domains, and women's crucial role in their organization.[29]

A shift in gender relations occurred during the nineteenth century, because of the introduction of export crops in Guinea Bissau. The gradual demise of the slave trade during the nineteenth century provoked reorganization of commercial patterns in West Africa. Local entrepreneurs were forced to seek alternatives by producing rice and maize. As a result, the need for land and labor made women's cross-cultural brokerage a valuable asset.[30]

> Partnership between African women and (mostly) Creole men with Cabo Verdean connections functioned as pivots. From far being confined to settlement perimeters these alliances permitted the actors involved to progressively penetrate the interior … These developments contrasted with the simultaneous decline of the *signares* in French settlements such as St Louis and Gorée whose room for manoeuvre was gradually limited by increasingly powerful French administration and French commerce.[31]

The nineteenth-century situation would continue to consolidate the advantaged position of Bissau Guinean women, who skillfully explored their unique position in the Afro-Atlantic conjuncture.[32] First, the development of plantation or agricultural factories showed the important role of women traders, especially with the introduction of groundnuts in the Senegambia region in the 1820s. Second, as most African communities on the mainland were resisting colonial occupations, the colonization process or colonial domination created another opportunity for women from the Bissau Guinean islands. Women in their own right entered into partnerships with outsider trader-officials to expand groundnut cultivation on the islands by negotiating arable land, and

> Acting independently from their trader partners, they headed their households, controlled large numbers of slaves and founded their own lineages in settlements. These *naras* [women traders from Afro-Atlantic settlements] were personalities of such magnitude that they were regularly referenced in Official Portuguese sources as a model for peaceful mediation by means of which territorial claims were reinforced. The attention paid to the impressive careers of a few stands in sharp contrast to the majority of anonymous free women from settlements.[33]

The women would have to re-adapt to the new conditions of colonial occupation and gender relations during the twentieth century. Between the 1880s and 1915, inter-ethnic conflicts, tension between African and Portuguese authorities, and an overall downturn in the regional and Atlantic economy led to the collapse of the export economy.[34]

Consequently, the positions of women within these trading networks were greatly affected. The developments of colonial policies contributed to the decline of influence of Bissau Guinean women in settlements. "In the meantime, legislation based on racialist and patriarchal preconceptions cast suspicion upon cross-cultural ties and limited the social mobility of local actors in general, and above all of women."[35] The events that occurred during the nineteenth and twentieth centuries eroded the base for women's participation in the political arena, and limiting their economic options.

> The fact that men from settlements were increasingly absorbed into wage labour and rapidly expanding colonial departments altered the gendered division of labour and circumscribed women's margin for manoeuvre. Portuguese legislation, imbued with patriarchal and racial precepts introduced by the new administration now independent from Cabo Verde, would anchor this shift into legislation. Although the ineptitude of government delayed their implementation, women's dependence on men, whether husbands, fathers or brothers, gradually increased, also with regard to accessing basic services and the exercise of their civil rights. Pushed into petty trade and domestic employment, their opportunities for income generation diminished.[36]

Colonial Administration and Gendered Roles

Major changes took place in the economic, social, and political organization of sub-Saharan Africa during the nineteenth century. By empowering men as heads of households and interlocutors in decentralized communities where African women formerly had participated in political and socioeconomic decision-making, the colonial system treated women as subalterns. The introduction of a cash crop economy, involving rice, peanut, cashew, cotton, palm oil, and others, and the imposition of colonial policies had an enormous impact on domestic relationships, in particular on the relationships between men and women.³⁷ The changes in gender relations in colonial Africa generally resulted in a decline in the social and economic positions for women relative to men. The increasingly disadvantaged position of women is partly reflected in statistics on mortality, unemployment, and illiteracy.³⁸ As African men received some kind of educational training or education that allowed them entry into colonial administrative departments, male conditions were better than African female conditions.

Portuguese Guinea was a small territory of around 36,000 km² and 500,000 inhabitants. The main ethnic groups were Fulas, Mandinka, Manjacas, and Balantas. The Balantas, essentially, were rice growers, the Fulas and Mandinkas dry rice and groundnut producers, and the Manjacas were rice producers. The four groups constituted 85 percent of the population, with two groups, Fulas and Balantas holding two-thirds of all land between them.³⁹ These groups were related to those in adjacent French-speaking countries, as the boundaries between them were at that time arbitrary.⁴⁰ Portuguese Guinea was administratively and politically neglected by Portugal, which failed to promote economic and social development, as it neglected all its African colonies (Angola, Mozambique, and Guinea-Bissau) during the nineteenth and twentieth centuries.

In Fula communities, women had no rights, and polygyny was a highly respected institution, according to Amilcar Cabral.⁴¹ The Portuguese used local chieftainship to consolidate Portuguese power in the northern and eastern sides of Guinea Bissau. For example, the Portuguese gave the Fula a large measure of local privilege and used their ruling class as an instrument of indirect domination over the decentralized or acephalous communities.⁴² Acephalous or decentralized communities found themselves under the control of one elected or nominated individual by the colonial powers.

The colonial powers became the main factor leading to the weakening of the position of pre-colonial African women who had previously had some or at least a little socioeconomic power, such as the Balanta women. Balanta women lost their economic power as brokers and entrepreneurs in the last quarter of the nineteenth century because of cash crop implementation.⁴³ The introduction of new cash crops in European colonies such as rice, peanuts, cashews, and palm oil changed gender relations and the sexual division of labor. Men benefited the most from these changes, acting as the colonialists' interlocutors and the ones in change of the cash crops' cultivations and trading, while women's burden in subsistence production increased in Guinea Bissau.[44]

The sociocultural structure forced women to work in their husband's fields, while husbands helped wives at their discretion. Women's indirect access to land did not give them the official status of field holders during the colonial period.[45] The consequence of this shift was that the colonial administration tended both to ignore women's rights to the land and to ignore them as partners in negotiations.

Men controlled most of the social political structures, and they transformed their controlling power into laws, policies, and masculine ideology, which gave different opportunities to men and women. In the colonial period, women remained outside the stream of major political and economic development. Colonial officials, coming from a male-centered sociocultural environment in their home country, had an interest in stabilizing domestic relations and strengthening male familial power; they solidified male authority in the home to solidify these aims in society. European colonial administrators also imagined men, solely, and not women, as wage labor. African men were hiring in colonial farms, mines, administrative departments, police and colonial armies.

The stage was thus set to subsidize indigenous men financially through the unequal distribution of state resources to foster male accumulation. Men dominated positions of political authority at the state and familial levels in overwhelming numbers.[46] Colonial state systems directly controlled men within the public sphere and made them actual and potential wage laborers or farmer producers; the state sought to regulate women indirectly through the structure of kinship and male authority. Elders and kin groups, in places where gender equality or neutrality existed, such as in the acephalous communities, insisted on state assistance in keeping women under control and in rural areas. Restricting women's freedom of movement was one of how the state and chiefs sought to control women. This collaboration happened at both the state and familial levels to ensure that men had authority and decision-making power over women.[47] In this manner, they limited the opportunity to understand or analyze the social, economic, and political roles that women had traditionally played in African social systems, recasting women as "by nature" belonging to the "domestic domain," dependent on their husbands or male relatives for representation in extra-familial matters, and unfit to exercise the functions of political authority.[48] Was the liberation of the country tied to the liberation of women?

It is important to consider that, even though colonial systems participated in reinforcing male dominance over women in places where women formerly had certain economic power and freedom during pre-colonial times, colonialism nevertheless provided opportunities for women and younger men to escape from senior male domination.[49] Women sought to take advantage of the opportunities offered by colonial economic systems, but in reaction, African chiefs and colonial officers combined forces in creating state and ideological structures to bring these women back under control.[50] Despite women's intensive participation in production and local economies, their status was consistently lower than men's, and their political contribution was minimal. Fula and Mandinka women faced the most exploitative situation, because their men refused to share any power or decision-making with them.[51]

One must recall that Mandinka women, during the pre-colonial period in Guinea-Bissau, used to play key economic, political, and agricultural roles in the Senegambia area. Mandinka women had their own fields and produced nutritious crops and abundant fruits; in the blacksmith clans they produced pottery.[52] Some Mandinka women exercised royal power.[53] By the early seventeenth century, some Mandinka women were living with Portuguese men.[54] In the Guinea Bissau region, intense economic and cultural exchange between Mandinka and Atlantic traders took place. "Most Bissau traders kept small trade houses there, usually administrated by their female Kriston partners, i.e. *tungama* of Mandinga origin."[55]

After being defeated by the Fula during the nineteenth century, Mandinka people dispersed along the Senegambia region, and eventually they were forced into submission by the Fula. They survived because of their traditional entrepreneurial skills, and their women, who were known for their dyed indigo cotton cloth, continue to exercise their talent in the Senegambia region.[56] Loss of power by Mandinka males made them more resistant to allowing their women any room to thrive during the colonial and postcolonial eras.[57]

If Mandinka males resented their perceived emasculation and loss of power, why did they then block Mandinka's women's opportunities to develop or expand? According to Philip Havik, the Fulas are one of the dominant ethnic groups in Guinea-Bissau. For centuries, the nomadic Fulas had settled among their Mande hosts, paying tribute in the form of soldiers, slaves, and cattle. By the late eighteenth century, tensions had arisen between Islamized Fula and the ruling class of the Kaabu states, which led to armed conflicts in which Kaabu was defeated and replaced by the Fuladu confederation.[58] Fulas experienced major population growth in the nineteenth century; by the middle of the century, they had begun to overshadow the Mandinkas and others in commodities trades such beeswax, hides, ivory, and gold.[59] Mandinka males refused to allow their women to develop economically and socially, because they did not want to lose control over their women. Also, as a centralized patriarchal community, women have been viewed as second-class citizens or subjects and not as independent agents.

Women and Anti-Colonial Organizations, 1938–62

During the nationalist struggle for independence, men maintained the same conception about women until after the 1959 events in Bissau. After 1959, the nationalist political parties realized the importance of women's participation in the liberation struggle, although they were still divided about integrating women's emancipation and social transformation into the independence struggle. It is important to recognize that women were accepted into the party during the early years of the struggle; however, after 1965 they were not allowed to participate in direct combat operations even though they were armed and served on the village defense committees.[60]

For the duration of the struggle, Amilcar Cabral kept reminding his followers of the importance of associating political with social emancipation to create a new egalitarian society. The struggle for political and civil rights for women in Guinea Bissau gained momentum after the formation of the African Party for the independence of Guinea and Cabo Verde (PAIGC).[61] The reason for that is because the PAIGC program action established equality between men and women.[62] The translation of these words into practice would only be possible if the women themselves realized that their emancipation and freedom depended on them and their will to fight the sociocultural and societal inequalities that kept them under the rug.[63]

The Guinean women joined the struggle at its earliest phase of clandestine organization, in 1959–60. Women in Guinea Bissau made valuable progress as they were allowed to participate in the political organizations and people's courts as jury members. Before 1972, women participated in military operations and militias and were an integral part of the military units in the war fronts.[64] Besides defining the emancipation program, the PAIGC created the UDEMU (União Democràtica das Mulheres da Guiné e Cabo Verde/ Democratic Union of the Women of Guinea and Cabo Verde) in 1961, with the main goal of mobilizing women on women's issues.[65]

Later, in 1966, the organization would be dismantled by the PAIGC leadership because of a lack of positive results and reconstructed again after independence.[66] Some keys facts or elements may be overlooked in the analysis of the women's situations during these years. Carmen Pereira was the first woman National Assembly President from 1984 to 1989, and in the Bijagos archipelago, women's spiritual leaders and economic activities are recognized by their male counterparts.[67] Evidence of women's participation in state-building during the post-independence era is somewhat meagre, even though change could be seen within the public sector as some women were recruited as teachers and administrative department workers. Today, women in Guinea-Bissau are still fighting against political instability and poverty.[68] However, the women's conditions must be nuanced because of the existence of many disparities in women's treatments and conditions, disparities mostly based on their socio-cultural or ethnic background. These varieties of treatment date back to the early period of nationalist movements' creations.

Women and Anti-Colonial Organizations, 1938–59

During the 1950s and 1960s, scholars of African nationalist struggles focused primarily on the Western-educated male elites who led the nationalist movements and assumed power after independence. However, in the 1970s, African farmers and workers as agents of historical changes became important subjects of historical inquiry. Later, scholars challenged the idea of having men at the center of historical processes and as the sole agents of African modernization.[69] These revisionist scholars reevaluated the absence of women from labor and nationalist struggles.[70] The incorporation of women's vantage points into analyses of labor and nationalist movements has altered our understanding of the dynamics of these struggles, particularly their premises, organization, and objectives.

We have come to understand, however, that much like their male counterparts, few female participants in nationalist movements were Western-educated Christians influenced by European ideas concerning individual rights and liberties, nor were most even generally aware of other nineteenth-century resistance movements against the colonial system. The vast majority of them had little, if any, formal schooling and virtually no contact with Westerners. As Susan Geiger has demonstrated in the case of Tanganyika, women did not "learn nationalism" from the Western-educated male elites; instead, they brought something that was already present in their trans-ethnic social and cultural organizations.[71] The women in Guinea Bissau did the same when they joined the political parties after 1959 and became extremely important agents for the PAIGC.

From the 1930s to the 1950s, most of the African political parties in the Portuguese colonies were clandestine or labeled "social associations." Under the Portuguese Colonial Act of 1930 and the Native Statute of 1954, officials enforced a legal distinction between the so-called *indigenous* or native Africans and the *Assimilados* (persons who had fully adopted Portuguese language and culture). Only the assimilated were considered citizens and were allowed to exercise the few democratic rights granted to the people of Guinea, such as belonging to social gatherings and organizations.[72] "According to the 1950 official survey, there were 8,320 Assimilados/Civilizados in Guinea Bissau, a mere 1.6 percent of the population."[73]

As a result, many Africans living in Portuguese colonies were not Portuguese citizens and not governed by Portuguese civil law. This also meant they were not granted political rights. Under these conditions, Cabral and the other political activists recognized the importance of developing or creating clandestine political parties. However, according to Carmen Pereira, one of the emblematic figures of the revolution, the reason for the PAIGC not having female members was based on some of the PAIGC Executive bureau male members' belief (during the period 1956–59) that "if you want to keep a secret, you should not tell your secret to a woman because women are talkative."[74] The impractical sexism in this statement justified leaving women out of the revolution and political processes and exemplified conventional Bissau Guinean patriarchal attitudes.

Carmen Pereira jokingly remembers how she found out about the existence of the PAIGC during its clandestine days in Bissau. She remembers that whenever her husband, Cabral, and other men were meeting at their house, her husband made sure she was out of the house. She became suspicious one day after they had finished their meeting, so she started to look around the house to find clues about what was going on. She found documents and a PAIGC flag under the mattress. When she confronted her husband Umaro Djalo, he responded that she should not pursue the issue further and that women should not be aware of political activities because women could not keep secrets.

Cabral and the PAIGC members did not explicitly say they did not want women members, but apparently some of them thought it was wise to exclude them for the sake of the movement. The response of Carmen's husband represented a stereotypical view about women, but it was not a response formulated by the party. It was rather a symptom of a more general societal issue. After the PAIGC relocation to Guinea Conakry in 1959, PAIGC leadership saw the important roles that the women of the newly independent country played within the Sekou Touré's party in terms of mobilization. The Guinean women's roles in Sekou Touré's party were not new. Sekou Touré and the RDA had witnessed women's capacity for mobilization and assistance during their 1953 seventy-day general strike.[75] This gave the PAIGC another reason for integrating women into the party.

In Africa, many early female nationalists in other colonies were Western-educated and influenced by European Enlightenment ideals concerning individual rights and liberties. These women were aware of the nineteenth-century nationalist resistance movements in Europe; however, this was not the case in Guinea Bissau. The percentage of Western-educated women in Portuguese colonies was very low compared to the rest of the continent because the Portuguese did not offer state education to most Bissau Guineans.

In Guinea Bissau, only members of the *Civilizados* or *Assimilados* class had access to state education. The majority of the population, the *Indigenous*, attended the indigenous schools sponsored by the churches. In 1951 and 1952 there were eleven official primary schools with twenty-seven teachers and

735 pupils and one secondary school in Bissau with seventy-eight students for the 1,478 *Assimilados* or *Civilizados*, who represented 0.39 percent of the general population of 502,457. During the same period, missionary education consisted of ten schools with full cycle (935 pupils) and forty-five schools with shorter cycle (1,044 pupils).[76] Statistics show virtually no indigenous African received a secondary education, which was in fact restricted to *Assimilados*. As Lars Rudebeck has pointed out, even Upper Volta (a West African French colony with the lowest record of education expenditures) spent more than twice as much on education as Portuguese Guinea.[77]

In the 1950s, 99.7 percent of the population of Guinea Bissau was considered illiterate (unable to write or speak Portuguese) in general, whereas 45.1 percent of the *Assimilados* were assessed similarly.[78] It is not surprising to realize that most of the early Bissau Guinean nationalists were from the *Assimilados* groups. It is also important to consider that less than 40 percent of the *Civilizados* and *Assimilados* were women. The data reveal that it was almost impossible to find Western-educated women in Guinea Bissau.

Many Bissau Guinean families sent their children and teenagers to Senegal and Guinea to be educated. These families believed giving their children a Western education would allow them to find jobs in the colonial system, given that the colony was importing Western-educated Cabo Verdeans to serve as administrative department agents, postal service workers, clerks, retailers, and lawyers. But education would also give their children opportunities to better understand the world. Some of the most prominent Bissau Guinean students to obtain Western education abroad or in the colony were Francisca Pereira and Carmen Pereira.[79] The sociocultural beliefs among the *Assimilados* made it almost impossible for young girls to obtain higher education. Carmen Pereira recalled that she left school after she finished the primary level because her father, a well-educated Cabo Verdean lawyer, believed that women did not need advanced education, but just knowledge of how to read, how to write, and how to take care of a household.

Regardless of their ethnic group, women lacked political power and real authority in their society at the exception of the Nalu or the Bijagos. As Cabral stated, "It is only rarely that they [women] take an active part in political affairs. In our country, women have almost always been kept out of political affairs."[80] Cabral does not single out any individual women, but rather refers to them as a group. One might claim that this essentialization of women, despite being rooted in social practice, is a stereotype. After the 1959 massacre, Bissau Guinean political activists faced new challenges that moved them slowly toward consciousness of the roles that women could play in the political movement.[81]

Women and the PAIGC, 1959–62

After 1959, Nationalist Bissau Guineans moved to Dakar and Conakry for security purposes, as the party leaders were targeted by the colonial police, PIDE. The PAIGC realized that the dream of organizing workers and urban nationalists had ended with the massacre of fifty-nine dockworkers in Bissau.[82] From this point on, the PAIGC leadership became increasingly conscious of women's roles and their participation in the resistance, contrary to what some scholars believe.

According to Stéphanie Urdang, the ideology of the PAIGC integrated the emancipation of women into the total revolution, emphasizing the need for women to play an equal political, economic, and social role in both the armed struggle and the construction of the new society. She asserts that the PAIGC understood that the liberation struggle needed to be waged by women as well as by men.[83] But she points to several reasons why it was very difficult for the PAIGC to have women as pioneers among the mobilizers and members, most importantly the issue of women's lack of personal freedom, in that they had virtually no economic and social mobility or agency. For example, farmers would be more receptive to a male foreigner coming into their village than to a foreign woman.[84] However, I believe the early refusal to recruit women involved more concrete ideological and social concerns, as was explained by Carmen Pereira.

My conception of why the PAIGC changed its policy toward women differs from Urdang's argument. Urdang underestimated the attitudes against women by the PAIGC leadership and misunderstood how men came to reverse their opinions as circumstances changed. The key elements in this change of behavior toward women came with the relocation of the Portuguese Guinea political parties. Because of colonial police harassments and imprisonments, Portuguese Guinean political parties relocated to Dakar and Conakry, where the party witnessed the important roles, women played in the nationalist movements of neighboring countries. In addition, they encountered small groups of exiled Bissau Guinean women who were involved in the smaller nationalist and liberation movements based in Conakry. In the French colonies, women's participation in political mobilization was not something new, especially in Guinea Conakry, the new home of the PAIGC.

Since the pre-Second World War period, under the leadership of Lamine Gueye, the Senegalese contingent of the French Section of the International Workers Organization, affiliated with the French Socialist Party *(Section Française de l'Internationale Ouvriére (SFIO))*, championed women's emancipation in the colonies, in recognition of women's support for Gueye's political career.[85] The Brazzaville Conference followed the creation of the Senegalese contingent of the SFIO in January of 1944. During that conference, delegates insisted on the need to protect and implement women's rights, condemn polygyny and the practice of marrying child brides, and recognized women's roles in resistance movements. They also made a proposal for equal rights for women in colonial society, a proposal that led to granting women the right to vote for the first time in metropolitan elections in 1945.[86]

In 1945, Fily Dabo Sissoko, a French Sudanese leader of the French-Soviet Union Association/French West Africa section *(Association France-URSS/ Section de L'AOF)*, mirroring changes in France, reiterated the same appeal for the emancipation of women.[87] In West African French colonies, women participated actively in nationalist and political struggles and helped to organize mass protests. For example, in Ivory Coast, on December 21, 1949, a group of women members of the Ivory Coast Democratic Party section of the African Democratic Rassemblement *(Parti Démocratique de Côte D'Ivoire/ Rassemblement Démocratique Africain* [PDCI/RDA]), under the leadership of Madame Ouezzin Coulibaly, organized a demonstration in Grand Bassam protesting the arrest of eight of their political leaders. The French colonial response to these women was brutal. They were beaten and arrested.[88]

Four years later, the French Guinean women showed their aptitude in participating in organized strikes by helping strikers and their families, by providing food, collecting financial donations and mobilization female market workers around the country. This crucial participation inspired the Democratic Party of Guinea/Section of the African Democratic Union *(Party*

Démocratique de Guinée/Rassemblement Démocratique Africain[PDG/RDA]) to mobilize and to recruit women into their party. This move was crucial, because female participants mobilized voters in the coastal areas in 1956.[89] This was a decisive move, and critical to the legislative victory of the PDG/RDA in 1954 and in the referendum in 1958. During the referendum, the population rejected the proposed constitution for the Fifth French Republic and opted for immediate independence.[90] According to Francisca Pereira, the PAIGC, newly relocated in Conakry, witnessed the ability of PDG/RDA women to mobilize the Guinean party and decided to attempt to bring about something similar with the women of Guinea Bissau living in Conakry.[91]

The relocation to Conakry ended some of the colonial state's obstructions and presented the PAIGC with new opportunities and visions. The party was able to develop and mobilize openly without having to deal with the Portuguese police. While dealing with new and more favorable conditions, the party accepted coordination with other organizations that had women members. The PAIGC joined forces with all of the anti-colonial movements and mobilized all the Bissau Guinean and Cabo Verdean immigrants in neighboring countries.[92]

In Conakry, there existed several anti-colonial and sociocultural organizations, such as the Movement for the Liberation of the Portuguese Colonies (*Movimento pela Libertação das Colónias Portuguesas* [MLCP]) and the Bissau Guinean Immigrants in Conakry Association (*Association des Ressortissants de Bissau Guinée Bissau a Conakry*). The MLCP members came from all the African Portuguese colonies (Angola, São Tomé e Princípe, Mozambique, Cabo Verde, and Guinea Bissau). Both political and social organizations had women members and participants.

Cabral and his followers were very sharp in analyzing present situations and reshaping their strategies in the new party regarding female participation. This suggests that the party understood at a very early stage the importance of recognizing and accepting the socioeconomic situation as the party moved to change directions and goals. In 1956, one of the PAIGC's goals was to organize urban workers and challenge colonial authority.

> On the Pijiguiti dock minutes at the port of Bissau, Portugais colonialist agents killed by gun shots in less than thirty minutes, fifty of the strikers and wounded hundreds ... Those dock workers of the Bissau port and

the river boats; in which many were our [parti] members and leaders, by their action and patriotism own a respectful place in our people's history ... This massacre told us, because of the violent and criminal character of the Portugaise colonialists, we should mobilize the people, unite it, organize it and prepare it for the struggle," We have learned because of the deadly weapons of the Portuguese, the only way for us to free the people from the Portuguese domination is through armed struggle."[93]

The PAIGC was formed in 1956 by six Africans from Guinea Bissau and Cape Verde Islands, including Amilcar Cabral, Aristides Pereira and Luis Cabral, now President of the new Republic. Because it was apparent that the Portuguese government which was dictatorial at home would not respond in a friendly way to any political opposition in the colonies, the organization was set up as an underground party. It was quickly extended from the capital city of Bissau to the other towns. It believed that it was possible to fight by peaceful means and with help of some underground trade union organizations it launched strikes protesting labor exploitation by the Portuguese and held demonstrations.[94]

But by 1959, the party realized it was impossible to attain these goals, not only because of Portuguese unwillingness to compromise politically, but also because conflicts of interest brought about discord and tension between the party and the labor unions. The labor unions' goals were to get better pay and working conditions, instead of liberating the country from its oppressors. After studying the political and sociocultural situations, in which the PAIGC saw that its goals were different from the labor unions' goals and being targeted by the colonial system and its PIDE, the party decided to "change gears" by mobilizing the countryside.

Most African intellectuals and higher-ranking political leaders, who formed the core leadership of African nationalist parties, came from the urban lower middle class and very often had little interest in the countryside.[95] After 1959, the PAIGC principal field of struggle became the countryside, and the party found it important to have political leaders who came from the countryside and to have their political education directly linked with local reality, rather than simply with political generalizations. The same process of analyzing and adopting new strategies led the PAIGC to accept women as members after

1959, and the party later developed an agenda that appealed to women and spoke to women's conditions (as will be explored in Chapters 3 and 4).

One of the most important factors in the decision both to incorporate women's participation in the liberation movement and to address topics of concern to women split the party leadership into two groups. For example, Amilcar Cabral genuinely understood that the liberation of the country and significant social change could not happen without liberating women. Several other party leaders, including Sekou Touré of Guinea and Lamine Gueye of Senegal, also accepted the integration of the ideas of liberating women and establishing women's rights as a way to make the party more attractive to women. Their acceptance of women's rights and emancipation was an opportunistic and pragmatic decision. The party subsequently struggled throughout the war and postwar period to develop a clear policy on the question of women's emancipation. As Cabral and the "pro-women" faction within the party structure worked to liberate women, other party leaders were reluctant to change their old attitudes and practices toward women.

One of Amilcar Cabral's fundamental strategies involved explaining to male mobilizers during the struggle why women's agendas must be included and how they must deal with this issue during their meetings with villagers. Cau Sambu, one of the first mobilizers, recalled that men and women did not understand the concept of liberating women from their double oppressions of male power and colonial power. For Carmen, reverberating Urdang's ideas or what she learned after her involvement with the UDEMU, women faced two oppressions or colonialisms: one by the Portuguese and one by men. Cabral had to explain these new ideas to them carefully and told them they needed to accept the new ideas.[96] At the same time, Cabral understood that women themselves must wage the struggle to achieve full emancipation. This led to the creation of the Democratic Union of Women (*União Democràtica das Mulheres da Guiné e Cabo Verde* [UDEMU]) in 1961, a female organization led by Bissau Guinean women living in Conakry and members of the PAIGC.

> When trained members of the PAIGC began the process of mobilizing the peasantry, the question of equal rights for women, of their emancipation and hence their full and equal participation in the struggle was discussed and pressed for. Women quickly responded and now the liberation of women,

while integrated into the overall program of the party, is seen as a struggle which must be essentially waged by women themselves—and it is "In Guinea-Bissau" says Carmen Pereira, vice President of the National Assembly, "we say that women have to fight two colonialisms. One of the Portuguese, the other of men."[97]

What impact would the UDEMU have on the lives of the Bissau Guinean women and in the PAIGC's structure? What help did the women's organization receive from the party? How did Bissau Guinean men respond to the UDEMU and the women's emancipation agenda?

Conclusion

One of the most important aspects of the nationalist movements in Guinea Bissau was that after the 1959 Pijiguiti massacre and the relocation of most of the nationalist organizations to neighboring countries, PAIGC, under the leadership of Amilcar Cabral, represented an exceptional break or discontinuity in the long-term history of Guinea Bissau. The massacre marked an important shift in the movement; the relocation process and the relocation in newly independent Guinea led to the re-examination of gender relation within the PAIGC and the Portuguese colony.

The relocation of the movement was extremely important, as the massacre leads to relocation which leads to reexamination of gender roles and development of a new approach. Then the colonial policy planted the seeds of its own destruction. For the first time, the PAIGC and Amilcar Cabral challenged the gendered social structure in Guinea Bissau and understood that political and social emancipation must go hand in hand. PAIGC members did not have a unified opinion about women's rights. This data challenges and undermines the oversimplified dichotomy between colonial powers and freedom fighters. Within the PAIGC, party members and freedom fighters did not all have the same views about women's rights and social equality between sexes.

Contested views about waging a war for independence and about women's socioeconomic and juridical liberation became major factors during the long liberation war. Amilcar Cabral, like most of the charismatic revolutionary movement leaders, understood that the country's social and political liberation must be waged on two fronts: against the colonial oppressors but also against the sociocultural beliefs that hold women under male dominance and control. However, throughout the revolutionary struggle, some male participants presented a different discourse; they considered the most important issue in the wider sociopolitical struggle to be the country's political liberation. Throughout the liberation war in Guinea Bissau, those two visions squared off, and Amilcar Cabral's view was never totally accepted or realized.[98]

Women combatants' discourses allow us to develop a new understanding of their reasons for participation, one that is far removed from abstract Marxist revolutionary ideas. Instead, women's participation resulted from the daily concrete challenges that women, as principal food providers, faced during the colonial period.[99] Women participated in many different aspects of the war. Even as they carried out the usual domestic household tasks, they also participated in direct combat operations, functioning also as weapon transporters, spies, and nurses, in spite of attempts by some in the PAIGC leadership to prevent or limit their participation. They suffered displacement, and they endured sexual harassment and other significant physical abuse from both sides in the war.

2

Female Work and Participation in the Armed Struggle in Portuguese Guinea

Reasons for Female Participation and Mobilization

While historians and male participants in the Portuguese liberation war focus on anti-colonialism, nationalism, and leadership in their accounts of the war, female participants explain that their reasons for participating were more personal and arose from the daily life struggles they faced because of Portuguese domination and exploitation. The primary reasons for women's involvement in the war were personal and tied to family matters linked to the conflict or related to the harsh conditions imposed by the Portuguese. For instance, Francisca Pereira, who was born on June 12, 1942, in Bolama (the former capital city of Guinea Bissau), was one of the first women to join the PAIGC in 1959 at the age of seventeen. She left her mother in Bissau and followed her uncle in order to continue her education because her mother could not pay her school fees in Bissau. She said she joined the PAIGC because she wanted to go back to Bissau and live with her family, but she believed the only way this could happen was by liberating the country. In her discussion of the struggle, family matters were the centerpieces of her explanation for her decision to join the PAIGC. Francisca's narrative closely resembles other women's narratives. All the women's stories highlight their motives for participating as personal and familial.

There are four major points that must be considered. First, it is informative to consider how historians and Bissau Guinean male combatants portrayed female combatants. From the time of the Guinea Bissau Liberation war to Stephanie Urdang's book *Fighting the Two Colonialisms*, social scientists interested in the Bissau Guinean nationalist movements focused on the big narratives, while male nationalists, with very few exceptions, focused on the notion of freeing their country from the Portuguese colonialists. These academic and local behaviors had major implications, such as dismissing the micro narratives.

Second, one must look at the way that female combatants narrated their war and the reasons for their participations. One of the major findings is that female participation was more closely linked to the deterioration of their daily life as mothers, wives, and food providers than to ideas of independence or nationalism. Third, I will analyze what were the daily life activities of female combatants in war zones, and finally, what were the different tasks performed by female combatants.[1]

Some young women joined the PAIGC and the struggle to escape the restrictions they faced in their societal organizations, such as forced marriage, polygyny, and male or elders' refusal to allow divorce, but in their narratives, they at first emphasized the need to liberate the country or join a family member who was involved in the liberation movement as dixit Carmen Pereira and Fatoumata Diallo. Nevertheless, PAIGC and the liberated zones clearly represented a sanctuary of safety and self-protection for the women who fled their original homes.[2] More frequently, historians and other scholars have focused on how very dangerous such spaces were, or how vulnerable and fraught were the lives of those who moved through or lived in them.

In the case of Fantam Kawsara, the liberated zone was more a safe zone than a space of danger. Fantam Kawsara came originally from the region of Gabu, and at seventeen she was not ready to accept the husband her parents had arranged for her when she was much younger. As preparations for the marriage progressed, she decided to contact the PAIGC and rejoin her brother.[3] She attempted to run away but was discovered; however, a second runaway attempt was successful. Walking through the forest during her escape, she was suddenly surrounded by a group of armed young men. They asked her what she was doing in the forest, and she responded, "I have come to join the party."[4]

Women followed husbands and sons to PAIGC bases and later became fighters after receiving political training or education from the PAIGC male activists. Wives joined husbands in order to lighten the burden of living alone with children and to defend against the constant threat of Portuguese police harassment. Mothers joined sons to make sure they were well nourished, and young women joined the guerilla bases to run away from Portuguese harassment and forced labor. Carmen Pereira recounted that Cabral, her husband, and other PAIGC members left Bissau for Conakry after the Pijiguiti massacre in 1959. Three months later, as she had been left with three children to raise on her own, she decided to join her husband. During those three months, she developed a strategy to leave Bissau with her children without the Portuguese police becoming aware of her decision. Her father, who was a lawyer, requested travel permission for her. As the PIDE or the Portuguese colonial police knew who her husband was, and that he was a PAIGC member, she was not allowed to travel anywhere without police permission or supervision. Families of known PAIGC members were heavily monitored, as a way to either find out about their family members or to see who else may be PAIGC sympathizers in their ranks or environments. First, she was allowed to leave Bissau without her children and was ordered to be back in thirty days with her husband. When she came back, she presented herself to the police station and told the police officers that her husband was very sick and needed to have surgery in Senegal. She requested permission for herself and the children to go to Senegal and assist her husband. She left Bissau for Ziguinchor (the southern region of Senegal), where the PAIGC leadership asked her to stay to set up a passage camp for newly recruited PAIGC members who were on their way to Conakry for military and political training. She agreed to do so to help her husband and his friends, even though she was not yet a member or even interested in fully participating. She later joined the party in 1961.[5]

Like Carmen, Fatoumata Diallo, a Fula woman from the Cacheu region, in her eighties when I interviewed her, joined the PAIGC almost by accident in 1964. Her son, Alpha Dabo, was one of the fighters in the northern and eastern fronts. He and other fighters often used to stop by her house, looking for something to eat or to rest after long marches and fighting. Alpha was a PAIGC sympathizer before he became fully involved in the party in 1962. Fatoumata decided to become fully involved because the Portuguese police pursued her son and others in Cacheu. "He came to me and told me he had to leave in order to avoid being arrested."[6] It was a sad moment because Alpha was her only son. She worried about her son's health and well-being. The PAIGC fighters' visits became rarer as the Portuguese army's presence in the region became heavier. To make sure her son had food, she started taking food to the *maquis* or places where guerilla fighters were stationed on a weekly basis. She walked through the forest for hours to do so. One day she asked herself, "Why not live with them and cook for them and save me from the risk of being arrested by the Portuguese army or police?"[7] So she stayed with them. She had always hated the Portuguese because of their heavy taxes, the requirement of passes to travel, and the forced labor Guineans faced, but she never thought Guineans could fight against them or that Guinea Bissau could be independent one day. She believed God decided for them, and that he might solve the Portuguese problem without Bissau Guineans having to do anything. As she was living with the *maquisards*/freedom fighters/PAIGC combatants and listening to their conversations, she started to have a different view of the situation and became gradually more involved in the party and the independence movement.[8]

Aside from reasons related to family unity, others left their homes because of Portuguese police intimidation and army exactions, such as burning villages and heavy taxes. Teodora Gomes, in her interview with Stéphanie Urdang, recalled that these reasons made her decide to join the PAIGC. Her father had been a PAIGC member since 1962. He had joined the nationalist movement because of heavy taxes and arbitrary bureaucratic fees. For example, the colonial administration charged him 5,000 escudos to replace a lost identity card. The 5,000 escudos would correspond in in 2010 to US$175.00. A brutal incident in 1963 persuaded Teodora to join the cause as well. The Portuguese army rounded up ten well-known people in her town, all supporters of the PAIGC, and executed them in full view of the townspeople. "That day, my whole family decided to join the guerillas, and we went to live in the forest," Teodora remembered.[9] Ule Bioja, a Balanta young woman from the Como Islands, assisted her village, supporting the PAIGC for several years before she joined the party. At age thirteen, she witnessed the Portuguese launching their massive attacks against the Bijagos islanders. "Many people went into the forest, under the protection of the PAIGC, and helped to fight off the 'Tuga' [Portuguese colonialists or Portuguese colonial army]. As the siege wore on, I joined the work in support of the guerillas. I helped the women cook for the guerillas."[10] Sandé NHaga, another Balanta woman, was born in NXeia in the southern region of Guinea Bissau. She joined the rebellion after the Portuguese killed her brother in a location called NTchalé.[11]

Portuguese bombings and imprisonments pushed many people to join the PAIGC. For instance, Ana Maria, Fina Crato, Titina Silla, and others joined the struggle because of Portuguese harassment and aerial bombing of PAIGC sympathizers' villages in the southern region of Guinea Bissau. Fina claimed that the early stage of bombings killed many people in her village. Later, villagers adjusted their lives around the raids, and casualties diminished. They woke up by five o'clock in the morning and by seven o'clock left the village, which was out in the open and highly visible, to hide in the mangrove swamps, where they would remain the whole day, in water up to their waists. The Portuguese then began to bomb the village with napalm before seven.[12]

Most of the women's involvement with the PAIGC resulted not only from the Portuguese imposing harsh conditions, but also from issues related to forced marriages, polygyny, and difficulties in obtaining divorces. Gender inequality continued to be present in contemporary Guinea Bissau because men often resist change, and most women still believe patriarchy is the natural order and that customs must continue to be respected.[13]

My interviews with former participants do not support this as a fundamental motivation. The recurrent themes that came out of many of the PAIGC women's narratives made it obvious that family separation, running away from Portuguese exactions, and seeking physical protection were the primary goals of most women participants and future female combatants. This could be seen also as cultural empowerment. These are the actual material reasons for women's participation in the liberation war.

Women's Roles

When asking to my I interviewees if women were to be found in all fields of work associated with the liberation war, the response was uniformly similar. For example, Eva Gomes responded, "Few women fought in combat."[14] A consistent reply to my question was that the male combatants did not think that arming the women was necessary, and most of the former female combatants I interviewed agreed. I asked about when it might be necessary for women to participate in armed combat. If the goal of the PAIGC was an equal society in every respect, as the party stated in 1961 during the creation of the women's organization within its structure, then how could something be considered necessary for men, but not for women? Or was the idea of an equal society just to make the PAIGC look good in the eyes of international communities such as the United Nations, activist organizations, and independent countries?[15] There were many different responses, but one central idea behind the responses was that Guinea Bissau was too small in demography and geography to enlist many soldiers.

According to Carmen Pereira, from the beginning of the war to the creation of the People's Revolutionary Army (*Forças Armadas Revolutionárias do Povo*, [FARP]) in 1966, women participated in all combat roles.[16] It was only after 1966 that women's involvement in combat operations was ended because Guinea Bissau had more than enough men to respond to the needs of direct combat operations, even though a number of women were already in the army. Interestingly, as reflected in Pereira's response, the PAIGC policy regarding women in combat contrasted sharply with the way in which the Mozambican nationalist and revolutionary group, FRELIMO, handled the issue of women combatants. In 1967 FRELIMO created a detachment of women combatants under the party General Command. Subject to the same training as men, several of them joined male guerillas and participated in direct combat operations.[17] With the creation of the regular army or FARP after 1964, the PAIGC leadership decided not to have women involved in combat operations and assigned them tasks related to security, communication, logistics, and nursing.[18] Indeed, Pereira's comment mirrors an earlier discussion by Amilcar Cabral on the issue. "From now on [1966] there are going to be only fighting men in the bases. The women and girls will go into the villages as nurses or teachers, or they will work in production or in the village militias."[19]

In spite of this statement, women participated in direct combat in large numbers at least until 1967. During the liberation war time, arguments differ as to why the party decided to end women's participation in direct combat. Some refute the party's argument, stating for example, that women could not keep up with the lengthy marching or were not courageous enough to participate in direct combat operations.[20] The decision had several implications, such as reinforcing ideas of inequality between the sexes in the eyes of men and thereby weakening women's struggle for social participation and decision-making equality. However, for Francisca Pereira, the decision not to have women participating in combat did not diminish their role in the struggle. For her, women were involved in all other aspects of the war, such as transporting weapons, spying, cooking, village defense committees, running the agricultural productions and their commercialization, and transporting and caring for wounded fighters.[21]

For Stéphanie Urdang, the PAIGC's decision to end women's combat roles reflected the population decrease after years of guerilla war. The PAIGC leaders wanted to preserve the female population to guarantee a rising birth rate.

> Luisa and her husband, Battista, both of whom were in the [PAIGC] diplomatic field, saw the central issue as the necessity to increase the population. When Cabral had been asked this question, Luisa said, he would stress that they have and extremely small population: "We cannot put women in our army and risk their death, because we want to increase the population when the war ends. We cannot work without people. To develop our country, we need as large a population as possible".[22]

However, this decision reinforced gender inequality and undermined the efforts to liberate women. This masculine ideological narrative sought to subordinate women, and it reinforced existing customs and views about women. Whatever the underlying motivation, the party's decision explicitly emphasized gender differences. Urdang claims that demographic issues guided the decision and explained references to "women as the mothers of the national ideology."

However, in 1972, the PAIGC Executive bureau or leadership reversed its policy and decided to recall female fighters into the battlefield. This decision was made based on its goal to defeat the Portuguese army as quickly as possible.[23] I see this reversal as a sign of struggle within the party regarding women's social and political roles. Some party leaders such as Amilcar Cabral showed strong support for female emancipation agendas from the beginning, while certain party leaders such as Luis Cabral refuted any effort to change the existing gendered social order. The changing positions corresponded to the struggle between feminist and masculinist orders within the PAIGC structure. This meant that the party leadership was struggling within their structure about women's positions and role; sometimes they championed women's equality, whereas at other times they retreated from doing so in the face of custom by not giving practical and full support to female emancipation.[24] During the whole process of the liberation war, the women's liberation discourse was articulated variously within the PAIGC leadership.

For Urdang, Fatimata Sibili's story had heavy consequences in the way in which several PAIGC officers characterized women in combat operations. Fatimata Sibili, a twenty-one-year-old Fula woman from Senta Saré, had been in combat at the age of sixteen as the only woman member of a unit of thirty young men: "During the period of training, both she and her instructor had felt she was equal to her comrades. But this was not the case in actual combat."[25] It was very difficult for Fatima Sibili to keep up with the speed of marching, so her comrades helped carry her heavy equipment. This she ascribed to physical femininity: "I am just not as strong as a man." And she never went into combat again. Urdang concluded that this "account seemed to corroborate what I was told on various occasions, that PAIGC experience had led them [women and men] to conclude that women could not fare as well in combat as the men. I wondered while listening to Fatimata, however, how much her performance could have been affected by attitudes, rather than by her inherent capability."[26]

The 1966–67 PAIGC decision of removing women from combat operations was very consequential. The decision effectively divided liberation war tasks and responsibilities by gender. The division may have fit Bissau Guinean sociocultural beliefs, but the cleavages within the PAIGC uncovered by this change revealed a contradictory attitude toward custom. After the decision, women participated in every field except physical combat operations. The PAIGC leaders, such as Luis Cabral and Umaro Djalo, recast combat operations as a space where transgressive women sought access in order to break traditional attitudes and customs regarding the inability of women to take part in war and carry weapons. Carmen Pereira recalled, "When I was nominated to be the Political Commissioner of the Southern front, Luis Cabral called and said, 'Carmen, it is safer for you, as a woman, to continue running the program of sending female fighters to foreign countries for nursing and military training. This would be safer for you, and the battlefield is too dangerous and risky for you.'"[27] In the sociocultural structures of Bissau Guineans and in colonial administration beliefs, guns were often equated with power, and as I interviewed the old rebels, I also began to wonder what psychological effect this might have had on girls and boys growing up in Guinea-Bissau.[28]

Fighters, Logistics Transporters, and Medics

It is clear based on my findings that the only time when women were not authorized by the PAIGC to be involved in physical combat operations was the period 1967 to 1972. Women were present in the FARP and Local Armed Force (*Forças Armadas Locais* [FAL]), in which women registered as defenders of liberated zones and assumed other social and educational functions. "All women who were participating in the struggle knew how to shoot and handle weapons," remembers Teodora Gomes.[29]

Most of the women who participated in direct combat operations did so in the first stage of the war, 1963–67, given that the war ended shortly. Several women combatants challenged the party's decision to restrict women's participation in direct combat between 1967 and 1972. For Carmen Pereira, Titina Silla exemplified the typical woman fighter; she refused to accept any restriction regarding participation in direct combat operations, making her an example for other women as liberation movement participants.

Amilcar Cabral began a program for the mobilization of girls and young women in 1959. One of these, Ernestina "Titina" Silla, was born in Cadique Betna, Tombali region, in April 1943. In 1961, she was living with her mother in Cacine. Two PAIGC recruiters, Nino Vieira and Umaro Djalo (Carmen Pereira's husband), contacted her. They recruited her to distribute clandestine literature. Later, she acted as a liaison between mobilizers living in the forest with farmers around Medina Boé in the southern region of Guinea Bissau. The leadership chose Titina to be one of those to study in the Soviet Union. Health issues forced her to return home in 1964 without having finished her training, and she resumed her political work. She attended the Cassacá Congress, February 13–17, 1964.[30] In 1965, she returned to the USSR with Carmen Pereira as co-leader of a revolutionary group of women. Back in Guinea, Titina went to the northern front, where she set up a militia training camp as assistant to the front commander. Later she became a political commissar for the whole northern region. Portuguese soldiers killed her in the first week of February in 1973, as she was on her way to pay respects to Amilcar Cabral at a funeral held in Conakry.[31]

> Crossing the Farim River on February 1, as part of an advance guard to prepare for the funeral, she and her comrades fell into a Portuguese ambush.

This was not the first (more likely the seventh or eighth) but this time her presence of mind and bravery could not help her as before. Titina was shot and fell into the water. The others managed to get away, but Titina, unable to swim, did not, and the revolution lost its political commissar for the whole north front.[32]

For Francisca Pereira, "Titina symbolized the kind of woman that the PAIGC was trying to produce."[33] Titina Silla and Fatimata Sibili represented women's participation in combat operations, but they were only the tip of the proverbial iceberg. Many other women, especially from the southern region, participated in direct fighting between 1963 and 1967.

Women's duties ranged beyond military operations. They became nurses, transporters of wounded soldiers, teachers, diplomats, and political cadres. The crucial roles played by women in the fight became apparent even to the strategists of the colonial army. The very presence of Carmen Pereira in the liberated zone prompted the Portuguese to design a special strategy for her elimination or capture. They spent six weeks bombing the area around her base in Donka. Carmen Pereira recalled that during six weeks in 1968, she spent more time in the trenches than anywhere else. Cabral sent a messenger to Carmen Pereira asking her to retreat into Conakry, but she refused to do so. "The Portuguese believed I was Cuban because of my skin and they wanted to stop the work I was doing," recalled Carmen.[34]

Carmen grew up in Bissau as the daughter of one of the few Bissau Guinean lawyers. She and her three sisters went to school up to the fourth grade before their father took them out of the educational system. Their father wanted them to learn how to be good wives and to do such lady-like activities as embroidering and sewing. Later she got married and gave birth to three children in the following years. Her husband joined the PAIGC, which she learned of only by accident. The secret police, responding to an escalation of the guerilla war between 1959 and 1962, conducted massive raids, which forced Carmen's husband to leave for Conakry. Later, Carmen followed his example and left for Senegal (Ziguinchor). In Ziguinchor, the PAIGC and her husband encouraged her to help the new recruits in their transit to Conakry. From there, she ran a small party house, where she and others offered help to rebels. They prepared meals and treated wounded fighters brought in from the Guinea war zones across the border.[35]

In 1963, the PAIGC sent Carmen to the Soviet Union to study nursing, and she left her children in the care of PAIGC supporters in her Ziguinchor house. Two years later, she returned from the Soviet Union with Titina Silla, Francisca Pereira, Eva Gomes, and other women. On her return, the party sent her to the south front to be in charge of implementing a public health program. She opened the first hospital in the liberated zones and became political commissar for the south front in 1967. Although she was trained to handle weapons in PAIGC military bases, Carmen, unlike other cadres, because of her personal beliefs chose not to carry them herself. One or more armed men always escorted her.[36]

Francisca Pereira became one of the first women to gravitate around the PAIGC in Conakry, and she and Titina Silla were sent to the north front as public health supervisors in 1967. The two of them became very close. Late in the liberation war, Francisca represented the PAIGC at the Pan African Women's Congress based in Algiers. This was very important, as most of the time the diplomatic aspect of nationalist movement was in the hands of men. The PAIGC leadership at least recognized the importance of sending women to these global spots, and in doing so, advocating an image that put women at the forefront of the liberation politics. Francisca, Titina, and Carmen carried on diplomatic missions and were members of the *Conselho Superior de Luta* (CSL) (Superior Council for the Fight) wherever they went.[37] The PAIGC accepted women's participation in all non-combatant aspects of the war. The only layer of the war in which their role was challenged was direct combat operations, and even though they proved their ability to fight, male combatants continued to challenge them by asking them, most of the time to stay behind or collect the wounded male fighters.

Women as Socio-economic Agents

As an agricultural society, women were dedicated to agricultural subsistence, trading, and housework. Women participated in cash crop production like men, but men oversaw commercialization. To sustain the war effort, the PAIGC needed women's help as central economic agents. Jacinta da Souza, director of schools in the southern region, explained the roles of women in liberated zones to a group of students, and reaffirmed that women took care of the bases as if they were their own houses. Whatever they were supposed to do in their houses, they did the same duties on the bases. They also performed other tasks for the good of the struggle, such as teaching, nursing, fighting, and farming.[38]

Women participated as agents in many facets of the liberation: the economy, education, propaganda, politics, and health care. They played an enormous role in health. At the beginning of the war, the PAIGC had no more than three male nurses, but by the end of the war there were more than ten doctors (one female), ten medical assistants (five of them women), and over five hundred nurses, with more than half of them being women. Most had undergone full medical training in PAIGC-sympathetic countries (Soviet Union, Ghana, and Cuba).[39] Nurses were well prepared to work at health posts, brigades, and hospitals.[40]

Women such as Fina Crato and Jacinta da Souza also became involved in the education system as teachers and school directors for the PAIGC in the liberated zones. Cabral attested that by 1966 the PAIGC had enrolled more than 4,000 children in schools in the northern region and 5,000 in the southern region, while under the Portuguese the number of indigenous children enrolled had numbered 2,000 for the entire country.[41] Eva Gomes affirmed this was only possible because of women teachers.[42] Women cooked for the fighters in bases and villages, usually providing rice for the guerillas. Later, they oversaw collecting quotas of raw rice from all the families in their respective villages, which they transported to PAIGC camps and military bases. The party made them responsible for the harvest and for rice stores in their respective villages.

The 1964 Cassacá Congress decided to create a regular standing army.[43] Subsequently, a selected number of 2,000 guerilla fighters were organized into new regular military units called the FARP. The party assigned the rest of the guerilla fighters, including women, to the mission of defending the liberated zones as militias.[44] The PAIGC asked women to focus on all aspects of the war except direct combat operations.[45] However, women established an important role for themselves in the success of the liberation war, and Cabral considered it important to have women involved in the struggle on every level.

Warfare and Female Sufferings

Arrests in and bombings of villages in liberated zones had destructive consequences on villagers in general, but more specifically on women. Men left for the fronts and PAIGC headquarters while women, old men, and children stayed behind. These groups of people suffered the most at the hands of the Portuguese army and the colonial police. Bombings made daily life in the villages harsh, as attested by Sito Sadio, a resident of Bafata:

> Bombings forced us to move out of our villages and take refuge in the forest. We moved our village several times to avoid bombings. We even sent our children to the PAIGC pilot school to avoid them being killed.[46]

Not only did women, children, and the elderly move away from their villages, they also had to strategize their daily lives around the activities of the Portuguese army and police. Another woman, Ndalla Mané discussed this situation:

> When we moved our villages, we had to be conscientious in how we organized and moved around. The little girls' and boys' roles had been to be on constant alert for Portuguese bombers, which were trying to find and destroy new villages or camps. Usually, we do not stay long in the same place. When it became too dangerous, the PAIGC decided to escort the boys and girls out of the country.[47]

Fina Crato likewise recalled how dangerous circumstances became during the war in Catchanga in the south. Her village suffered daily raids over a period of four to five months. To avoid causalities, they also had to adjust their lives around the raids. Women worked hard during this period. They cooked and carried ammunition for the fighters under difficult circumstances. For example, they had to find ways to cook so the smoke would not alert the enemy, and they had to hide their cooking utensils.

The Portuguese army or the colonial police would occasionally arrive in villages and surround the villagers; they arrested and interrogated both men and women. Brutality and torture occurred both in prisons and in front of the villagers. Police and army officers used sexual harassment as a method of getting information from women.[48] It is important to note that women not only faced sexual harassments and assaults at the hands of the Portuguese police and army, but also at the hands of some PAIGC officers during the early stages of the liberation war. The occurrence of rape was so frequent that Amilcar Cabral thought the issue was important enough to be addressed during one of his interviews in the African Union Organization Conference in Khartoum, Sudan, in January of 1969.[49] In the early years of the fight, the Cassacá Congress punished some PAIGC military commanders for sexual crimes against women.[50] Punishments varied in severity, from revocations from the movement to jail time and executions of offenders.[51]

Bombings had a negative impact on agricultural production, and when the Portuguese army or colonial police invaded villages looking for PAIGC members or sympathizers, they often destroyed food supplies and farms. They seized livestock as a punishment or as a contribution to their war effort, adding to the economic loss. These practices frequently led to hunger and famine in the villages. The first PAIGC mobilizers used the issue of hunger and famine as a starting point for discussions in the villages. Custom required villagers to give a meal to a foreigner, so when an undercover PAIGC cadre visited, the villagers often presented him with bowl of rice with palm, but neither meat nor fish. The first question coming from the PAIGC cadre was, "Why do you present me only rice and palm oil?" The usual response from the villagers: "I lost all my livestock from the Portuguese Police and taxation methods; my son, life is not what it used to be."[52] Women belonging to the PAIGC generally suffered more during the struggle.

Conclusion

As presented here during the Guinea Portuguese liberation struggle, female participants or PAIGC members participated in all aspects of the struggle. From mobilizing themselves and their husbands to direct combat operation participations from the early stage of the war to the end. Even though at some point their direct combat participations was limited. On top of the traditional roles of Guinean women such as cooking, fetching water, educating the children, they transported weapons, carried wounded fighters, spied the Portuguese armies and PIDE police, organized the economic sectors in liberated zones, participated in the village defense committees.

Instead of fully recognizing the roles of women in support positions and in their narrative of the war, male fighters referred to the female combatants as "heroines," while defining the nurses and logistical transport supporters as simply women who had been doing their regular tasks as women. Mary Ann Tetreault argues that, "What any group gets after the revolution is at least in part a function of what that group is perceived to have earned by the blood of its members."[53] Male fighters in the liberation war saw women combatants as engaged in housekeeping tasks as well as occasional, unique, or isolated cases of heroism, so men left them out of the discourse of the liberation and just gave them a small piece of the pie without sharing the whole pie with them. Women participated fully in the war, but conventional narratives of the war minimize and underrepresent their roles.

Amilcar Cabral intended for women's participation in the war to be the transitional phase leading to their full participants in the future liberated country's socioeconomic and political life. Their participation, he felt, would also change men's views of women as second-class citizens, a view he associated with the perspective of colonizers. To further his belief and convince his male followers, Cabral, via the PAIGC leadership, assigned a group of women to run the UDEMU. But Amilcar Cabral's view was not widely shared among the male PAIGC members, and female participants continued to be challenged and female participants viewed themselves as subalterns, reinforcing what I call the women's self-paradox agenda.

It was important for the female fighters to participate in the struggle as the Portuguese destroyed their daily lives. The Portuguese occupation meant less food for their families, as they were forced to use their daily meals of rice to pay Portuguese taxes; they also lost important amounts of time because of Portuguese forced labor and the Portuguese implementation of commercial cash crops. Women viewed their roles and participation as crucial for the survival of their families, communities, and societies. However, it must be acknowledged that the idea of the women challenging sociocultural and traditional beliefs, as seen in their fighting for gender equality and women's rights, after the PAIGC created the UDEMU, was not a very popular approach, especially among the male leadership of the revolution.[54]

3

Female Combatants and Portuguese Guinea National Liberation War Narratives: Do They Tell the Whole Story?

The relationship between women and war is obscured and mystified on one side by sexism, which maintains that women are physically inferior and unsuitable for important work, and on the other side by some feminist scholars' designation of women as nurturers and pacifist by nature.[1] Many women have indeed been antiwar and anti-military.[2] In contemporary discourses of war, it is frequently assumed that women should not want to have anything to do with war. This is often based on the stereotypes that women are incapable of fighting or are essentially nurturers, who "should be involved in life-supporting rather than life-destroying activities."[3]

Gender-sensitive lenses are useful theoretical tools for highlighting the roles of women in contemporary discourses about war.[4] The problem facing a gendered analysis of war is that, until most recently, war was an event that had always been given prominence over the question of gender identity.[5] Women have always participated in war, but discourse about war often fails to mention women's wartime roles, regardless of whether they were participants or not. This exclusion in part reflects the social dichotomy that isolates women in the private, household, and family spheres. This gendered division "is commonly treated as a natural function of the physical differences between men and women, although it is in reality no more than a human-made device."[6] Women's discourses enable us to see how gendered concepts, practices, and institutions shape the world.[7]

However, several scholars believe that there are direct links between nationalism and feminism. After pointing out the connections made by analysts between nationalism and feminism, Allison Drew argues that some

African feminism results from "the inability of nationalism to liberate women from the shackles of domesticity after wars of national liberation." Most movements toward women's emancipation arose out of nationalist movements that aimed to achieve political independence, asserting a national identity and modern society. The homegrown women's emancipation movement resulted from women's participation in nationalist struggles.[8]

Women were perhaps excluded from war narratives because nationalism and anti-colonial sympathies have often led historians to omit from their narratives the very perspectives of the excluded. The reasons for this exclusion lie in the prevailing narratives of nationalism, anti-colonialism, and Marxism. These narratives place nation building as the highest priority, to the detriment of small communities, villages, and families.[9] James Giblin and Ranajit Guha both help us understand how women combatants participated in their own double exclusion: female combatants were excluded both in the way the story of the liberation war was told by male combatants and in the way their own recollection of the war reinforced this exclusion.[10] This is an extension of Urdang's argument in the case of female Bissau Guineans having to fight "two colonialisms."

Downplaying Their Roles in the War

Francisca Pereira and Carmen Pereira both talked about the war in ways that made the issue of gender invisible. They started to talk about their own roles as women only after I had raised specific questions regarding women's roles in the liberation war. All the women combatants I interviewed had the same approach until I directly asked about their own roles. It was at those points that the narratives of the liberation war changed from the official state and nationalist points of view to different and more complex narratives.[11]

Women combatants underestimated and undervalued their own roles in the liberation war, which contributed to their absence from the official narratives of those wars. They frequently emphasized heroic male actions and the charisma of Amilcar Cabral. The reasons for the behavior of these women can be found in traditional sociocultural structures and customs. This is what I call the self-paradox agenda. The self-paradox agenda is the fact that women combatants minimized their own roles in the war despite their heavy involvement. It seems they did not want to highlight their significant participation consciously or unconsciously. When women talked about themselves, they presented their participation as supportive of the males. They presented themselves as secondary participants in the liberation war, whereas they in fact did very important work, serving as fighters, nurses, weapons transporters, and cooks. Their tasks were integral to the success of the military campaign. If female combatants had not been involved, these tasks would have had to be executed by male combatants or, very possibly, the war might have been lost.

Why Women Were Downplaying Their Roles

After several discussions, I concluded that women combatants did not view their roles as important both because of the social structure of the Bissau Guinean society and because of the conventional ways in which others have presented the liberation war. As James Giblin, Toby Green, and James Giblin argue, exclusion breeds a feeling of deprivation.[12]

In my initial interviews with Francisca Pereira, Carmen Pereira, and other women, they gave me the "official" narrative of reasons for, and the goals of, the liberation war and praised Amilcar Cabral's leadership. They all talked about the war in ways that made the issue of gender invisible. They started to talk about their own roles as women only when I raised specific questions regarding women's roles in the liberation war. All the women combatants I interviewed took the same approach until I redirected my questioning to their own roles. It was at that point that the narrative of the liberation war changed from the standard nationalist point of view to a different and more complex perspective of the war.[13] During my interviews with male combatants, the situation was not dissimilar. They presented the war as a male enterprise and emphasized the roles of men in the success of the war. I had to reformulate my questions by asking specifically about roles of women in the war in order for them to talk about women.[14]

It is important for historians to be aware of this phenomenon in terms of interviewing and recalling the roles of women in history. It was only when I directly asked for women's actual roles using gender-focused questions that they started to mention their specific participation in the war. Thus, gender lenses are essential theoretical tools for highlighting the roles of women in contemporary discourses about war.[15] However, the problem facing a gendered analysis of war is that war is an event that has always been given prominence over the question of gender identity.[16]

Women have always participated in war in a variety of ways, but discourses about war often fail to mention women's wartime roles, regardless of whether they were participants in the fighting or not. This omission in part reflects the social dichotomy that isolates women in the private, household, and family spheres. Women's discourses enable us to see how gendered concepts, practices, and institutions shape the world.[17]

How Women Viewed Their Roles

In the Guinea Bissau liberation war, Bissau Guinean women participated in a wide range of roles, from the traditionally assigned female roles to the most progressive. They cooked, fetched water, transported weapons, spied on the enemies, transported, and cared for wounded fighters, participated in direct combat operations, and protected the frontlines and liberated zones. On top of all their direct involvement in the war, they were also the main economic agents, producing rice and in charge of the trading systems during the war. As critical as their roles were, Bissau Guinean female fighters tended to downplay their roles before later expressing their importance.

Women saw their participation in the Guinea-Bissau war of liberation as something normal and of no special importance, parallel to the ways in which take they would care of their families under ordinary circumstances. Quinta Da Costa, a seventy-four-year-old Balanta woman recruited by Nino Vieira in the village of Katungu, reported that after mobilization and training, the PAIGC military commanders sent her to the Como islands with other women. There, they cooked and transported war material to different areas of the battlefields. Later, she joined her husband Danfa Mendy in Cumbukaré as "wives do." During one of the many Portuguese bombings of the Cumbukare camp, she was hit in her leg by a bullet.

The female fighters in the Guinea Bissau Liberation war believed that what they were doing was normal. Their roles seem to echo the relationships between the Namibian and Zimbabwean freedom fighters and women villagers.[18] The resemblance between their tasks in the house and in the camps in Guinea Bissau made women see themselves as not doing anything out of the ordinary. In the household, patriarchal and colonial settings deepened the ability of men to compel women to oversee cooking, childcare, nurturing the sick, fetching water, doing the laundry, and transporting familial goods. In the PAIGC military bases, women in surrounding villages or living on the bases had always overseen the fighters' laundry, meals, logistics, and caring for the wounded.[19] To the female fighters, their tasks in the PAIGC bases resembled their usual household tasks, and these were nothing new or unusual for them. What is important to see is that even though female fighters viewed their participation as routine, it was in fact, revolutionary to cook, fetch, and do laundry in military or guerilla base settings, rather than in households, because military or guerilla bases had always been considered exclusively male environments.

Ordering women to participate in combat operations repeatedly involved discussions about whether they were suited for those roles. Women who challenged general beliefs and customs by joining male fighters in combat have been depicted as "superwomen." Specific women's names were mentioned to me without my directing the discussions toward women's roles only during my interviews with Barnaté Sanha, a Balanta male fighter, and Teresa NQuamé. Barnaté Sanha joined the PAIGC in January 1963 and participated in military operations for the first time in 1965 in the village of Mores, in the northern front. In June 1966, he left Mores with "176 guerilla fighters, with guns and bazookas" to open a new front. When he received the order from the Commander in Chief Amilcar Cabral, he recalled that a female fighter named Titina Silla was present.

> Cabral visited Mores in 1966, in the north front to boost morale and give the order to open a new front in Nhacra in the north. It seemed that Osvaldo Vieira told Cabral he had the right fighters for that task. At this moment, I was serving in Biandy. I got a message that I should come to Mores. When I got to Mores the next day, I was called into a meeting room where Chico Mendes and Osvaldo Vieira explained to me my new mission to me. It was to open a new front in Nhakara. I accepted the mission in front of Cabral, Vicenté Candi and Titina Silla. I left Mores in June 1966 with 176 guerilla fighters heavily equipped with AKs and Bazookas.[20]

Barnaté mentioned Titina as someone who happened to be present in that meeting. However, he minimized her participation as a woman because he was a fervent defender of the idea that women should not take part in combat operations, fearing that they would jeopardize the missions and put male fighters' lives in danger.[21]

Teresa NQuamé is a Balanta woman. She joined the PAIGC in 1963, and the PAIGC trained her as a *sapadura*, someone who set mines in water and on land to destroy Portuguese naval embarkations, bridges, and roads. After training in PAIGC's facilities around Boé, the PAIGC military commanders sent her to the northern front. NQuamé affirmed that she was not the only woman who specialized in mine setting in the northern region. Two women specialized in those tasks in the groups of men. Teresa NQuamé mentioned Titina Silla as one of the many militaries and political trainers she had in the northern front. She had personally worked with Titina Silla. Recalling with emotion the day Titina died, she described how Titina drowned when she jumped out of the pirogue that was transporting some PAIGC members to Amilcar Cabral's funeral. She jumped to avoid being arrested by a Portuguese naval patroller, even though she did not know how to swim.[22] I realized from the way Teresa was talking about Titina that she held a deep admiration for her and wanted to make sure I understood how courageous and admirable Titina had been during combat.

Presenting women who participated in direct combat as heroines or superwomen illustrates the unconscious tendency to minimize women's roles and participation in the Guinea Bissau liberation war. In most of the women combatants' minds, participation in combat operations was something that only distinguished, or "special" women could do. This belief further also led women participants in the liberation war to consider all their war work as unimportant and routine. With both men and women not recognizing women's roles as significant, it became difficult for women themselves to see, and much less to highlight, their roles as important.

Without someone doing the work that women accomplished in the war, the revolution would have been ineffective and unsuccessful. According to Quinta da Costa and Juditi Gomes, all the different tasks assigned to women in the war were familiar to them, since they had performed similar roles in their daily chores at home. As Juditi said, what was new to female war participants were military training, daily sentinel or guard duty in the camps, and participating in combat operations.[23] They continued to do domestic work during the war, such as cooking, fetching water, cultivating, collecting and pilonning (i.e. processing with large pestle and mortar) or grinding and collecting rice, taking care of the wounded, and serving as sentinels. As the liberation war needed fighters, spies, cooks, caregivers, and weapons transporters, the female combatants were essential to the success of the liberation war. As the war was being waged, the female fighters nourished, cherished, and fed the nationalist fighters. They worked as economic agents in charge of rice cultivation and commercialization in liberated zones. They were also part of the village defensive forces. Even then, during the period 1966–72, some women participated in combat operations, thereby challenging orders and directives. As one of them said, without the women combatants and combatants, the PAIGC would not have won the war.

Filling these critical roles meant that the women were essential parts of the revolution. Even though some of the tasks such as cooking, fetching, and cleaning seemed to be mundane to female combatants, they were not performing them in familial or private spheres. Women performing these tasks in war environments, far from their households, facing Portuguese bombing campaigns and living the harsh lives of guerilla camps and military barracks, was a revolutionary occurrence and critical to the success of the nationalists. Being defined as "routine" simply because women were performing these tasks does not diminish their revolutionary value.

The Self-Paradox Discourses

This oral history project was initiated during the summer of 2008, at which time I started to meet female Bissau Guineans who had participated and fought during the Guinea Bissau Liberation war. Meetings were organized at mutually convenient times, until my interviewees thought their responses to my questions were completed and well transcribed. During the first hours of my interviews with Francisca Pereira and Carmen Pereira and other female war participants and members of the PAIGC during the liberation war struggle, they all talked about the war in ways that made the "official narrative" of the liberation war a centerpiece of their narratives or discourses. Gender issues or women's emancipation questions were initially not at all mentioned. After several days of my collecting female fighters' narratives without being able to convince them share their own personal accounts of the struggle and their reasons for participating, I started to question myself. Is it because I am a stranger to them? Is it because I am a man and they do not want to tell me about their "female" roles in the war? Are they aware of their key roles in the war? Are they consciously or unconsciously avoiding talking about their roles and participation in the war?

Since my decision to move away from my initial research interest and focus on re-writing the Guinea Bissau Liberation war through female fighters' perspectives and narratives, I, with the valuable help of Carlos Gomes Junior "Cadogo," then-president of the PAIGC, Juliao Mané, and others started to focus more on interviewing female veterans of the liberation war and members of the PAIGC during the war. After a long period of visiting the female fighters' houses and interviewing them, I started to ask myself why the responses of my interviewees all revolved around the "official" narratives of the liberation war, that is, centered around Amilcar Cabral's leadership and notions of independence and nationalism.

During my first year of research in Guinea Bissau, I was almost not able to persuade the female war participants or PAIGC members to share their personal stories and reasons for participating. It was only when I had become more familiar with some of the women, almost at the end of my first field trip, that they started to open and give more personal accounts of their participation. The first time it happened it was with Carmen Pereira. It was a simple conversation, not even a formal interview. After listening to her for a while, I asked her why only now she is telling some personal stories without my asking? She responded, "I do not share our personal matters with foreigners always." A light went on in my mind, and I thought to myself, "Yes, even though I was introduced to her by Carlos Gomes Junior, the then-PAIGC president, I was still a foreigner to her. This may be the case with all of them." Since then, I understood that the process of interviewing must be a long one, and patience must be key when the interviewer is an outsider. Over time, the interpersonal relationship between Tia Carmen and me evolved positively, with increased warmth and openness.

From that point on, Carmen, Francisca, and others became more inclined than before to explain or tell me things I did not know before or did not ask. From that time, sharing mealtime with some of the interviewees became routine, or my being introduced to other female fighters by some of my interviewees became normal.[24] Since I was a foreigner, it was a slow process for me to be able to get into the "real" female narratives about female participation, roles, and narratives of the struggle periods. Being a male interviewing woman was not without challenges also, as Binetou Seydi recalled, after a couple of weeks of our discussions at the PAIGC headquarters. She believed that discussing what I called female perspectives of the liberation war would be very difficult for me to understand, as I am not a woman. She said,

> Aliou, you can understand what we women have to go through in this male dominant society. Because of that, we [women] prefer just to discuss about our female issues between us or with other women who, for sure, may be facing the same challenges. Now, as we are familiar and you seem to be really interested in knowing what we went through, I will tell you, but I am still in doubt if you can understand what I will be saying and referring to.[25]

Throughout the discussions I sought first, my female interviewees were not aware of the important roles they played and how their participation contributed to the success of the liberation movement. What made me aware of this was their constant recollection of what I called the "official narrative" of the war. The commonality between Carmen, Binetou, and most of the other female participants and fighters I interviewed was their automatic recall of the official narratives of the national liberation and setting male fighters, Cabral, and independence as the focus of the struggle.

But over time, some of their doubts about my ability to understand their discourses were eased, and most importantly, I became more accepted or familiar to them. As I focused my questions on more personal matters, their responses started to become more personal and more revealing. It was only at that moment certain of them, such as Joacinta Da Silva Rosa, said, "without us [female combatants] they [male fighters] would not easily win the war. We fought, transported weapons, spied, cooked, farmed, ran the village stores, produced rice, protected the villages in the liberated zones etc."[26]

When asked about the war, the female fighters' first instinct was to give the traditional narrative, the official discourse of the national liberation war, and to highlight the men's participation and roles in victories. All my female interviewees emphasized heroic male actions and the charisma of Amilcar Cabral.[27] During my discussions and interviews with women veterans of the Guinea-Bissau liberation war, in formal or informal settings, among educated or illiterate former combatants, they almost always recalled the same names as the architects of victory in the liberation war. These victors are all men: Amilcar and Luis Cabral, Nino and Osvaldo Vieira, Domingo Ramos, Constantino Teixeira, Rafael Barbosa, and Chico Mendes.

When women mentioned other women during our discussions and interviews, they would mention them furtively, without specific names, and refer to them as performing tasks related to women's traditional roles (for instance, cooking for the male fighters, washing their clothes, or fetching water for the camp, in other words, playing traditional familial and wifely roles). I interviewed Na Ndjati in the Boé, and she used the term "we" to refer to women. When she told me about women's participation in direct combat operations, she mentioned "two women" without naming them, but referred to her camp commander by his personal name.

> We as women were allocated to collect rice for the meals of the fighters; others of us cooked the meals, while others pilonned rice, and washed clothes. In our camps only two women used to participate in combat operations and were both killed. Malan Sanha, our camp commander, believed all men and women are equal, but we could not do the same tasks. After the death of the two women combatants, he decided to stop women's participation in combat operations. But in every combat operation, women were present as nurses and logistic transporters.[28]

In the Guinea Portuguese colony, women believed men's voices represented the community at large. For this reason, women often unconsciously accepted their lot and viewed men's history as the conventional representation of the community's history. For Eva Gomes, the PAIGC represented the voice of the people of Guinea Portuguese during the colonial and postcolonial era.[29] During the colonial period, the PAIGC was a group of male activists who had always been the decision-makers. They had the power to decide when and how women participated in the war,[30] what would be the women's agenda, and how women would accomplish their tasks.[31]

Men also had the power to control media and personal communication. They could channel the communication process for their own benefit and to the detriment of women. This fact is not specific to Bissau-Guinean society. This characterizes the relationships between powerful and marginalized groups across cultures. Marginalized women's groups often end up accepting the situation stoically and do not feel concerned about the macro sociopolitical and economic issues that seem to fall within the sphere of male power. If they accept the situation unconsciously, they see it as the norm within which their society should function.

Women's behavior vis-à-vis the men reflects the dichotomy of the specific occupations into which the sexes are classified in modern Guinea Bissau society. Women oversee household management, while men oversee the outside world, managing the community in general. The tendency to keep women outside of the decision-making sphere appears normal to most of the communities in Guinea Bissau. Controlling all the components of the society gives men the power to control politics and all other sectors of the society.

The fact that men have traditionally been viewed as representatives of the communities gave them the power that they needed in order to cast the history of the communities as they saw it. As in the past, they continued to silence women's voices in order to focus on male narratives of glorious male participation in the historical progress of humankind. I believe because of that, some Bissau Guinean female fighters seemed to lack interest in challenging the "official narrative" or "official discourse" regarding the liberation war, finding it easier to adopt the male-centered version of events as their own. However, by the time most of the women had finished recounting their stories of the liberation struggle, they were able to admit or to recognize their importance and the pivotal roles they had played in the war victories. I believe the self-paradox behavior has a great deal to do with the traditional or present sociocultural beliefs and structures of the Bissau Guinean communities and with colonial rules and policies.

Bringing Women's Roles and Voices Back into the Official Discourses

My research and the women's own narratives contradict traditional gender stereotypes of women's roles in the Bissau Guinean liberation wars. The view that all war—and especially this one—is the exclusive domain of men is fallacious. Pronatalist policies in which women's sole responsibility is to reproduce the new nation as mothers and wives to compensate for lives lost in the struggle are not necessarily natural. After the wars, women are sent back home because "war is understood as totally a male affair."[32] But internationally, changes have occurred over the last decades of the twentieth century; female soldiers have reached higher ranks and played increasingly important roles in the militaries of several countries. However, in the past, when women were needed to support the war, they were given assigned roles designed to serve the needs of male participants: as wives, prostitutes, entertainers, cooks, launderers, spies, and sympathetic nurses, but in almost every case as subordinates.[33] These supportive and nurturing roles are presented in "official" narratives as secondary to the main events of combat.

Historically, African women were able to directly or indirectly influence the production and allocation of strategic resources prior to the implementation of colonial systems, as they played important roles in the political, religious, and economic spheres.[34] However, it is important to acknowledge, as mentioned by Philip Havik, that in "segmentary" or acephalous communities women's roles were less glamorous "but noteworthy" than women of "centralized" communities.[35] Changes occurred during the pre-colonial and colonial periods.[36] Through time, women developed strategies to stop the erosion of their rights and privileges or to "enhance their marginal position."[37]

In the Algerian war, women participated fully as fighters. Frantz Fanon saw them not only as the centerpiece of the colonial setting, but also as equally important participants in the anti-colonial war.[38] Algerian women fought as freedom fighters, carried arms against the French colonial system and its army, and planted bombs in Algiers. The revolutionary phase of the war occasioned transformations in sexual relations and women's status, because the leaders considered it a priority.[39] From my findings, I realized that Guinea Bissau women combatants were more focused on concrete issues than on abstract political ones; in short, the idea of women's emancipation had been accepted by a very few women, who mostly followed the party line. In order for these women to deal with the idea of women's emancipation, what I call the self-paradox agenda of the Bissau-Guinean women combatants needed to be overcome.

Bissau-Guinean female interviewees readily discussed the reasons for the war, the denouement of the war, Cabral as a visionary, and the leadership and heroic actions of many male fighters without discussing women's roles. Sano Seydi, for example, was the wife of Musa Diamba. They both joined the liberation struggle in 1963 and served under the command of Innocentio Cani in the eastern front, who was involved in the killing of Amilcar Cabral later. Musa was killed during a combat operation in the village of Kankefala on January 1, 1965. Sano stayed on the eastern front as a cook and transporter until the end of the war. She returned to her village, Dialakoto, sick and without medical care, and later she joined her sister in Gabu.[40] Na Ndjati was the wife of Famara Djassi; she was recruited by Malan Sanha, in the southern region. Her husband, like Malan Sanha, organized weapons transport convoys composed mostly of women from Guinea Conakry to the different fronts in Guinea-Bissau. In the case of Guinea Bissau, just because of that contribution, women' voice should be heard. And to do so, the official narrative must include them to make them feel comfortable and to enable them to move away from what I called the self-paradox issue.

So, what did I learn as scholar? First, in most of African liberation movements, women have been left out of the narratives of the struggles. Second, when presenting the struggles, most of male participants' discourses and social scientist's discourses have focused on the macro-narratives about nationalism, charismatic leadership, or class struggles. In these narratives, it is the struggles of the colonizers vs. the colonized, the applications of Marxist theories, and comparisons between different nationalist struggles around the world that are the focal points. After several years of discussion with female participants in the national liberation war in Guinea Bissau, I understood there were several different struggles within the fight for independence in Guinea Bissau.

The reasons why some of those underlying struggles have not been viewed by social scientists was because of their interest in comparing different struggles, or in fitting the Bissau Guinean struggles into pre-conceived paradigms or macro-narratives. In other words, scholars come with a preconceived theoretical framework and want to make sure the Guinea-Bissauan case fits their understanding of a national liberation movement or of decolonization struggles. These precepts have led to the silencing of subaltern groups such as women. During the years of the liberation war in Guinea Bissau, Stephanie Urdang was the only one focusing on recalling women's involvement in the struggle for independence, while others, such as Gerard Chaliand and Basil Davidson, mentioned or interviewed female combatants as a side affair.

Conclusion

By focusing on female fighters' narratives, what I discovered and learned was this: At first, female fighters/combatants/participants did not want to discuss their personal involvement or roles. They would do that only after gaining a sense of familiarity, often first discussing personal matters that seemed to not have anything to do with the war. When they started talking about their involvement, they presented their concerns as more related to the deterioration of their daily life activities, the destruction of their family lives. They presented the war narrative in a way that was different from the traditional discourse. Even though they faced some gender-based challenges, they participated in all aspects of the struggles, in addition to accomplishing their duties as women. They trusted their leader Amilcar Cabral implicitly, and they still believe if he were alive, they would not have been shut out after Portuguese Guinea became the Republic of Guinea-Bissau.

4

Gendering War Space and Heroinization of Female Fighters

The Gendering of War Zone Space

Historically, war zones have always been gendered in the general historiography and "official" narratives of war; however, in the female combatants' narratives of the Guinea-Bissau liberation war, they view themselves as having participated in or witnessed all actions throughout the war from 1963 to 1973. They see women as having been engaged in a true struggle on all battlefronts. Carmen Pereira claimed that women participated in every combat for the liberation of the country from the time when the PAIGC moved to Conakry in Guinea after September 1959 through to the Medina Boé declaration of independence in 1973. She stated that during the early stage of the mobilization, women villagers were the first to volunteer.

Even when women combatants had been asked to stop participating in combat operations, some of them refused, and a large number of other women continued to witness the battles as they worked as nurses, weapons transporters, spies, and cooks in the combat zones.[1] The decision of the 1964 Cassacá Congress regarding women's involvement in combat operations did not keep them all from fighting.[2] Carmen believed that the person who best exemplified women's participation in the war was Titina Silla.[3] As political commissars, women such as Titina Silla and Carmen Pereira participated in political meetings as well as in battles.[4]

In the Guinea Bissau liberation war, female fighters were very involved in their liberation war. But that fact did not mean that they did not face gender-based challenges on the battlefield. Male fighters in this war, as in others, saw direct combat operations as properly male space. However, PAIGC women as nurses, and eventually transporters of the wounded, were never far away from combat zones, often waiting until the end of hostilities to enter the field, when combat operations were likely over and male fighters had moved on to another place.[5] Thus, the same space, at different periods of time, belonged to male fighters and to women.

Each group, at the time they "owned" the space, had total control of it, and the other group was not allowed to enter, even though it happened sometimes that the women entered the field at a point when their group was not yet in full control of it. The interaction of the two sexes on the battlefield contributed strongly to PAIGC success, because without women's roles as weapon carriers, wounded transporters, and fighters at different periods, it would have been very difficult to achieve victory. Transporting wounded fighters, weapons, and information are key factors in winning a war. And women combatants did all of that, even when they were forbidden to participate in direct combat.

Another revolutionary action involved how women, in addition to their familial duties, worked as sentinels and guards during the day, but not at night. At night, male fighters took charge of the security of the camp or village.[6] Hence, the process of guarding the camp was gendered. The decision about which gender group would mount guard depended on the risk of attacks and perception of courage. Making women guard during the day and sleep at night was based on the idea that women might not be able to face the emotional and physical insecurity of the dark. Thus, the division of guard duties between women and men, between day and night, was culturally defined.

Places never mentioned in conventional narrations of the war became important parts of the narratives collected from women combatant; these included places such as those allocated for cooking, fetching water, washing clothes, and caring for babies. This is exemplified in an anecdote from Juditi Gomes. Juditi remembered preparing meals with other women when they were informed about the arrival of the "Tuga." They hid the rice and pestles and ran away. A *homem grande* (elder man) called to them and let them hide in his huts, and he took away the rifle Juditi was carrying. Juditi and the other women started cleaning the house. Later that day, after the Portuguese had passed, the women went back to what they were doing. As Commandant Lucio and his group of guerilla fighters were passing around the rice field where the women worked, he yelled a remark about Juditi having a rifle and pilon at the same time.⁷ Men never cooked, fetched water, or washed the camp members' clothes.

At first, male fighters did not want to share the "manliest" space of the battlefield. In the general view, combat operations required courageous, physically and mentally tough, solid men. Men saw battlefields and combat operations as their own spaces; they did not want to share this space or appear to be sharing this space with women combatants. By accepting a shared battlefield space and the PAIGC's request in 1961 about ending polygyny and authorizing women's right to divorce, male combatants and men in general felt as if they were losing control and thus power over women.

In order to maintain their space and power, male combatants defined two spaces in the war zones. The first space was male, occupied by those who were doing the shooting and fighting (male combatants and very few female combatants). The second space was female, occupied by those who were responsible for military logistics, nursing wounded combatants, and militia (liberated zones' security agents). Women taught and cooked in the liberated zones and villages (all were women combatants). In the male narratives of the war, all the sources focus on the fighting space, a space occupied by male combatants, and ignore the space occupied by the women in the front lines. By separating the spaces, the women combatants' history becomes disconnected from the rest of the war. Women's participation as active agents in the war becomes the "her-story" of the war.⁸ "Her-story" was not included in the "official" discourse of the war, in which male agencies constituted the complete war history.⁹

Even though female fighters showed what they could do during the early years of the nationalist struggle, from 1961 to 1967, they faced discrimination in direct combat participations. Fatu Turé confirms that women and male fighters lived together in the camps and villages. "They [women] were cooking and washing clothes for the camp's members. They [women] all participated in military and political training, and all worked for the success of the war."¹⁰ Sandé NHaga confirms this view:

> We were cooking, washing clothes. We were doing all the womanly tasks because if we as women do not do it who will do it? It was our job to take care of all the women's tasks. While doing all this work we have to be alert and avoid being located by the Portuguese. In cases of attack, our base

commander in Ballacounda, Mamady Kamara, ordered us women to run into the mangrove swamp, the rice field, or the forest to protect ourselves.[11]

Most of the PAIGC male members and fighters supported the idea that women had to stay behind the front lines. Each of them had specific explanations about why women should stay behind. Barnaté Sanha said, "Women got scared easily and always put the life of the fighters in danger. They are not suited for combat operations."[12] Hutna Yala, another Balanta man and combat veteran, believed that a woman's place was in the house, and not to fight with the Portuguese. According to him, "men are suited to fight. Women are suited to take care of the family and their husband, not to fight."[13]

War and Manhood from Female Fighters' Perspectives

Guinea Bissau female fighters had different views in regard to women's participation in direct combat operations. While some claimed women were suited to take guns and fight, others disagreed. Juditi Gomes claims that it is not only that men do not believe women can take up arms against invaders but also that most women do not believe they can do that. She continued, saying that in Guinea Bissau men have overseen defending the territory. Women do not fight because they are supposedly not physically strong enough to defeat an armed enemy. During the colonial period, it was always men who fought the Portuguese forces.[14] When men went to fight, women stayed in the villages and prayed for their safety.[15] It was only with the arrival of Cabral that women were asked to take an active role in the war. And many did what they could to help men win the war.[16]

In the case of the Guinea Bissau liberation war, Juditi Gomes and some participants testified that women were not suited to participate in wars. Historically, in most African societies, men are caricatured as warriors, while the few female warriors are equated as heroines and their actions are idealized. For example, Titina Silla, a female fighter, had been portrayed as heroine and personified as a "superwoman." In any conversation regarding women's participation in active combat operations, men and women combatants will cite her name. In most ways, she acted the same as the male fighters acted, but the fact that she was a woman, in Guinea Bissau, for the general observer unaccustomed to seeing women participate in combat operations, she was idolized and became the representative of all the women who participated in combat operations in the Bissau-Guinean liberation war. In other words, Titina did not appear to be a typical woman.

The idolization of the women who participated in combat operations, in fact, reinforced the idea that war was exclusively for men. However, it is important to attest that the *heroinization* of female participants in direct operations as a way to keep women out of the revolutionary and essential roles they played in the war did not diminish the importance of their participation. Despite male portrayals, female participation was equal to and as important as male participation for the success of the liberation war.

Societal Structure in War Narratives

Guinea Bissau societal structure shaped the way in which communities explained or decided who would participate in war. In communities in which women were not allowed to participate in wars, even if this conception or belief was challenged, it could never be fully overcome. For example, some of the women combatants seemed surprised when I asked if they participated in direct combat. Fatu Turé responded, "No, no, no, we women have not been part of combat operations. Our tasks were cooking, washing clothes, etc."[17] Fatu Turé is a Mandinka woman. Cau Sambu, one of the first mobilizers of the PAIGC, recruited her in 1963. Turé is from the village of Cicior, and she moved between different military bases or barracks near the southern front. She and other women cooked and washed the clothes of base members. As members of the militia, women worked as guards, weapon transporters, and military logistic transporters from Kandiafa to all the fronts under the supervision of Bacar Konté using baskets, walking for long distances without shoes.[18] Fatu Turé attests that even though women were trained by the PAIGC instructors militarily and politically, and on several occasions carried AKs, they did not participate or were not authorized to participate in combat operations by the PAIGC decision-makers after the Cassacá Congress in 1964. The only circumstance in which they might fire a gunshot would be for defensive purposes. Ndalla Mané, surprised by my question, likewise responded, "No, and none of us as women, in our barracks, were called to join combat operations."[19]

It was mostly at the exception of the Bijagós' women who accompanied their men into battle, men who told the narratives of wars in Guinea Bissau because they were the ones who fought and participated in military campaigns. Indeed, even though women may have been present in some of the wars, the official narrators of the war continued to be men. In many African traditions, a male narrator is present during military operations between different political entities.[20] The presence of male narrators in wars corresponded to the general belief that only courageous, strong, and emotionally and physically tough male fighters can tolerate the harshness and violence of war. The presence of a male narrator or *griot* responds to the desire to have someone present who will narrate the story of the battle, not just for those who were not present, but also for future generations.[21] Thus, a link is established between participation in the war, war narratives, and men's narrations. As male griots transmitted stories of wars and courageous behavior, in most of West African societies such as the Balanta in Guinea Bissau, the Fulani in Senegal, and the Mandinka in Mali, women have overseen the education of children through stories, myths, and legends. This teaching is organized within the familial sphere and happens inside family homes. It has occurred in what some scholars call the familial or private sphere, to emphasize the fact that only family members will witness women's performances as narrators or teachers. Outside the house in general, male narrators (*djalli* in Mandinka and *gauulo* in Fula communities) have been the "griots." Women singers, who sang and danced in between the male master of the parole's speeches, have sometimes accompanied them.[22] So men's roles as narrators are not simply as oral or written authors, but also as the transmitters of tradition.

The Balanta and Diola in Guinea-Bissau have been socially egalitarian, in contrast to the Fula and Mandinka. A council of elders made decisions. Although Balanta and Diola have been less stratified and without a hierarchical power, male figures have been charged with the representation of the community and the narration of the community's history. For example, in Bijagos people in the Bijagos islands, even though the society is egalitarian, it was almost impossible to see women speaking during meetings or in large crowds of people. Women are present, but they are guided by the masters of the ceremony who are, most of the time, male figures.[23]

Some women's discourses reinforce men's desire to control the narratives of the war. Teresa NQuamé observed that women never competed with men for power, because each of the groups was assigned specific tasks in the liberation war. Women and men shared some tasks and power, even though most of the time the male group was the one leading the discussions, work tasks, defense, and rituals. In the case of war narratives, as the men were the ones always defending and fighting for the community, it was normal for them to oversee the war narratives.[24] This is the origin of men controlling the narrative of the war. The same thing is happening now; even though women participated in the liberation war, they let the men narrate the war. When the men told the stories, they focused on themselves, neglecting to mention all of the combatants. Men unconsciously took control of the narratives without integrating women into their recitations, and they consciously took control because they believed they were the important actors in the victory.[25]

One-sided narratives of the war are not something new in Guinea-Bissau. After the liberation war, male fighters just followed the same patterns and practices as their ancestors had followed in the past. And when the men omitted women participants from the story, women did not react, because they accepted and respected the traditional culture. Women, at the exception of female societies, and the young have been accustomed not to discuss or challenge men's or elders' power, decisions, or narratives anywhere in Guinea Bissau.[26]

Female fighters participated in combat operations during most of the wartime. When they were asked to stay behind, many of them refused. "Titina is pictured as the model of women the PAIGC was trying to create in Guinea-Bissau," said Francisca Pereira. She was a fighter who participated in direct combat operations in the northern region. Significantly, Titina represented a large group of women who refused to follow the directives regarding how women should act or not act. Another woman who took part in the fighting, Joanita Da Silva Rosa, lost her right eye in direct combat operations around Medina Boé, and Teresa NQuamé, as a naval fusilier, sunk two Portuguese boats in the northern region.[27] Many more female fighters refused to stay behind; these women cited represent the tip of the iceberg, as confirmed by Joanita da Silva Rosa.[28]

It is accepted that in the early years of the struggle, everyone, both men and women, fought. It was only later that roles changed because first, the population numbers dropped, and second, the idea of having a national army emerged. There was a desire to protect women, as mothers of the nation, in order to ensure future population growth. Hence, the women were exempted from participating in operations that might expose them to a high risk of injury and death. However, the plan was in place and women started to train for combat, but they did not participate in combat operations at that time, because the PAIGC declared unilateral independence a year later.[29] It is also important to note that even though the party decided to stop women's participation in combat operations in the middle of the war, many women did not respect this decision. A number of them, and on all fronts, continued to participate as naval fusiliers, nurses, and fighters, such as Joanita and Teresa.

Gendered Liberated Zones

A very important addition to village life was the decision in 1964 to place women on every village committee. The village committee was a group of five elected persons in the villages of the liberated zones. Regarding the village committees, most of my interviewees and the documents I have consulted affirm that the committees were composed of five members, but in Gerard Chaliand's book *Tchico Té* (Francisco Mendes), the political commissar for the northern inter-region, speaking to Chaliand, states that "we have held elections for a Party committee in each village of the liberated regions. We call it a *tabancas* [Creole for village] committee. In general, it is composed of three men and three women, and is elected by the village assembly, in other words, by the entire adult population of the village."[30] Until the decision was made by the PAIGC, the five elected officials were men. In 1964, the Cassacá Congress directed that two of the five elected must be women. In a certain way, this decision was a step forward in the visibility of women on legislative committees.[31] However, it was not enough to achieve complete gender equality because, as was confirmed by Eva Gomes, the women were never able to challenge male power because they were only two against three men.[32]

Female combatants were divided into three different groups, each associated with the typical roles' women had occupied before. The three groups were composed of female officers with political and military roles, women with household duties and limited military roles such as surveillances or defensive military roles, and finally women with lesser military roles such as transporters and economic agents.

The first group of women was those who mostly lived in the camps as political officers, such as Carmen Pereira, Teodora Gomes, and Titina Silla; they were political commissars who were mandated to supervise political training in liberated zones. They also participated in all the military meetings regarding battle plans and the activities of nurses and "sapadura," whose tasks were respectively to follow the male fighters to provide medical care for the wounded and to set mines. Some of these women also participated in combat operations, like Joanita da Silva Rosa. These women completely challenged traditional notions of roles of women in the public sphere as they participated in political decision-making or in military operations, which had never been considered as women's roles.

The second group was composed of women living in the camps or villages who were responsible for cooking, washing clothes, fetching water, and working as daily sentinels or guards under the supervision of male fighters, but who never joined the combat operations or participated in the militias. This was also revolutionary, as having women living in military environments, other than to cook or fetch water for the nationalist fighters, was unprecedented. In military settings men, not women, traditionally accomplished these tasks. In addition, having women working as sentinels or guards at night was completely a challenge of the military sphere as male space.

Women Defining Their Roles and Participation in the War

Many women combatants valorized their own feminine roles in the liberation war. Fanta Sané was a proud cook in Kandiafara on the eastern front, and the figurative mother of the combatants, whom she called "sons."[33] Fatoumata Diallo, who was never interested in politics, was also very proud of her participation.[34] They viewed their roles as natural and normal without bragging about it or emphasizing the political aspect of their participation. This begins to explain why they were left out of the official narrative of the war. However, many of the women I interviewed spoke harshly about how the country has been handled since independence. Most of them believed that the PAIGC's ideals during the war have been rejected or forgotten by the current party leaders and the government. For example, Segunda Sambu remembered the suffering they went through as women. She, her husband, and husband's brother participated in the war. Her husband's brother was killed. As former combatants, her husband and his late brother were never paid as war veterans.

> We do not have either house or money. My husband and I live on the 15,000 XOF [US $30] I receive monthly from the war veteran services. We women did our share in sending the Portuguese back to their country. Now do you think [asking me] the men could win the fight without us women fighting with them? No, because empty stomachs will not help in combat operations.[35]

At the starting point of the liberation war, it was believable that the PAIGC leadership moved away from its earlier vision of what must be done in order to build a suitable independent country. It is possible that the decision to integrate women into the struggle after 1959 was not fully accepted and understood by all the PAIGC leadership. Perhaps Amilcar Cabral's progressivist views on gender relations and establishing sociocultural equality were in the minority within the organization he helped build.

The combination of women and men working together was the reason for victory, but most of the men did not understand or recognize that.[36] The slow recognition of women's participation in "official" narratives of the war reminded me of Maria Santos' opinions in Stéphanie Urdang's work. Maria Santos was a young woman under thirty, who after independence came back from Portugal to take up a responsible position on one of the UDEMU commissions. Urdang accompanied Santos to a women's meeting organized by the UDEMU in 1974.[37] Santos said:

> We are fighting for a piece of the pie. The men control the pie, and we don't want men to give us a piece of their pie. For if we accept something that is given to us, even if it is half, we will never have the same power as those who gave it. They will still control it. What we want to do is to destroy this pie so that men and women, together, can build a new pie where women will be totally equal with men.[38]

Maria Santos' assertion is still valid for today's women in Guinea Bissau, because women are still struggling to get their part of the pie, while men are refusing to share. When talking to Bissau-Guineans such as Joanita, Segunda, and Fanta, it would seem as if almost nothing has changed. Urdang concludes her book by writing that women will have to wait at least one generation to measure the progress made regarding women's emancipation.[39]

All of these women present their participation as crucial. Responses to the question "could male fighters have won the war without women?" varied depending on the person's place in the contemporary sociopolitical structure of the Bissau-Guinean society. One interesting response from a woman was:

> We should not look at your question in terms of whether if women did not participate in the struggle, could men alone win the struggle, because both groups played crucial roles in the war, and both of them are benefiting from the success and the liberation of the country by living free; women have the right to decide for themselves, and forced marriage is not allowed anymore.[40]

Former women combatants who are now very close to the government and the party leadership gave me similar answers. Francisca Pereira cited for me all the benefits that women got from their participation. She talked about the number of women in village councils, the participation of women in the national popular assembly, and their roles in the UDEMU.[41] Carmen Pereira discussed women in the executive bureau of the PAIGC and the government, as well as how the male fighters and the PAIGC executive bureau valorized the women's participation and roles in the war.[42] Their responses led me to ask, "Why, then, are women under-represented in the narratives of the war?" Their responses were almost identical. Women are under-represented in the narrative of the war because those who recall the war narratives asked only men, and only for what they want to know.[43] What the women who made this type of argument have in common is that they have or had high positions in the party or in the governments that have ruled the country since independence, or they have been or are representatives in the popular assembly. In a certain way, they all benefitted from defending the party, and wanted to show the positive side of the war and the party. Of them all, only Eva Gomes criticized the slow process of liberating women in Guinea-Bissau.[44]

The second main response to my question revealed the frustration of women veterans about having their contributions minimized and being left out of the political and economic systems since the country was liberated. "We women were never recognized for the roles we played in the liberation war, and we are left outside of the system. We gained no political recognition, and we are out of the economic system. We live with difficulties. Even the ones who got sick from the work we were doing during the war are not being taken care of," said Segunda Sambu.[45] In another form, NDo Mané says the same: "The men are egotistical. They do whatever it takes to get the help they need by promising that things will change for the better for the women, but when they get what they want things get back to the usual."[46] This response reflects the views of most of the women I interviewed in Guinea-Bissau. I sensed bitterness in the voices of these women. Some of them recognized that the party did accomplish something, but they didn't consider to be enough, because forced marriages still occur, and in a society where very few people request or get civil marriage certificates and most live in "common law" arrangements without any official document, it is almost impossible to control polygyny.[47] Others, such as Dialan Diamba, also claimed that traditions and customs never go away, or else go away very slowly, because the ones who are making laws are the ones benefiting from polygyny and forced marriage.[48] When I said, "A few women said the party recognized women's roles and participation, and that the party did improve women's conditions during and after the war," the response was unanimous: "Are we blind?"[49]

> What is very clear is that very few groups of women are profiting from their involvement in the war. Those who have been involved in the party at a high level and in the government since the beginning of the struggle for independence and today are still the ones who are the beneficiaries of political and governmental positions. If you look, they do not represent twenty women. They can say whatever, but we all know the truth.[50]

The common denominator among these women is that all except a few of them are excluded from the current political and economic systems, or they are far from where decisions are made. Of all the women I interviewed, fewer than five said men had recognized their roles; the large majority said their roles had never been recognized. The male fighters think about woman fighters mostly as mothers, wives, and sisters, but not as guerilla fighters or freedom fighters. In order to protect their power, men divided the space and tasks along gender lines, and women accepted the spatial division, even though some simultaneously challenged this role definition. The women let the men decide what the official narrative of the war would be, but women combatants, without saying anything, understood that their participation was crucial to the success of the war. Furthermore, their participation was not linked to women's emancipation or "liberation," as Urdang wanted to define their involvement. Their participation responded to their needs and desires to take care of their families and protect their family life. The next chapter will address the following question: What are the consequences of having women excluded from the "official" narrative and of the female self-paradox agenda in the postwar attempts to eliminate inequality between women and men?

Conclusion

As we see, initially in Portuguese Guinea, both male and female members of the PAIGC tended to underrepresent and resist the role of women combatants in the nationalist struggle for independence. Most importantly, this initial underrepresentation of female fighters and their roles and participation in the movement and war became part of the official male-based narrative of the war. However, when female fighters are given an opportunity to express "their" narrative of the war, more and more women resist and challenge the traditional or official male-centered narrative of the war. The new, female-based narrative presents women participants in the Portuguese liberation war as active in every aspect of the national struggle, ranging from traditional female roles to active participation in military and hostile environments and engaging in direct combat operations, in spite of facing tough male resistance in many aspects of their involvement. This new, female-centric narrative repositions and revalues the role of these women in our current understanding of the war.

5

Gender Roles and the First Republic

Women played key roles in the liberation war, even though male fighters considered them subaltern participants. Male views of women's roles and the official narrative of the war affected how women perceived and valued their participation. In a sense, women combatants minimized their roles and participation, even though the part they played was quite significant.

Among its other goals, the PAIGC sought to emancipate women and establish gender equality, so it is important for us to ask whether women achieved their goals of political and social equality. If not, how do we uncover the postcolonial hopes and ambitions of the participants of a failed gender revolution? One answer is that the success of the revolution itself masked the failures of gender liberation. Men did not allow real change to take place, so the goals and hopes of the independence struggle were not realized. Many of the former male fighters easily slipped back into their old misogynistic and sexist attitudes, while most women gave up the struggle for equality as they surrendered their importance in the liberation war narrative. Women took active political and social roles in the new republic, but they were marginalized as workers and as elected officials. The consequences of the behavior toward women led to the emergence of an elite group composed mostly of by Bissau Guinean individuals with Cabo Verdean backgrounds. Many women refused to challenge old sociocultural behaviors and laws. Those who were ready to challenge conventions or to implement laws promoting equality faced male resistance.

Old Societal Structure: Back to Normal

During the period in which the PAIGC controlled some liberated zones and after their declaration of independence and implementation of the new government and new policies, it was clear that men did not want gender-based changes. For example, in the education sector, 13,361 primary school students lived in liberated zones during the war in 1965–66 (9,821 males and 3,540 females).[1] Yet, the number of female students decreased by 1970–71 (male students: 10,898 and female students: 2,155).[2] According to Cabral, the party did not succeed in increasing the number of female students in liberated zones, because the teachers (only 2 percent of them women) as educators and as political agents did not perform their educational and political duties properly, and what they were doing did not support the political work of the party.[3] The recruiting officers very rarely selected women to be teachers for two reasons. Few women qualified for the work, and the party tried to make the schools more acceptable to traditional and hesitant minds by not recruiting a lot of women teachers.[4]

The sources indicate that the problem of education also involved other factors such as a lack of interest in educating women or a disinterest in challenging the overall traditional sociocultural behavior or views about women and school. Also, since most of the teachers were men, the tendency to replicate old views about women's education became greater. Only 25 to 30 percent of primary school children and one-quarter of secondary school students were female, reflecting the families' refusal to release their female children for a formal education. The low representation of women in the education system resulted in a lack of commitment by male leaders and most of the components of Bissau-Guinean society, including many women who refused to challenge the traditional sociocultural fabric of their society.

Politics is arguably the arena in which gender inequality remained most pronounced even after the declaration of independence. Although women have entered educational institutions and the labor force in significant numbers around the globe, women hold only about 17 percent of the world's parliamentary seats today. In Guinea Bissau, women's representation in the National Assembly is even lower than the worldwide female representation percentage.[5]

> Women rarely occupied positions of crucial political leadership. Although women were free to run for political office, they did not hold many significant political positions. The discrepancy between the official policy of gender equality and the low representation of women in political leadership has inevitably aroused several interpretations and speculation about the

seriousness of the Bissau Guinean commitment to gender equality. By 1977 the number of women in top leadership positions remained low. A breakdown of women in some of the leadership positions was as follows: National Popular Assembly, 19 women among 150 delegates (including Carmen Pereira as vice president), State Council, 2 women of 14 members (Ana Maria Cabral and Francisca Pereira); Regional Presidents or Governors, 1 woman (Francisca Pereira) of 8; Permanent Commission of PAIGC, 0 woman of 8 members; Executive Committee of the Struggle, 1 woman of 26 members (Carmen Pereira); Superior Council of the Struggle, 2 women of 90 members (Francisca Pereira and Carmen Pereira). As Urdang points out, the figures were not enhanced by the fact that there was an overlap in the positions occupied by women, reducing the absolute total.[6]

The party Congress was the basic institution of sovereignty in Guinea-Bissau. The first Congress in Cassacá gave birth to the party organization. The second Congress, in September 1973, declared the existence of the state. The third Congress (November 15–20, 1977) proposed policy guidelines. Women were under-represented or not represented at all of the Congresses. For example, only 6 percent of the 303 Third Congress delegates were women.[7] The relatively small percentage of women delegates reflects their relatively peripheral role within the party.

Some scholars, such as Joshua Forrest, look at this discrepancy as an indication of the lack of serious commitment to certain social issues by the male PAIGC leaders, who were often cynical regarding the aims and practices of the revolution. Forrest states that postcolonial society was unsupportive of women's causes, and the Women's Commission was simply a social club centered in Bissau. The Women's Commission played a symbolic role at best, perpetuating the myth that there was a genuine commitment to prioritize the progressive emancipation and equality of women.[8]

Several women I interviewed confirmed Forrest's view. Udé Camara and NDo Mané saw the under-representation of women in political and governmental affairs as the result of the disinterest of male political decision-makers in women's agendas or their well-being. Since the independence, the PAIGC leaders and government officials referred to women's issues only when they wanted a large mobilization during meetings, when foreigners were visiting the country, and during political elections. During those periods, they would say whatever women wanted to hear, such as emphasizing the issues of civil rights, job creation, and financing women's small businesses.[9] Afterward, they forgot about their promises until circumstances again required.[10]

The under-representation of women in the Bissau Guinean political and governmental spheres is not something new or surprising, given the fact that during the war, even though the party made clear its desire to end the sociopolitical exclusion and exploitation of women, it did not do much to make it happen. The reason rested within the party structure, in which there was a great deal of opposition to women's emancipation. After independence, with the death of Cabral, it became obvious that women's emancipation was not one of the main concerns of the state. The women chosen to lead the emancipation movement were mostly not interested in the issue of emancipation or were simply not ready to take on the fight that was needed to convince the party to focus more interest on women's issues.

After independence, the hard-won unity achieved by Amilcar Cabral soon started to disintegrate. President Luis Cabral reinforced his power by imposing his will on all the country's structures, and many of the war participants suffered because of it.[11] Luis Cabral started to develop controversial constitutional reform which allowed Cabo Verdeans to hold political posts in Guinea Bissau, although Bissau-Guineans were not permitted to hold offices in the archipelago.[12] Christoph Kohl states that most "Bissau-Guinean Cabo Verdeans" are part of the Bissau-Guinean's middle and upper classes who participate in the "country's politics, bureaucracy, civil society, intelligentsia, and economy," and they represent a "very small proportion of the country's total population."[13] Historical sources suggest that Cabo Verdeans living in the coast of Upper Guinea can be traced back to the seventeenth century. Later, during the nineteenth century, these Bissau Guinea Cabo Verdeans dominated public services and trade.[14] "A census revealed that there were 1,703 citizens of Cabo Verdean origin in Guinea-Bissau in 1950. Half of them resided in Bissau."[15] These people with Cabo Verdean background were called the *assimilados* or "civilized," while the rest of the population; 98 percent, were viewed as Indigenous or "uncivilized."[16]

In the summer of 1979 in the Bissau-Guinean archipelago, a population estimated at 800,000 inhabitants, 250,000 to 300,000 were Bissau-Guineans with Cabo Verdean descents.[17] For Bacar Cassama, the party leaders were more interested in setting up their followers and positioning themselves in regard to the different factions within the party and were not interested in developing Amilcar Cabral's vision of an "African" identity.[18] In Cassama's view, women and youth suffered the most, but all sections of the country likewise suffered: "Amilcar Cabral would not be happy if he came back to see what happened to his country. The ideals of the revolution were forgotten because of opportunism and corruption within the party and state."[19] Joacinta da Rosa Silva states that if she had known this was what was going to happen after the liberation war, she would not have joined the movement.[20] Joacinta was not the only woman to express such an opinion.

The health services seemed to be the only sector where the PAIGC fully accepted women's participation as workers. Several hundred nurses and auxiliary nurses, both male and female, belonged to the PAIGC. Their number, in 1972, was reported to be at least 410.[21] However, during the Superior Council meeting in 1971, Cabral recognized that keeping women nurses in their respective posts while pregnant or dealing with other familial issues caused them difficulty:

A solution needs to be found to the problem of female nurses leaving their jobs after having their first child. From the point of view of the party, it was pointless to recruit and train a nurse who then would not work.[22]

In order to fix the problem, according to Cabral, the party needed to convince women to delay having babies until after the war.[23] In Guinea Bissau, only women who were trained in the field of health care were able to find jobs in the newly independent country, while the others were demobilized and sent back to their villages without employment. The fortunate ones were able to become registered as combat veterans in order to receive monthly pay.[24] Most of the women with whom I spoke to at the Former Combatant Ministry in Bissau believed the government did not keep all of its wartime promises to women after the war.[25] Even though the health sector was the one place where women were accepted most of the time because their participation fit within traditional practices, they were not recruited as intended and their possibilities of practicing in health professions were limited because of traditional beliefs and familial roles.

Female Participants in the First Republic

The attempt to realize the goals of the revolution in general failed because policies and conditions within the newly independent country brought about the development of a new elite composed mostly of those with Cabo Verdean backgrounds, according to Fodé Cassama:[26]

> The truth is most of the people who profited from the liberation war were people with Cabo-Verdean or Portuguese family names. Because the Portuguese brought a lot of them from the Cabo-Verde islands to run the colonial administration and because we were autochthones, most of us were not educated or went to the indigenous schools, while Cabo Verdeans went to the "civilized" and missionary schools in Cabo Verde.[27]

For Cassama, the post-independence policy of Luis Cabral was not a very great departure from Portuguese colonial policies. Luis Cabral built his government and administration around the Cabo-Verdeans and those of Cabo Verdean descent.[28] It did not matter if they were on the side of the Portuguese or the PAIGC.

It is important to understand that the relationship between Guinea-Bissau autochthons and those with Cabo Verdean background was the source of many discussions in scholarly and political circles, at least since 1959, although for the most part the debates were minor.[29]

> Upon the rise of nationalism in Guinea Bissau, several divisions among nationalists became apparent. A crucial one concerned the question of whether Guinea-Bissau and Cabo Verde should form one state together once independence was achieved or if Guinea Bissau should go its own way. Here, anti-Cabo Verdean feelings played a role, as PAIGC rivals like Francois Mendy and members of other clandestine parties that opted for a "mono-national" solution criticized the Cabo Verdean-dominated PAIGC for its binationalist project.[30]

Ideological divisions in PAIGC between the Cabo Verde faction and the Guinean nationalist faction over the ties between the two countries, as well as discontent in the armed forces over a new promotion system resulted in a military coup against President Cabral in 1980, led by the famous war commando Joao Bernardo (Nino) Vieira.[31]

As President Cabral promoted trusted soldiers who were close to him, and who were mainly Cabo Verdeans, Balanta liberation fighters demanded that they should be compensated for their sacrifices with higher positions and better pay. As early as 1959, there were reports of tensions between Bissau-Guinean Cabo Verdeans and the remaining population, leading to divisions among nationalists once independence was achieved.[32] Some historians believe that the assassination of Amilcar Cabral on January 20, 1973, reflected "the inner tensions and ideological divisions within the PAIGC, particularly over the dominance of the Cabo Verdean leadership and possible unity between the islands and Guinea-Bissau."[33] As a result, all the following administrations have shown the same pattern of privileging the Cabo Verdeans over the autochthons or indigenous citizens, and the same privileged group also controlled all of the businesses.[34] For Antonio Tomas;

> Cabral, a revolutionary of Cape Verdean origin, was killed at the hands of his own men from Guinea. Cabral had not taken the resentment between Cape Verdeans and Guineans seriously, but at a deeper level, this shows that Cabral was incorrect in his explanation of the social process in Guinea. He was convinced that a process of cultural osmosis would make the Cape Verdeans and Guineans into a community; in reality, Guineans took advantage of the anti-colonial war to advance their own agenda of power. But it also shows that Cape Verdeans and Guineans, pushed apart by colonialism, were culturally irreconcilable.[35]

For example, in 1980 there were about two hundred Cabo Verdeans in important government and administrative positions.[36] Some had participated in the armed struggle, but many more had come from the colonial administration. In theory, the National Popular Assembly (ANP) was the highest authority of the state, followed by the Council of State and the Council of Ministers or Commissars.[37] The majority of the Council of State and ministers were also members of the Permanent Commission (CP), the Executive Committee of the Struggle/Conselho Executivo da Luta (CEL), or the Highest Council of the Struggle (CSL). Most members of these groups were of Verdean descent. In the 1977–78 Council of State, only Umaro Djalo was not of Cabo Verdean descent, and he was not an officer. The other members were Luis Cabral as the President of the State and Head of the Council, Francisco Mendes as Prime minister, Nino Vieira as Commissar of the Armed Forces, and C. Teixeira as Commissar of National Security and Public Order.[38] The 1977–78 Council of Commissars and Ministers of the period were mostly of Cabo Verdean descent, with the exception of Joao Bernardo Vieira (Nino), and Samba Lamine Mané (two out of twenty ministers).[39]

The favoritism that benefited the Cabo Verdeans and those of Cabo Verdean descent was not new in Guinea Bissau. Looking at the colonial history of the country, the Portuguese policy of assimilation was an integral part of the colonial policy. The Portuguese considered the indigenous members of the African colonies as racially inferior and needing to be dragged gradually from their "primitive" and "savage" condition into the modern world. However, the Portuguese did not consider Cabo Verdeans to be "savages" and "primitive."[40] Consequently, they set up a dual system of education in Guinea, one for the so-called civilized Cabo Verdeans and Portuguese children, and one for the children of the natives or indigenous peoples.[41]

Most Bissau Guineans believe that the greatest national problem in the country is not the under-representation of women or the existence of gender inequalities, but rather the confiscation of political and economic power by Bissau Guineans of Cabo Verdean descent. For Mamady Kamara, whom I interviewed in front of a large crowd of PAIGC veterans as they were waiting for their monthly veteran's pension in Bissau, the problem was not that women were under-represented in the political and economic structures, but that the autochthons were under-represented, while people of Cabo Verdean descent were over-represented.[42] He and others went into extensive explanation about the origin of the issue. According to Mamady, the central factor involved the fact that the founding fathers of the PAIGC were all Cabo Verde descendants, and that the Cabo Verdeans were the most highly educated in Guinea Bissau at that time. When the country became independent, Luis Cabral did not hesitate to use them as the core of his administration and as a way to secure his position as the president of the country.[43]

While Mamady responded indirectly to my question regarding the under-representation of autochthonous women in the political and economic structures after independence, Barnaté Sanha was listening. As soon as Mamady finished his explanation, Barnaté intervened. For him, the under-representation of women autochthones was not the issue, but rather the under-representation of Bissau Guineans was the point I needed to focus on: "In this country you need to have connections to find a job. As the Cabo Verdeans and those of Cabo Verdean descent were already in the political and economic structures, that makes it easy for them to use their connections and find jobs, and that was not the case for us autochthons."[44] Although the question of the under-representation of autochthons in the socioeconomic and political spheres is a cause for concern, it should not result in overlooking or underestimating the under-representation of or bias again women with Bissau Guinean background in the processes of job recruitment and law.

The question of the under-representation of autochthonous Bissau Guinean women in political and economic spheres was sensitive and even frustrating for people with Cabo Verdean background in general, but particularly for women with Cabo Verdean background. I received many explanations, depending on the political and economic interests of the interviewees. People such as Carmen Pereira, Eva Gomes, and Francisca Pereira responded in one way; they turned the issue around and argued that the party and the government have always seen the natives of Guinea Bissau and Cabo Verde as one and indivisible. Hence, the problem was not about background or origin, but about competence and education level.[45]

For Quinta da Costa, the under-representation argument is misleading because not all people with Cabo Verdean descent benefited from the newfound independence. Many people with Portuguese or Cabo Verdean names do not have jobs and live equally as miserably as most Bissau Guineans. A small group controls the country, and you have to be part of the group in order to get the benefits you want or need.[46] Joanita Da Silva Rosa said if the administration were truly based on background or family name, then she should not suffer. She is of Cabo Verdean origin and lost one of her eyes during the war. Her late husband, Eusebio da Costa Ribero, was a Cabo Verdean, and he was killed during the war.[47] She is surviving now with the help of her church, which provides her a one-bedroom apartment and a monthly pension of 14,000 in local currencies (USD30).

While I was listening to Quinta da Costa arguing that the problem was the elite and exclusive leaders or executives, I recalled a situation that I witnessed in July of 2008, when I interviewed Carmen Pereira for the first time in her home. Her phone rang while I was interviewing her in the presence of my interpreter Juliao Mané Junior. She asked us to excuse her and to stop videotaping our conversation. As soon as she finished her phone conversation, she asked us to come back the next day. The reason she gave was that one of her relatives was ill at the hospital Simon Mendes, and the doctor was the one who called her in our presence to explain the severity of the illness. The doctor told her it was imperative for her to find a way to evacuate the patient to Lisbon in Portugal as soon as possible. When Juliao and I went back the next day, I asked her how her ill relative was doing. She responded that the patient had been sent to Lisbon on the late-night flight with the help of the health minister.[48] I was surprised at how quickly it happened. Connections or not, it was very quick.

Why No Changes and Continuation of the "Old Behavior"?

Certain social scientists studying Guinea Bissau, such as Jonina Einarsdottir, stated that it would be untruthful to claim that social and cultural changes had not taken place in Guinea Bissau over the last fifty years, but those changes are not readily visible, or else they are minimal regarding the issues of forced or arranged marriages. "Times are changing. Today no young girl has cuts made on her body as traditional practices. Adult women who have scars often feel ashamed and try to hide them with clothes," said Apili, a Papel woman in her forties, during an interview with Jonina Einarsdottir.[49]

> "During my fieldwork, I [in post-independence Guinea Bissau] was often confronted with contrasts," wrote Einarsdottir. "I could see it with my own eyes: these women were unhappy, exploited, oppressed and powerless."[50]

Many of the reasons for their unhappiness involved polygyny, forced marriages, and poverty.

Polygyny and arranged marriage are prevalent among several ethnic groups in Guinea Bissau, but the demography for the practice is not always consistent. In the region of Biombo, 29 percent of the chiefs have four or more wives, compared to less than 7 percent for all the other regions.[51] According to Einarsdottir, one-fourth of all married men have more than one wife that they have married themselves, and most of them also have inherited wives from their dead brothers in the region she studies.[52] Einarsdottir also provides evidence for the existence of forced or arranged marriage in the region.[53] The only recent change regarding forced marriage is that the marriage of a girl will not be arranged before her birth, as it used to be during the pre-independence period. However, parents still want to decide whom their daughters will marry, since they have both economic and social interests in their children's marriages.

In Guinea Bissau, people have various opinions regarding arranged marriage. I asked whether the laws of the newly independent country and the PAIGC policy were intended to liberate women and reject forced marriages.[54] The group of women with whom I was discussing this in Bairro Luanda, one of Bissau's neighborhoods, laughed, and Faniara Mballo responded,

> The fact that you decide whom your daughter is going to marry is not something bad, because you as parents have a better view about what is good or bad for your daughter. You will never put her in harm's way. This is not something new, because our parents were choosing husbands for us; why not do the same for our daughters?[55]

Female subordination is obviously evident in Guinea Bissau. Famara Mballo is a Fula woman who was born in 1959 in Farim (in northeastern Guinea Bissau). She was fifteen years old at the end of the liberation war. In Farim, she remembered helping her mother and other women transport foods and military supplies to the PAIGC soldiers or to the FARP. She attended the PAIGC schools and learned how to read. After six years of schooling, she decided to stay home and help her sick mother in the house. She married her cousin, Bacary Seydi, at the age of sixteen. The heads of the two families made the arrangements for the marriage. She still lives with her husband in Barrio "Militar" in Bissau, and they have three daughters and one son.

However, not all women agree about the custom. Some of the women in the audience nodded their heads in agreement with Famara, while Felicidad Mané seemed not to agree with her. For Felicidad, it was not right to have parents choosing husbands for their daughters. The daughters should be allowed to marry whom they want because it is their future, not the parent's future. When I asked her, "what would you do if your husband decides to choose your daughter's husband?" She responded, "I will do nothing, but I will not like it. But he is the father of my daughter and my husband. I will have to respect his decision." I responded by asking, "Why wouldn't you refuse, because the laws forbid arranged marriage and the laws will be with you?" Felicidad said, "I will never take my husband to the court; if I do, I will be disrespectful and I do not want that."[56] During all the discussion, the men who were present had a smile on their faces when Felicidad, who at first seemed to challenge their power, affirmed it was her duty to respect her husband because he was the decision-maker in the house.

Felicidad Mané was thirty-nine years old at that time; she is Mandinka, born in 1971 and raised in Bissau. Her father was a merchant with several wives, and he owned a small shop in the Bandin market in Central Bissau. Her mother was the first wife, and she is still alive, although Felicidad's father passed away in 1999. Felicidad stopped her studies at primary school level and never went back. She did not like polygyny because of what she saw in her personal family; in conflicts between co-wives, the father always took the side of the younger wives to the detriment of her mother. Coming from a Mandinka background, where respect for male authority is not negotiable, she told me that she is accustomed to accepting and following social rules, even though she may not like them.

The arrangement of marriages is obviously an important economic issue for parents. I asked most of the women about whether parents should arrange marriage for their daughters. The women who were against arranged marriage believed the solution to stop this traditional behavior would be to allow young girls to attend school. If young girls attended school, they would most likely refuse arranged marriage, because marrying early would stop their schooling. They would be more inclined to decide for themselves whom to marry and when to get married. Some women do not hesitate to run away, but they are also the ones most likely to come back home pregnant as a consequence of being away from home and seeing themselves as more independent in their decision-making, according to Laidy Costa.[57] For the women who are against forced marriage practices, schooling could be the solution, but at the same time, they believed that schooling could lead to problems within families. Therefore, schooling appears to them to be both a solution and a problem for those who oppose forced marriages in Guinea Bissau.

The issue of arranged marriage represents an important area of discord between Bissau Guineans. Cira Diallo maintains that, without parental input, young girls just follow their desires, desires that most of time are not the right ones. Girls who choose their own husbands sometimes are not very lucky. The husband could be violent or not appreciate his wife's family. The parents know better than their daughters, she said:

> I was lucky because I married against my will, but my husband and his family accepted me, and my marriage is going as well as I want it. Everything is not perfect, but I am not complaining. When my parents choose for me a husband, they will not sacrifice my interest or my life because they love me and may know what is best for me based on their own experience.[58]

Cira Diallo is a fifty-six-year-old Fula woman from Gabu. Her father was Alfouseyni Diallo, who migrated from Labé (French West African Guinea). Her mother was Fandima Dialan Kouyaté; a Mandinka woman born and raised in Gabu. Cira's father had three wives and seventeen children. She said that instead of being married against her will, she had wanted to marry her boyfriend, Seikou Sané, a Diola migrant, who was viewed in the community as a foreigner and outsider.

In contrast to Cira, Ndella Dialan married her longtime boyfriend. She is a Balanta from the Bijagós islands. She was born in 1974 and moved to Bissau to go to school when she was ten years old. In Bissau, she lived with her uncle. She said, "I was born in an independent country, and I went to school and graduated in 2001. Now I work at the state house as a secretary."[59] She met her future husband at her college, Liceu João XIII, in Bissau in 1996. They dated for three years before deciding to be married in 1999. They lived together two out of the three years they dated. The couple has three children, and Ndella has been the only one working since 2005. The two women, Cira and Ndella, held sharply contrasting views, based on their very different personal experiences.

The views exemplified above illustrate the situation in postwar Guinea Bissau. The newly independent country has enacted laws against forced or arranged marriage, but the enforcement of the new laws faces several challenges. The challenges come from both men and women, because many do not see the issue of arranged or forced marriages as a problem, and most find a way to circumvent the laws. As many women and men refuse to challenge traditions, the few women who reject arranged marriage face a dilemma, because they do not want to challenge their husband's authority, while at the same time, they also do not want to challenge traditional behavior by requesting arbitration in the case of an arranged marriage. They prefer to accept the situation rather than to request court arbitration.

In daily life, married women must get along with their husbands, but also with a varying number of co-wives or mistresses. From my discussions with women and men in Guinea Bissau, very few men were polygynists. However, a large number of married men (with one wife) had mistresses, especially in the cities. "Men want many women. Men have a sexual need for women during their whole life. Most of the men who have one wife also have several mistresses," said Adama Sy, one of my interpreters who is in his late thirties. He continued, "Having mistresses and polygyny are seen as the same. They are an adaptation to the Catholic tradition and life in urban areas."[60]

Being polygynous or having mistresses is very common today in Guinea Bissau. Opinions about polygyny vary. Some people I interviewed find it unjustifiable under any circumstances, while others say it depends on the situation. Still others also believe women do not have a choice, because it is in men's nature to want many wives. Many women also viewed polygyny as desirable because it alleviated their burden of domestic work, especially in the villages.[61] Ideally, co-wives treat each other as sisters or best friends and assist each other. In case of need, they help each other and take care of each other's children. According to Casey Lifton, the senior wife has the authority to interfere in the economic and practical matters of her co-wives, and she has the right to order them to sleep with the husband.[62] Ideally, the young co-wives cook, and the senior wife serves the food. However, relations between co-wives are not always amicable. Rivalry, jealousy, and animosity are often problems.[63] In urban areas, men circumvent polygyny by having secret mistresses. Some men tend to have several houses called *kasa-um, kasa-dus, kasa-tres* ("first house," "second house," "third house," etc.). The "first house" was the house of the legal and official wife, while the others were those of the man's mistresses.[64]

Women interviewed by Jonina Einarsdottir did not consider the ideas of polygyny or of men having mistresses as a problem, but for those women, the practices represented anarchy, without obligations and rights. Some women condemned the practices of polygyny and keeping mistresses because they felt the right of the official or first wife was not respected, while others worried about the rights of those women in the extra houses, the mistresses. In the end, the consensus on polygamy was that it was natural for men to have many women, and that co-wives should have friendly and mutual supportive relations. When co-wives argued among themselves, they most often blamed the husband, who, they believed, should respect tradition; he should recognize his senior wife's superior position within the group of co-wives and distribute all material and emotional favors equally.[65]

Those interviewed by Jonina Einarsdottir believed the issue of polygyny should be dealt with by forcing men to take responsibility for their actions in respecting the rights of the first wife and the wives in the extra houses. Some of those with whom I spoke totally rejected the idea of having "co-spouses" in their lives. However, many stoically accepted the idea of their husbands being polygynists or having mistresses, because the sexual stereotype of heterosexual men normalized such habits, and because women could do nothing about it: "Why fight with my husband for having a lot of wives? If he does not have many wives, it means he is having affairs somewhere. All men are like that," said Quintara Sanha.[66]

Quintara is a Manjack, born in Sao Domingo in 1948. She was fifteen when the liberation war began. Her father, Arfang Sanha, was a clerk in a shop owned by a Portuguese landowner in Cacheu. Her mother was a housekeeper for the same Portuguese family. Her father had three wives, and they all lived in the same compound. In addition to her father working as a clerk, he owned land where the family cultivated rice and vegetables. Quintara migrated to Bissau after the war. She was opposed to polygyny or having mistresses but affirmed no one could stop it because it was the natural order of men's sexual behavior.

Most of Bissau Guinean women seem uninterested in challenging the social order. For Anna Maria Naneira, a twenty-eight-year-old Balanta woman working for one of the two telephone companies in Bissau, the problem is not about choosing her own husband, or her parents choosing him, but rather how responsible her husband would be in matters regarding family life. She told me, "You can choose your husband and have a difficult married life, or your parents can choose your husband and you can have a decent married life."[67] She continued, saying, "If we want to challenge all the matters someone may think are wrong or unfair in our way of living, then we will cause a lot of confrontations in our communities. It would be very difficult to decide what to change and how to change it. Second, who should be allowed to make the changes?"⁶⁸ Her argument made me aware of how social change happens and led me to add to my series of questions, "How do gendered changes happen and who should advocate those changes?" The responses were quite interesting but often contradictory.

Women often refused to challenge the social order because they did not want to be stigmatized by society, and they would prefer to accept whatever sacrifices were necessary in order to keep family life as stable as possible for the sake of their children and their children's future. I spoke with D. B., a thirty-five-year-old Mandinka woman from the Mansoa region who teaches in Bissau. She told me, "My husband, M. T., after five years of us living together, decided to marry a second wife; I was not happy at all, but I have to accept it." I asked her why she felt she had to accept it, especially since polygyny has been against the law since independence. She responded,

> My choices are to divorce him, something I do not want to do because of our two kids, or to take him to the court and I will be seen as a bad wife because I took my husband to the judiciary system. Our community would view this as a very bad thing; I do not want my children to be cursed because of my doing [it]. Also, as we did not do the civil marriage as most of the couples in Guinea Bissau, so the law can't legally sanction him.⁶⁹

Few of the women I talked to affirmed that, in a situation where the judiciary institutions were strong enough to protect them, they would challenge polygyny and a forced marriage. As it is now, a woman can challenge her husband's decision to have more than one wife, because the law rejects the practice and she could easily win the battle. However, the cost might be high, especially when governmental institutions do not follow up to make sure their decisions are being respected. Nothing could really force the husband to respect the judiciary decision, and if the woman keeps challenging her husband for failing to respect the judiciary decision, in the end she will be the one to blame as "she does not want peace."⁷⁰ The most important aspect of this situation is that women will always have to confront husbands who are the household decision-makers. For Maria Gomez, time will solve the issue of arranged marriage and polygyny through better education and larger numbers of people being educated. With improving economic conditions, and the implications for family responsibilities, social views will change, and these two matters will disappear. "But it will take time before we get there."[71]

PAIGC and the Failure to Respect the Gender Equality Promises in Postwar Guinea Bissau

Much like the first UDEMU, the postwar UDEMU has failed to attain its objectives because of a lack of organization and the absence of policies that could mobilize and develop awareness regarding the socioeconomic position of women. The need for equality between men and women was made an explicit and integral part of the overall revolution from the beginning of the political mobilization for the war of liberation.[72] The PAIGC did not create a "women's wing" during the revolutionary period, as happened in other African revolutions, but the situation changed at independence. The party created the Women's Commission three months after independence to represent women. Within a few years this organ became the Democratic Union of the Women of Guinea-Bissau (UDEMU).

In the 1977 declaration of the PAIGC's Superior Council of the Struggle at the third Party Congress, the party affirmed that the UDEMU was committed to eliminating the conditions that created inequality for women vis-à-vis men. The UDEMU promised to encourage Guinean women to participate in socially useful activities such as entrepreneurship. The Commission was led by ten women: Teodora Gomes, Francisca Pereira, Carmen Pereira, Ana Maria Soares, Lilica Boal, Satu Djassi, Lucette Andrade Cabral, Satu Camara, and two women from a peasant background.[73] Their mission was to mobilize women to participate in development projects such as trading and cash crop production, to implement PAIGC policies, to campaign against illiteracy, prostitution, and alcoholism, and to promote women's artisanal cooperatives and maternity and childcare centers.[74] Most of the laws particularly benefited urban women who were themselves or whose husbands were in salaried work.

Since independence, peasant women have been legally guaranteed access to land by the government, but gender inequalities have still resulted in women being denied access to capital, technology, and training. In semi-urban areas, women have in some cases lost access to their personal plots of arable land when the land has been sold or leased.⁷⁵ In the urban areas, gender-specific roles and responsibilities in the family have been major obstacles to the educational and occupational advancement of women.

More broadly, the practical implementation of government policy paid little attention to the specific needs of women. For example, regarding the "integrated rural development projects," projects with the goal of improving and diversifying agricultural production, the government was not aware that women needed independent access to capital, tools, and training.⁷⁶ Women have rarely been targeted for specific development programs, and they have generally not been given the financial or structural independence necessary to organize effectively or to improve their working lives. Most development projects have benefited men and increased the labor burden of women. The lack of attention to the role of women in production has resulted in women being excluded from the development agenda.

With very few exceptions, the creation of the UDEMU, progressive legislation, and development programs have had little positive impact on the lives of women, largely due to traditional social structures.⁷⁷ At its inception, the women's organization had a small office behind an army post (from 1974 to 1985) and lacked staff. The UDEMU executive structure remains very small (twelve members) and has received insufficient funding to promote its official goals. By the early 1980s, the UDEMU had become more of a social club than a center for mobilizing women in support of their legal rights. Women who might have been persuaded to be politically active have found the battle against male political control impossible to fight without stronger support from the party leadership.

As a result, the UDEMU remained centered in Bissau and only played a symbolic role in perpetuating the myth that there was a genuine commitment to prioritizing the emancipation and equality of women during the first republic.⁷⁸ Women's organizations and organizations such as the Amilcar Cabral's African Youth (JAAC/Juventude Africana Amilcar Cabral) and the National Union of Workers of Guinea-Bissau (UNTG/União Nacional dos Trabalhadores de Guine) have been marked by inefficiency, lack of democratically motivated leaders, and the persistent efforts of PAIGC elites to assert hegemonic control over youth, labor, and women activists and to create support structures for the personal power of President Luis Cabral (until the 1980 military coup).⁷⁹

Presently, the UDEMU office is located inside the PAIGC headquarters in Bissau. As in the past, the organization is still under-equipped and under-funded. The only persons regularly present are the president Eva Gomez (elected in 2009), an unpaid secretary, and Binetou Seydi, who has been in charge of the cleaning of the PAIGC headquarter for at least three years now. Most of the time the UDEMU president will receive women in her office, and their discussions revolve around issues other than those that are gendered. The present-day UDEMU appears not greatly different from the one described by Joshua Forrest during the years after independence.[80]

When I asked Dianké Mballo, a Fula woman from the village of Kendiale in the Northeastern region of Guinea Bissau, how she viewed the role of the women's organization after independence, she fiercely responded that the women's organization existed only in name because it never really defended or helped women in need. Titina Silla recruited Dianké Mballo during the war years. She went through military and political training, and she was a member of her village committee during the early years of independence: "As the women's organization was not effectively fighting for our emancipation, our work, me and another woman (Fanta Baldé) was tougher because we did not receive support from the women in the village and from the women organization. At the end, we just do what need to be done and follow the male members' agenda."[81]

Conclusion

Women did not participate in the liberation struggle to emancipate themselves. The most common reason that women gave for their involvement was that, as Fatu Turé stated, "We wanted to take care of our families and children. This was not possible with the presence of the 'Tuga' who were beating our husbands for many reasons, forcing them to work, and taking the food from our children's mouths."[82] The next most common reason for their participation was "to liberate and develop our country." It is important to note that women usually offered this explanation as a reason for participating after they had gone through some political training or had been in contact with the PAIGC cadres. I viewed this response to be more a mechanical or automatic rationale in the case of most of the women.

However, I will not argue that all the women who referred to nationalist reasons for their participation were merely reflecting political indoctrination by PAIGC leaders, since few of them had a precise understanding of Bissau Guinean nationalism and larger colonial issues. For example, Francisca Pereira said if she had a choice now about whether to work for the success of the PAIGC again, she would not do so because of the social and familial sacrifices that go with being both a woman and a political activist in Guinea Bissau. She was divorced three times because her husbands' families did not understand the idea of her leaving her familial and social duties and "abandoning" her husband for months for the war.

It seems that after years and years of struggle for so-called women's emancipation, even the most committed women gave up because of the lack of support from the state, the party, and their social environment. It is possible that the pro-emancipation militants were not fully prepared for the reality of the emancipation struggle, or perhaps those who opposed it were stronger. The party and its participants were simply not prepared for how difficult it would be to take on the social habits and traditions that had been in place so long with respect to arranged marriages and polygyny. Additionally, many of the men in the country, and indeed in the party, were unwilling to make changes in the gendered aspects of their lives.

Conclusion

Bissau Guinean women had been promised, both during the mobilization prewar period and again during the liberation war, that they would be able to free themselves from the shackles of sociocultural constraints and traditional beliefs that keep them exploited from "above and below." Women's emancipation was meant to give women access to the economic, political, and social advantages that had been limited to men by traditional sociocultural beliefs and reinforced by a male-dominant colonial system.

By the 1980s, it was apparent that Stephanie Urdang's positive review (from 1974) of the newly independent state had faded away, as what was meant to happen to free the women of Guinea Bissau had not, in fact, taken place. Good ideas were left on the shelves and never materialized. Promises to free women from two colonizers, traditional sociocultural beliefs and the colonial state, were never kept. After the assassination of Amilcar Cabral, the new Bissau Guinean government did not fully support the women's emancipation agenda.[1] It was more interested in preserving the advantages of the new male elite and solving the internal bi-nationalist and ethnic divisions.[2]

The women's leadership became less interested in advocating for women's advancement in order to avoid being cast out and also because of lack of support from Luis Cabral's government. Along with external pressures and prejudice, this brought about the ultimate failure to free women both from the traditional sociocultural and economic order of the Bissau Guinean societies and also from the burden of the colonial and postcolonial systems. The Bissau Guinean women who participated in the struggle for independence said, in effect, "Men, instead of sharing the pie they received after years of fighting for independence, just decided to give women a small slice of the pie. And women did not demand their fair share, just because they were afraid of being outcasts and labelled as bad women who wanted to destroy the foundation of the Bissau Guinean family."[3]

In Guinea Bissau, the 1950s agitations for independence had been severely reprimanded by the Portuguese colonial system. The Portuguese obsession with total control of the colonial situation was demonstrated in the suppression of the Pijiguiti dockworkers' strike of August 3, 1959. The Portuguese colonial police PIDE had forced all the nationalist movements into exile in Senegal and Guinea-Conakry after the massacre.

The revolt of the dockworkers, which had been mobilized by the African Party of Independence for Guinea and Cabo Verde (PAIGC), proved ultimately unstoppable as in 1961, Amilcar Cabral and his allies launched the general insurrection that led to the independence of the colony.[4] Twelve years later, the PAIGC unilaterally declared the independence of Guinea-Bissau. Bissau Guinean freedom fighters achieved victory nine months after the assassination of their charismatic and revolutionary leader on January 20, 1973.

Throughout the political struggle, Amilcar Cabral clearly understood that the people did not join the struggle for purely ideological reasons but also in order to gain material advantages and to have a better life, living in peace. Cabral also understood that the war for the liberation of the country needed to be waged at the same time as the fight for sociocultural and economic transformation of the country's society. In Amilcar Cabral's vision, the liberation of the country and the liberation of women from societal oppression must be achieved together, because liberating the country without liberating women would not allow the development of a transformative and successful society.

The liberation of the colonial state did not, however, lead to the radical transformation of the Guinea Bissau economy and society as envisioned by Amilcar Cabral. Officially, the explanation given by the newly independent government was that the imperative to exercise effective control over society and the economy forced them to be realistic and pragmatic. Pragmatism meant that deviations from the radical agenda were inevitable. These departures led to the erosion of institutions, factional struggles, greater political instability, and a return to old societal behaviors.

"Obsessed with exercising effective control over youth, labor, women, and society in general, an over-zealous national security force intimidated and silenced almost all dissenting voices."[5] Arbitrary arrests, imprisonment, and summary executions were some of the most severe measures taken by the new government. Free expression and public debate became largely muted. The situation required self-censorship for the preservation of life, reinforcing disillusionment with independence and encouraging withdrawal from participation in politics and social transformations.

With the leadership of the PAIGC no longer subject to pressures from below, an environment more propitious for factional struggles and political instability was created. A new sociocultural environment based on origin and background became the determining factor regarding who belonged to the ruling elite. In 1980, the then-Prime Minister Joao Bernardo "Nino" Vieira put down President Luis Cabral, half-brother of Amilcar Cabral, and accused him of "deviation from the line of Amilcar."[6]

The "deviation from the line of Amilcar Cabral" had, in fact, already occurred under the leadership of Amilcar Cabral, as most of his followers believed that the liberation of the country was more important than having a radical and transformative society in which all members were equal and had the same opportunities to be successful. The consequences of the deviation were that "factional struggles within the party and the armed forces continued to generate political tension throughout the 1980s and 1990s, culminating in the armed confrontation which flared up on June 7, 1998, notwithstanding the accusation, and indeed the involvement, of high-ranking army officers in the supply of arms to the Casamance independence fighters in Southern Senegal."[7]

It should be emphasized that the internal power struggles and conflicts of interest among the country's rulers reflected deepening economic, social, and educational crises, the solutions for which led to the adoption of the International Monetary Fund and World Bank measures. The measures imposed by external institutions have had very high social costs and economic impact.[8] As a result of the tenuous economic conditions, the health care and educational systems deteriorated. Teachers and nurses would often receive their miserable salaries four to six months late, leading to strikes by high school teachers and nurses.

Among the most impoverished were the liberation war veterans who, like schoolteachers and other low-level public sector workers, would go months without receiving their meager salaries. In contrast, the ministers and senior government officials, high-ranking party members, and a few top military officers lived lavish lifestyles. This situation was far removed from what Amilcar Cabral had envisioned for his country. As Quinta Da Costa and most of the former women combatants said, "Amilcar Cabral would not be happy if he came back today in Guinea Bissau."[9]

As PAIGC members deviated from the line of Amilcar Cabral since the early stage of mobilization for the insurrection, so Marxist historians deviated from Karl Marx's concept of Marxist revolution in this movement. Marxist historians set starting points for analyzing so-called Marxist revolutionary movements by laying down first the theoretical framework of Marxism and they trying to fit nationalist and revolutionary movements into Marx's analysis of revolutionary movements. They went from a general or international analysis of Marxism to the particulars of individual national revolutionary movements.

The consequences of this analytical methodology are the perception of Marxism as dogmatic, the use of the state or movement and its leadership as the central point of analysis, and the marginalization of other important participants and actors in the revolutionary struggles and their exclusion from national liberation movement narratives, discourses, and analyses. Another consequence of this methodological approach is that women participants faced what I call the self-paradox paradox, that is, they tended to minimize their own roles.

A new historical methodology is needed, one that focuses on the excluded discourses and on developing a methodology that allows women combatants and other marginalized participants to understand that their discourses and narratives are equally as important as the "official" (male) participant narratives and discourses. These marginalized discourses lead to discourses and narratives far from the theoretical approach of Marxist historians because they are based on concrete facts of daily life. But they can also be interpreted as what Amilcar Cabral defined as the feeding ground of his revolutionary analysis. Others see such narratives as a reason to qualify him or his movement as Marxist.

Listening to women combatants' discourses and narratives, I discovered that women participated in all aspects of the armed struggles, even though they faced restrictions and gendered spaces and downplayed their own roles. Their participation was essential to the success of the war, but instead of sharing the fruits of the victory with them after independence, the men gave them token rewards and asked them to return to their habitual space and to resume their traditional roles.

Very few women benefited from their participation in the war of liberation. Instead, they witnessed the emergence of a small class of wealthy and powerful women with Portuguese names. The postwar independence was so difficult for most of these former women combatants that they believed the PAIGC leaders had abandoned them. They still believe that if Amilcar Cabral were alive, their situation as women would be better.

Most male former fighters believed that the conditions of the women former fighters were not just a result of their being women, because most men believe that all the former fighters have been left out of the newly independent political structure. In the end, the only one who is still in the heart of the former fighters is Amilcar Cabral. The failure of Cabral's vision of total and radical change of the Bissau Guinean societal structure, along with the addition of new layers of division based on family origins, have led to the development of conditions in which social and political stability was almost impossible, civil wars became unavoidable, and new external negative issues arose, such as drug and arms trafficking.

To move Guinea Bissau into an era beyond conflict, several problems need to be resolved. First, the second component of Amilcar Cabral's vision must be achieved. That is, women and other marginalized groups must be fully integrated into the existing social, economic, and political structures. Second, a new national army must be created based on republican principles, and not on the ideas of former freedom fighters. Officers with the mentality of freedom fighters still believe the country owes them and belongs to them, instead of thinking about how they can best serve the country. Because the economic situation is disastrous, some of them do not hesitate to become involved in arm and drug trafficking. Finally, national institutions must reform to avoid the perpetual confrontation between the prime minister and the president.

The passing of Amilcar Cabral left unsolved two major issues. One was gender-based inequality. The other was related to the bi-nationalist members of the PAIGC, that is, the opposition between PAIGC leaders (mostly of Cabo Verdean descent) and the PAIGC base (mostly local Bissau Guinean peasants and autochthons).[10] Cabral believed that changing traditional gender inequality was the greater revolution that needed to happen in Bissau Guinean society. But what happened between 1974 and 1980 was that the division between local Bissau Guineans and Bissau Guineans with Cabo Verdean background became the greater and more challenging problem, leading to the 1980 military coup.[11] The coup was organized by a Pepel who was given a Balanta pseudonym during the war; Nino Vieira, who viewed the Luis Cabral government as favoring people linked to Cabo Verde.[12] The coup led to the secession of Cabo Verde and a declaration of independence for the Cabo Verde Islands. This newly opened door enabled Nino to lead the country into more ethnic and bi-nationalist divisions, relegating the gender inequality question to lower importance, since without a stable country no discussion of woman's emancipation was possible. As social scientists, we should clarify and highlight the opposition in Guinea Bissau between people who call themselves locals or autochthons and those with Cabo Verdean descent, even though the latter group has always refused to see this opposition as part of the problem the country faces. Future studies of the revolution must integrate the questions of how these two groups interacted during and after the war.

Within the general study of the Portuguese Guinean liberation war, the most important contribution of my research is the re-writing of the liberation war narrative by integrating female participants' discourses, clarifying their reasons for participation, how they participated, and how their expectations were not met after the war. It adds to the general historiography of the newly independent country by focusing on the micro narratives of women participants, thereby moving away from more general presentations of nationalist movements and liberation wars that tend to ignore female involvement. In this presentation, women combatants and participants are not ignored, but shown to be full participants in a wide variety of ways, even though they continue to be undervalued or left out of the "official discourses." The consequence of the women's underrepresentation in official discourses has led to what I call the self-paradox agenda, meaning women participants themselves voluntarily dismiss their roles and understate their participation in the liberation war.

Cabral realized that for women to become emancipated, they needed to feel the urgency and to dedicate themselves to the success of the movement. That did not happen; in fact, the women's agenda was swept under the rug once the actual fighting stopped. But that does not diminish the fact that the women who were involved in the struggle contributed greatly to the success of the liberation movement, and it is safe to say that without their efforts, the outcome would have been quite different. Perhaps the most important thing, in the final analysis, is that their contribution is finally able to be recognized.

Figure 1 PAIGC Headquarters in Bissau (Photo Aliou Ly 2008).

Figure 2 Joanita Da Silva Rosa. During a direct combat operation in the southern front she lost her right eye and was sent to La Havana for medical treatment (Photo Aliou Ly 2010).

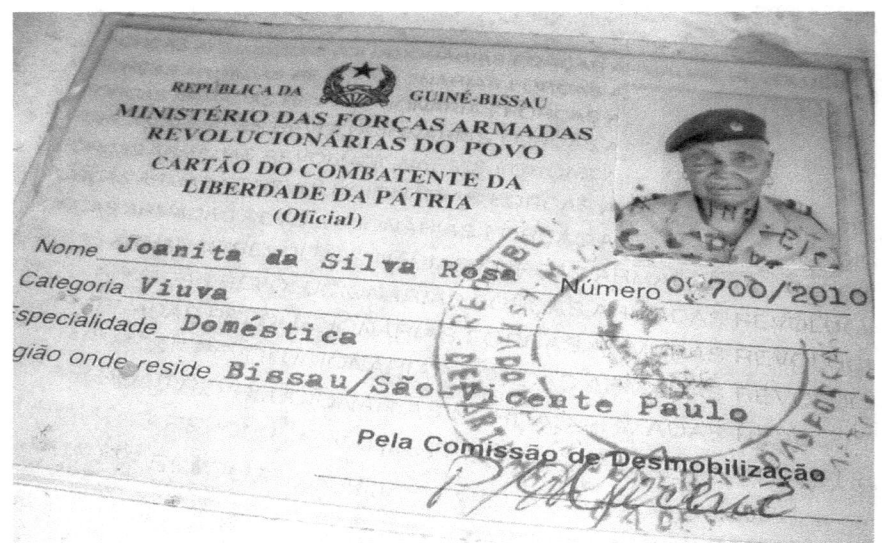

Figure 3 Joanita Da Silva Rosa, ID card as veteran of the liberation war (Photo Aliou Ly 2010).

Figure 4 NDo Mane, Na Ndjati, and Udé Camara, veterans of the liberation war, waiting to get their veteran pension in Bissau (Photo Aliou Ly 2010).

Figure 5 Quinta Da Costa and Segunda Sambu, both veterans of the liberation war, waiting to get their pension in Bissau (Photo Aliou Ly 2010).

Figure 6 Quinta Da Costa, veteran who was shot in her left leg during the liberation war. After the war she was nominated Captain in the Bissau Guinean Army (Photo Aliou Ly 2010).

Figure 7 Barnaté Shana was under the commandment of Osvaldo Vieira in the eastern front. He lost his eye during combat. He was one of the fierce opponents of female participation in combat operations (Photo Aliou Ly 2010).

Figure 8 Remembering the 1959 Pijiguiti Massacre in Bissau, August 3, 2010 (Photo Aliou Ly 2010).

Figure 9 Remembering the 1959 Pijiguiti Massacre in Bissau, August 3, 2010 (Photo Aliou Ly 2010).

Figure 10 Remembering the 1959 Pijiguiti Massacre in Bissau, August 3, 2010 (Photo Aliou Ly 2010).

Selected Interviews in Guinea Bissau

Gaitano Barboza, interviewed in English and translated Crioulo, August 8, 2008.

Dalanda Biaye, interviewed in English and translated in Crioulo, September 5, 2010.

Pauletta Camara, interviewed in French, June 22, 2009.

Udé Camara, group interviewed in English and translated in Crioulo August 2, 2010.

Bacar Cassama, interviewed in English and translated in Crioulo, August 14, 2008.

Mario Augusto Ramalho Cissokho, interviewed in French, August 8, 2008.

Laidy Costa, as participant of an informal group discussion in French, July 30, 2010.

Quinta Da Costa, interviewed in English and translated in Crioulo, August 12, 2010.

Joanita Da Silva Rosa, interviewed in English and translated in Crioulo, July 15 and 30, 2010.

Ndella Dialan as participant of an informal group discussion in French, July 30, 2010.

Cira Diallo interviewed in Pular, July 12, 2009.

Fatoumata Diallo, interviewed in Pular, July 27 and September 1, 2009.

Dialan Diamba, interviewed in Pular, July 1, 2010.

Aliu Fadia, interviewed in French, June 10, 2010.

Diabira Gassama, interviewed in English and translated in Crioulo, July 27, 2010.

Eva Gomes, interviewed in English and translated in Crioulo, August 13, 2008.

Juditi Gomes, interviewed in English and translated in Crioulo, July 28, 2010.

Mamady Kamara interviewed in Pular, August 23, 2010.

Fantam Kawsara interviewed in Pular, July 16, 2010.

Felicidad Mané, as participant of an informal group discussion in French, July 30, 2010.

Ndalla Mané, interviewed in English and translated in Crioulo, July 17, 2010.

NDo Mané, interviewed in English and translated in Crioulo August 2, 2010.

Dianké Mballo, interviewed in Pular, July 20, 2010.

Famara Mballo, as participant of an informal group discussion in French, July 30, 2010.

Anna Maria Naneira, interviewed in French, June 29, 2010.

Victor Naneira, interviewed in English and translated in Crioulo, August 15, 2009.

Na Ndjati, interviewed in English and translated in Crioulo, August 2, 2010.

Sandé NHaga, interviewed in English and translated in Crioulo, August 28, 2010.

Theresa Nquamé, interviewed in English and translated in Crioulo, July 28, 2010.
Carmen Pereira, interviewed in English and translated in Crioulo, August 21, 2008.
Francisca Pereira, interviewed in French, August 9 and 16, 2008, and July 12, 2010.
Sito Sadio, interviewed in English and translated in Crioulo, July 17, 2010.
Segunda Sambu, interviewed in English and translated in Crioulo, August 2, 2010.
Fanta Sané, interviewed in Wolof, July 27, 2010.
Barnaté Sanha, interviewed in English and translated in Crioulo, July 28 and August 23, 2010.
Quintara Sanha, interviewed in French, July 26, 2010.
Binetou Nankin Seydi, interviewed in French, June 20, and August 25, 2008.
Sano Seydi, interviewed in Pular, June 28, 2010.
Adama Sy, as participant of an informal group discussion in French, July 30, 2010.
Fatu Turé, interviewed in English and translated in Crioulo, July 27, 2010.
Hutna Yala, interviewed in English and translated in Crioulo, August 16, 2010.

Notes

Introduction

1 For more on Portuguese Guinea, see Chaliand, *Guinée Portugaise et Cap Vert*, 1–36; Pelissier, *Naissance de la Guiné*; Kohl, *A Creole Nation*, 3; Sousa, *"Amilcar Cabral (1924–1973)"*; and Dhada, *Warriors at Work*, 139–48. For Cabral's background, see De Andrade, *Amilcar Cabral: Essai de Biographie Politique*, 11–78; De Braganca and Wallerstein, *The African Liberation Reader: Vol. 1*, 6–37.

2 PAIGC: *Partido Africano da Independencia da Guine e Cabo Verde*: African Party for the Independence of Guinea and Cape Verde.

3 For more on Carmen Pereira see Chilcote, *Amilcar Cabral's Revolutionary Theory and Practice*, viii.

4 For more on nationalism and statehood in Guinea-Bissau, see Chilcote, *Emerging Nationalism in Portuguese Africa Documents*; Lars Rudebeck, *Guinea-Bissau: A Study of Political Mobilization*; Galli and Jones, *Guinea-Bissau: Politics, Economics and Society*; Lopes, *Para Uma Leitura Sociologica da Guiné-Bissau*, 230–1; Bull, *O Crioulo da Guiné-Bissau*, 78, 116–19; Couto, "Politica e Planeamento Linguisto na Guiné-Bissau," 52; Filho, "Rumores: Uma Narrativa da Nação"; "A Construção e o Fim dos Projetos Crioulos," 95–120; "Some Problems with the Creole Project for the Nation: The Case of Guinea-Bissau," Paper Presented at the Powerful Presence of the Past: Historical Dimensions of Integration and Conflict in the Upper Guinea Coast Conference, *Max Planck Institute for Social Anthropology*, (Hall [Saale], October 19–21, 2006); Nassum, "Politica Linguistic Pós-Colonial: Ruptura ou Continuuidade?"; Silva, *A Independência da Guiné-Bissau e a Descolonizaçao Portuguesa*; Scott, *Seeing Like a State,* 34; Askew, *Performing the Nation,* 182; Eriksen, "Creolization in Anthropological Theory in Mauritius," 174; Knorr, "Towards Conceptualizing Creolization and Creoleness," 4–5, and 13–14; "Contemporary Creoleness; or The World in Pidginization?" (*Current Anthropology,* 51, 2010), 747; Wicks, "Manifestations of Nationhood in the Writings of Amílcar Cabral," 45–70;

Embalo, "O Crioulo da Guiné-Bissau: Língua Nacional e Factor de Identidade Nacional," 105; Amado, *Guerra Colonial e Guerra de Libertação Nacional*.

5 Chabal, "Litterature et Liberation Nationale," 457–8; PAICV, *Continuar Cabral*, 135–463; Davidson, *Liberation of Guiné*, 77; Van Der Drift, "Democracy Warfare in Guinea Bissau," 229–30; Solodovnikov, "The Theoretical Legacy of Amilcar Cabral," 110–12; McCulloch, *In the Twilight of Revolution*, 49–56; Young, "Patterns of Social Conflict: State, Class and Ethnicity," 24; Womack, *The Foundation of Mao Zedong's Political Thought*; Wylie, *The Emergence of Maoism*; See Marx, "Theses on Feuerbach," 403; and Lenin, *Materialism and Empirio-Criticism*, 136–42; Solodovnikov, "The Theoretical Legacy of Amilcar Cabral," 110–12; McCulloch, *In the Twilight of Revolution*, 49–56; Young, "Patterns of Social Conflict: State, Class and Ethnicity," 24; Rudebeck, *Guinea-Bissau: A Study of Political Mobilization*, 78 and 103; Chabal, "National Liberation in Portuguese Guinea," 78. See also Krautsova, "Amilkar Kabral," 76–87; PAIGC, "Notes on AC's [Second] Visit to London," April 5, 1965, 2. It is important to note that Henriksen also paints the Guinea Bissau revolution as Marxist, even though Amilcar Cabral had always refused to call the revolution a Marxist revolution. Henriksen, "People's War in Angola, Mozambique, and Guinea-Bissau," 377–99; Chabal, "The Social and Political Thought of Amilcar Cabral," 56; Knutsen, *History of International Relations*, 251; Mao, *Four Essays on Philosophy*, 1.

6 de Andrade, *Amilcar Cabral*, 6. See also Raeburn, *Black Fire: Accounts of the Guerilla War in Rhodesia*, 9; PAIGC; Cabral, "Nkrumah," 1; PAIGC. *Amilcar Cabral's Letter to Kwame Nkrumah (handwritten rough draft by himself)* no date.

7 Idahosa, "Going to the People," 30.

8 Chilcote, "The Political Thought of Amilcar Cabral," 374.

9 Luke, "Cabral's Marxism," 308; Davidson, *No Fist Is Big Enough to Hide the Sky*, 15–16; Rabaka, "Contours of Cabralism," 15; Saucier, "Returning to Cabral," xvi.

10 For more on Cabral's agronomic work, see McCulloch, *In the Twilight of Revolution*, 59–82; Schwarz, "An Agronomist before His Time," 79–93.

11 Basil Davidson, *The Liberation of Guiné*, 30, 56–75.

12 PAIGC, "Notes on AC's Visit to London," [Date?]; Vice President, Senegal, 00144: Ministére des Affaires Etrangéres; Actualités Politiques et Informations diplomatiques concernant Guinée, Maroc et Vietnam: coupures de Presse et Correspondances (1958–1961). Tomas, *Amilcar Cabral: The Life of a Reluctant Nationalist*, 105–8.

13 PAIGC; Cabral, "Le Crime de Colonialisme," 12–13; PAIGC; Amilcar Cabral, Le Peuple de Guinee "Portuguesa" devant l'Organisation des Nations Unies.

[Declaration du Secretaire General du PAIGC, Ingenieur Amilcar Cabral.] Conakry, June 1962, 85 [French]; PAIGC; "A Nosse Luta pela Educacao das Masses e Pela Formacao de Quadros." Conakry, September 1965, 1-18; Chabal, "National Liberation in Portuguese Guinea," 82.

14 Byrne, *Mecca of Revolution*, 3. For more on ALGERIAN roles in the sub-Saharan revolutions or nationalism, see Byrne, *Mecca of Revolution*, 111, 164, 175, 189-92, 199, 248-9, 255, 266, 295; Ahlman, "The Algerian Question in Nkrumah's Ghana"; Christelow, *Algerians without Border*; Robert Malley, *The Call from Algeria*. For more on Chinese and African revolutions and nationalism, see Weigert, *Angola; A Modern Military History*, 15-30 and 69-105; Adie, "China, Russia and the Third World"; Hutchison, *China's Africa Revolution*; Jackson, "China's Third World Foreign Policy"; Larkin, *China, and Africa*; Edmundo Rocha, *Angola: Viriato da Cruz*. For more on CUBA and African revolutions and nationalism, see Guimaraes, *The Origins of the Angolan Civil War*, 136-60; Gleijeses, *Havana, Washington and Africa*; George, *The Cuban Intervention in Angola*; Fontanellaz and Cooper, *War of Intervention in Angola: Volume 2*; Mesa-Lago and Belkin eds., *Cuba and Africa*, 1-63; Castro, *Cuba and Angola*, 9-72; Marshall, "Cuba's Relation with Africa," 47-68; Villegas, *Cuba & Angola*, 29-44; Villafana, *Cold War in the Congo*. For more on Soviet Union roles in African revolutions and rebellions, see Morison, *The USSR and Africa*, 4-58; Fernando Andresen Guimaraes, *The Origins of the Angolan Civil War*, 161-96; Andrew and Mitrokhin, *The World Was Going Our Way*, 423-94; Roy Allison, *The Soviet Union and The Strategy of Non Alignment*, 105-7 and 227; Duncan, ed., *Soviet Policy in the Third World*, 135-55, 196-211; Iandolo, "Imbalance of Power," 32-55 " The Rise and Fall of the Soviet Model of Development in West Africa," 783-804; Katsakioris, "L'Union Sovietique et les Intellectuels Africains"; Mazov, *A Distant Front in the Cold War*; Klinghoffer, *The Angolan War*, 42-81.

15 Idahosa, "Going to the People," 32; Young, "Patterns of Social Conflict"; Tamarkin, "Culture and Politics in Africa."

16 Chabal, "National Liberation," 86; Dhada, *Warriors at Work*, 5-6; Davidson, *No Fist Is Big Enough to Hide the Sky*, 34; Maddox and Welliver, *Colonialism and Nationalism in Africa*, 153-65.

17 Chabal, "National Liberation in Portuguese Guinea," 86; Cabral, *Palavras de Orden Gerais* and *Alguns Principios do Partido*. For more on Amilcar Cabral, his leadership and theoretical works on early literatures: Andelman, "Profile: Amilcar Cabral," 18-19; Blacky, "Fanon and Cabral," 191-210; Gerard, *Armed Struggle in Africa* and *Revolution in the Third World*; Chilcote, "The Political

Thought of Amilcar Cabral"; Davidson, *The Liberation of Guiné*; Mugbane, "Amilcar Cabral: Evolution and Revolutionary Thought," 71–87; McCollester, " The Political Thought of Amilcar Cabral"; Morgado, "Amilcar Cabral's Theory of Cultural Revolution," 3–16; Urdang, "Towards a Successful Revolution."

18 Hubbard, "Culture and History in a Revolutionary Context," 70; Ferreira, "Amilcar Cabral: Theory of Revolution and Background to His Assassination," 52–3; Maddox and Welliver, *Colonialism and Nationalism in Africa*, 181–202.

19 Chabal; "Revolutionary Democracy in Africa," 84. For more on Angolan nationalist movements, see Guimaraes, *The Origins of the Angolan Civil War*, 85–113; Millar, *Forms of Disappointment*, xiii–xli; Weigert, *Angola; A Modern Military History*, 15–30 and 69–105; Marcum, *The Angolan Revolution, Vol. 1*, 200–65 and *The Angolan Revolution, Vol. 2*, 121–3, 169–79, 263–75; Angolan National Seminar, *Toward Angolan Independence*, 4–31; James III, *A Political History of the Civil War in Angola*, 1–88; Spikes, *Angola and the Politics of Intervention*, 1–48; Ingles, "The MPLA Government and Its Post-Liberation Record in Angola," 43–56. For more on Mozambique nationalist movements and revolution, see Nuvunga, " From Former Liberation Movement to Four Decades in Government," 57–71; Marcum, *Conceiving Mozambique*, 17–55; Dinerman, *Revolution, Counter-Revolution and Revisionism in Postcolonial Africa*, 32–114; Mondaini, Darch, and de Colin, *Independence and Revolution in Portuguese—Speaking Africa*, 43–57, 89–107, 147–60; Chabuca, *Self Determination in International Relations*, 36–82; FRELIMO, *Lusaka Agreement*, 1–7; Vines, *RENAMO, From Terrorism to Democracy in Mozambique?* 11–15, 73–146; Munslow, *FRELIMO and the Mozambiccan Revolution*. For more on Zimbabwe nationalist movements, see Staunton, *Mothers of the Revolution*; Raeburn, *Black Fire*; Norma J. Kriger, *Zimbabwe's Guerilla War* and *Guerilla Veterans in Post War Zimbabwe*, 1–34; Maddox and Welliver, *Colonialism and Nationalism in Africa*, 204–44; Sadomba, *War Veterans in Zimbabwe's Revolution*; Baxter, *Bush War Rhodesia*, 10–60; Ranger, *Peasant Consciousness and Guerilla War in Zimbabwe*; Moore, "Democracy, Violence and Identity in the Zimbabwean War of National Liberation."

20 David A. Adelman, "Profile Amilcar Cabral," 18.

21 Nyang, "The Political Thought of Amilcar Cabral."

22 For more on definition of the word "revolution" and "revolutionary," see Colburn, *The Vogue of Revolution in Poor Countries*, 6.

23 Chabal, "National Liberation in Portuguese Guinea," 75.

24 Ibid., 88.

25 Ibid., 89.
26 Idahosa, "Going to the People," 31. For more on Cabral/PAIGC/Portuguese Guinea Nationalism, see Weber, *Peasants into Frenchmen*, 9; Gellner, *Nations and Nationalism*, 1; Anderson, *Imaged Communities*, 47; Hobsbawm, *Nations and Nationalism*, 22–3, 137; Askew, *Performing the Nation*, 12–13, 182; Kennedy, "Religion, Nation and European Representation of the Past," 120–1; Kohl and Schroven, "Suffering for the Nation"; Chabal, " The African Crisis, Context and Interpretation," 48; Schmidt, *Foreign Intervention in Africa*, 79–102.
27 Tomas, *Amilcar Cabral*, 6.
28 Chilcote, "The Political Thought of Amilcar Cabral," 387; Jock McCulloch, *In the Twilight of Revolution*, 3–6.
29 Peterson, *Dubois, Fanon Cabral*, 116.
30 Solodovnikov, "The Theoretical Legacy of Amilcar Cabral," 110–12; McCulloch, *In the Twilight of Revolution*, 49–56; Young, "Patterns of Social Conflict," 24.
31 Mao, *Four Essays on Philosophy*, 3–5.
32 Idahosa, "Going to the People," 42.
33 Lyon, "Marxism and Ethno-nationalism in Guinea-Bissau," 156–7.
34 Magubane, "Amilcar Cabral: Evolutionary Thought," 71.
35 Ibid., 73.
36 Hubbard, "Culture and History in a Revolutionary Context," 70.
37 Bockel, "Amilcar Cabral: Marxiste Africain," 35–9.
38 Nigel C. Gibson, "Some Reflections on Amilcar Cabral's Legacy," 284.
39 Luke, "Cabral's Marxism," 317.
40 Ibid., 309.
41 Ibid., 317.
42 Ibid.
43 Chaliand, *Revolution in the Third World*, 70.
44 McCulloch, "Amilcar Cabral, a Theory of Imperialism," 509.
45 Peterson, *Dubois, Fanon, Cabral*, 117.
46 Rudebeck, "Reading Cabral on Democracy," 91.
47 Idahosa, "Going to the People," 29–58 and 36.
48 Ibid., 36. See also Carreira, *The People of Cabo Verde Islands*, 173; Moser, "The Poet Amilcar Cabral," 176–8; De Andrade, *Amilcar Cabral*, 14–20 and "Amilcar Cabral: Profil d'un Revolutionaire Africain"; Chabal, *Amilcar Cabral*, 32–4; Idahosa, "Going to the People," 37; Antonio Carreira, *Migracaoes nas Ilhas de Cabo Verde*, Praia, Institto Cabo-Verdiano do Livro, 1983, 36; Andrade, *Les Iles du Cap Vert de la Decouverte a l'indépendance Nationale (1460–1975)*, 164.

49 Cabral, *Our People Are Our Mountains,* 22. See also Chabal, "The Social and Political Thought of Amilcar Cabral," 32; Cabral, *Our People Are Our Mountains,* 21-2; Reiland Rabaka, "Contours of Cabralism," 15; Saucier, "Returning to Cabral," xvi; Cabral, "Friends and Allies," 4; Davidson, *Liberation of Guiné,* 73. See also Forrest, "Guinea-Bissau since Independence"; Rudebeck, "Conditions of People's Development in Post-Colonial Africa," and Milton, "Ecologies: Anthropology, Culture and the Environment."

50 Ibid.

51 Cabral, "Friends and Allies," 4.

52 Davidson, *Liberation of Guiné,* 73. See also Forrest, "Guinea-Bissau since Independence"; Rudebeck, "Conditions of People's Development in Post-Colonial Africa," and Milton, "Ecologies: Anthropology, Culture and the Environment"; Ferreira, "Amilcar Cabral: Theory of Revolution and Background to his Assassination," 52-3. Tomas, *Amilcar Cabral: The Life of a Reluctant Nationalist,* 109-10; Chaliand, *Lutte Armée en Afrique,* 114; Mao, *Four Essays on Philosophy,* 37; Cabral, *Palavras de Ordem Gerais do Camarada,* 23.

53 "For Cabral, the political education of freedom fighters was more important than their military qualification." Embalo, "From Cabral's Liberation movement to Power Struggle and Ideological Erosion: The Decline of PAIGC in Guinea Bissau," 86; Cabral, *Palavras de Ordem Gerais do Camarada,* 23.

54 PAIGC, Amilcar Cabral, "Structure Social de la Guinee 'Portugaise,'" 18-19 [French].

55 Cabral, "The Weapon of Theory," 92. See also PAIGC, "Statutes and Program." Conakry, 1960. 1-16 [French]; Chabal, *Amilcar Cabral,* 45; Cabral, "Recenseamento Agricola da Guine," 50; Cabral, in *Boletin Cultural da Guine Portuguesa (BCGP),* 11, 43 (July 1956), 229-43; Chabal, *Amilcar Cabral,* 45. Cabral, *Boletin Cultural da Guine Portuguesa (BCGP),* 11, 43 (July 1956), 229-43.

56 Chabal, *Amilcar Cabral,* 45. Cabral, in *Boletin Cultural da Guine Portuguesa (BCGP),* 11, 43 (July 1956), 229-43; Chilcote, "The Political Thought of Amilcar Cabral," 375; PAIGC, "Les Fondements et les Objectifs de la Liberation Nationale en Rapport avec la Structure Sociale," [Extrait du Discours pronounce au Comité des Peuples des Colonies Portuguese, par le Camarade Amilcar Cabral, Secretaire General du Parti, a la Premiere Conference des Peuples d'Afrique, d'Asie et Amerique Latine, La Havana, Janvier 3-14, 1966], Conakry, Departement de Secretariat, Information, Culture et Formation de Cadres Collection, " Discours et Interventions," [French], 1-12; Chabal, "National Liberation in Portuguese Guinea," 81-2; Davidson, *The Liberation of Guiné,* 33.

57 Cabral, *Return to the Source*, 54.
58 Luke, "Cabral's Marxism," 323; Davidson, *The Liberation of Guiné*, 83.
59 Luke, "Cabral's Marxism," 61. See also Tomas, *Amilcar Cabral: The Life of a Reluctant Nationalist*, 99–104; For more on Pascoal Alves and Antonio Bana, see Davidson, *The Liberation of Guiné*, 35.
60 Tomas, *Amilcar Cabral: The Life of a Reluctant Nationalist*, 102–4; Antonio E. Duarte Silva, *A Independencia da Guiné-Bissau e a Descolonizacao Portuguesa-Estudos de História, Direito e Política*, Porto, edição Afrontamento, 1997, 52–3.
61 Mendy, *Amilcar Cabral; Nationalist and Pan-Africanist Revolutionary*, 113, 114.
62 Laranjeiro, Arma Diplomatica e Ficçao, 51.
63 Ibid. See also Amilcar Cabral, *Revolution in Guinea*, 127–9; Pereira, *Uma Luta, Um Partido, Dois Paises*, 145; Chabal, *Amilcar Cabral*, 66.
64 PAIGC, "Um Encontro Marcado em setembro de 1959." (Recordações de Chico Te, *No Pintcha*, II, 225 [12 September 1976]). Ferreira, "Amilcar Cabral," 53–4.
65 Davidson, *The Liberation of Guiné*, 52–5, 64–5.
66 W. Luke, "Cabral's Marxism," 63.
67 Ferreira, "Amilcar Cabral: Theory of Revolution and Background to His Assassination."
68 Idahosa, "Going to the People," 46.
69 Gomes, "The Women of Guinea-Bissau and Cabo Verde in the Struggle for National Independence," 76.
70 Chabal, "National Liberation in Portuguese Guinea," 94.
71 Chaliand, *Armed Struggle in Africa; With the Guerillas in "Portuguese" Guinea*, 30, 31–2, 53–7; Vice President Senegal. 00208: Ministére de l'Interieur: Affaires Politiques, Problémes Frontaliers entre Guinée Bissao, le Sénégal et la Guinée; Arrestation d'Agitateurs au frontier de la Casamance. Declaration du PAIGC relative's aux Iles du Cap Vert, Correspondences et Rapports (1962); VP 00203: Ministére de l'Interieur: Activités, et Incidents á Ziguinchor et á Ngoudiane Peye; complot anti-nationalist (1957–1962).
72 Ibid., 45; Davidson, *No Fist Is Big Enough to Hide the Sky*, 9.
73 Chaliand, *Armed Struggle in Africa*, 58–9.
74 Davidson, *No Fist Is Big Enough to Hide the Sky*, 9.
75 Davidson, *Liberation of Guiné*, 33–7, and *No Fist Is Big Enough to Hide the Sky*, 20.
76 Davidson, *Liberation of Guiné*, 46.

77 Chilcote, *Amilcar Cabral's Revolutionary Theory and Practice; A Critical Guide*, viii.
78 Ibid., 134.
79 Urdang, *Fighting Two Colonialisms*, 85–92, 123–5.
80 Sarrazin, "Carmen Pereira: Woman Revolutionary," 41–7.
81 Sarrazin and Gjerstad, *Sowing the First Harvest*, 61–6.
82 Gomes, "Amilcar Cabral and Guinean Women in the fight for emancipation," 281; Sheldon, "Colonialism and Resistance: Protests and National Liberation Movements," 81–2.; Patricia Godinho Gomes; "Mindjeris di Guiné, ka bô m'pina, Ka bô burgunhu 1: narrativas de mulheres na/sobre a luta de libertação na Guiné-Bissau (trajetórias, construções e percursos emancipatórios)" in *AbeAfrica: Revista Brasileira de Estudos Africanos*, v. 6, n. 6, Octubro de 2021, 81–106, 82–90; Ines and Catarina, "Gender Struggle in Guinea-Bissau," 85–123
83 Ibid., 284.
84 Lundy, Fernandes Jr., and Lartey, "The Integrity of Women in Re-making a Nation," 59; PAIGC, "Guinea (B) on Verge of Victory," 1; PAIGC, "Amilcar Cabral Demande L'Etat Independent de la Guinee-Bissao," 3.
85 For more on African women's involvement in politics see Sheldon, *African Women*, 36–61 and 132–206; Bastian, "Vultures of the Marketplace," 260–81; Matera, Bastian, and Kent, *The Women's War of 1929*, 32–9; Presley, *Kikuyu Women, the Mau-Mau Rebellion, and Social Change in Kenya*; Elkins, *Imperial Reckoning*; Walker, *Women and Resistance in South Africa*, 194–7; Byfield, "Taxation, and the Colonial State," 250–77; Seferdjeli, "French 'Reforms' and Muslim Women's Emancipation during the Algerian War," 19–61; Lippert, "Algerian Women's Access to Power," 209–32.
86 Maloba, *African Women in Revolution*, 19.
87 Kanogo, "Kikuyu Women and the Politics of Protest: Mau-Mau."
88 Wipper, "Kikuyu Women and the Harry Thuku Disturbances," 300–37.
89 Decker, "Women and National Liberation in Africa," 3546; Bastian, "Vultures of the Marketplace"; Van Allen, "Aba Riots, Or Igbo Women's War?"
90 Decker, "Women and National Liberation in Africa," 3545.
91 Ibid., 3546. For more cases of women's involvement in nationalist struggles in Africa see Chapter 2. See also Stucki, *Violence and Gender in Africa's Iberian Colonies*, 255–80; Machel, "The Role of Women in the Revolution," 24–7; Sheldon, "Women and Revolution in Mozambique," 42–3; Scott, "'Men in Our Country Behave Like Chiefs,'" 95; *Liberation in Southern Africa*; Chingono, "Women, War and Peace in Mozambique"; Sheldon, "Colonialism and Resistance: Protests and National Liberation Movements," 81–103.

92 Mitchell, *La Condizione Della Donna*.
93 For more on African liberation Movements and revolutions, see Byrne, *Mecca of Revolution*, 111, 164, 175, 189–92, 199, 248–9, 255, 266, 295; Guevara; *The African Dream*; Galvez, *Che in Africa*; Geisler, *Women and the Remaking of Politics in Southern Africa*, 39–87; DeFronzo, *Revolutions and Revolutionary Movements*, 381–427; Ageron and Thiebault, eds., *La Guerre d' Algerie*; Cooper, *Africa since 1940*, 133–55; De Braganca and Wallerstein, *The African Liberation Reader*, 33–135; De Braganca and Wallerstein, *The African Liberation Reader; Vol. 3*; Friedman, "Reviving evolutions"; Iandolo, "Imbalance of Power," 32–55; Vitalis, "The Midnight Ride of Kwame Nkrumah and Other Fables of Bandung," 261–88; Raeburn, *Black Fire*, 1–54; Bereketeab, "Introduction," 3–16; Salih, "Varieties of African Liberation Movements," 17–32; Markakis, "Liberation Movements and the 'Democratic Deficit,'" 33–41; Roessler and Verhoeven, *Why Comrades Go to War*, 27–52.
94 Scott, *Gender and the Politics of History*, 25.
95 Stucki, *Violence and Gender in Africa's Iberian Colonies*, 1.
96 Marie-Helene Lefaucheux: "Le Role de la Femme dans le Development des Pays Tropicaux et Subtropicaux," 432. See also in *Women's Role*, 9, 16, 27.
97 Andreas Stucki, *Violence and Gender in Africa's Iberian Colonies*, 2.
98 Ibid., 3. See also Midgley, "Introduction," 1–18.
99 Stucki, *Violence and Gender in Africa's Iberian Colonies*, 3; see also Malia B. Formes, "Beyond Complicity versus Resistance," 629–41; Hansen, ed., *African Encounters with Domesticity*; Stoler; *Race and the Education of Desire*; Levine; *Gender and Empire*; Allman, Geiger, and Musisi, "Women in African Colonial Histories: An Introduction," 2–4; Martin-Marquez: *Disorientations*; Moorman and Sheldon, "Gender in the Lusophone World," 35–41.
100 Stucki, *Violence and Gender in Africa's Iberian Colonies*, 4.
101 Ibid. See also Bush, "Feminizing Empire? British Women Activist Networks in Defending and Challenging Empire from 1918 to Decolonization" and "Nationalism, Development and Welfare Colonialism," 2.
102 Stucki, *Violence and Gender in Africa's Iberian Colonies*, 4. See also Salma, "Provinces Portugaise d' Afrique," 110, 120, and 122; UN, *The United Nations, and the Advancement of Women*, 5, 22, 78.
103 Stucki, *Violence and Gender in Africa's Iberian Colonies*, 12; See also Spivak, "Can the Subaltern Speak?" 297; Bush, "Motherhood, Morality, and Social Order," 271.
104 Stucki, *Violence and Gender in Africa's Iberian Colonies*, 12.
105 Guha, "The Small Voice of History," 1, 7.
106 Ibid.

107 Giblin, *A History of the Excluded*, 5.
108 See Chaliand, *Armed Struggle in Africa*; Davidson, *The Liberation of Guiné*.
109 Davidson, *The Liberation of Guiné*, 34–6, 64.
110 Ibid., 33. PAIGC. Amilcar Cabral; Communiqué Final Sur L'Agression Portugaise du 22–3 Novembre 1970 contre La Republique de Guinée par le Secretaire general du PAIGC, 18 Janvier 1971.
111 Ibid, 46.
112 Chaliand, *Armed Struggle in Africa*, 29–101.
113 Ibid., 29, 50.
114 Ibid., 31–2, 92.
115 Ibid., 59.
116 Ibid., 97.
117 Malan was then a young PAIGC member, and later after independence ran as a Presidential candidate in several elections before being elected in 2009. Before that he was president of the National Assembly from 1999 to 2000. For more on Malan, see Kohl, *A Creole Nation*, 34.
118 Mario Augusto Ramalho, interviewed in French, August 20, 2008.
119 Gaitano Barboza, interviewed in Crioulo, August 8, 2008.
120 Lerner, *Creation of Feminist Consciousness*, 10–14.
121 McCall, "Introduction," 18–19.
122 Sheldon, *African Women*, 21.
123 Lyons, *Guns and Guerilla Girls*, 19.
124 Ridd, "Powers of the Powerless," 1–2; See also Thompson's edited book *Over Our Dead Bodies: Women against the Bomb*; and Ruddick, *Material Thinking: Toward a Politics of Peace*.
125 See also Thompson's edited book *Over Our Dead Bodies: Women against the Bomb*; and Ruddick, *Material Thinking: Toward a Politics of Peace*.
126 Lyons, *Guns and Guerilla Girls*, 20.
127 For more on African women and liberation wars, see Lyons, *Guns and Guerilla Girls*; O'Gorman, *The Front Line Runs through Every Woman*, 15–69; Staunton, *Mothers of the Revolution*; Kristof, *Half the Sky*; Mugabe and Nhiwatiwa, *Women's Liberation in the Zimbabwean Revolution*; Simoque, *MaFuyana: Mother of the Zimbabwean Revolution*; ZANU Women, *Liberation through Participation*; FRELIMO, *April 7, 1972, A History of FRELIMO*, and *The Mozambican Woman in the Revolution*; Welch, Dagnino, and Sachs, *Transforming the Foundations of the Family Law in the Course of the Mozambican Revolution*.
128 Cleaver and Wallace, *Namibian Women in War*; Urdang, *And Still They Dance*; Fanon, "Algeria Unveiled"; Saadi, *La Femme et les Lois en Algerie*.

129 See also books on African women and war such as Turshen and Twagiramariya, eds., *What Women do in Wartime*; Muthoni, *Passbook Number F47927*; Cock, *Colonels and Cadres*; Tetreault, ed., *Women and Revolution in Africa, Asia and the New World*; Sekai Nzenza, *Zimbabwean Woman*; Mahamba, *Woman and Struggle*; Leda Stott, *Women and the Armed Struggle for Independence in Zimbabwe*; Josephine Simbanegavi, *Zimbabwean Women in the Liberation Struggle*.

130 Decker, "Women and National Liberation in Africa," 3547. See also Liberation Support Movement, *The Mozambican Woman in the Revolution*; Sheldon, "Women and Revolution in Mozambique, A Luta Continua," 33.

131 Maloba, *African Women in Revolution*, 53; Knauss, *The Persistence of Patriarchy*, 96; Stowasser, "Women's Issues in Modern Islamic Thought," 6; Hatem, "Toward the Development of Post-Islamist and Post-Nationalist Feminist Discourses in the Middle East," 38.

132 Maloba, *African Women in Revolution*, 145.

133 PAIGC; "Amilcar Cabral and Aristides Pereira. Rapport sur la Lutte de Liberation des Peuples de la Guinee Portugaise et des Iles du Cap Vert," 51; Urdang, *Fighting Two Colonialisms*; Urdang visited Guinea-Bissau twice. The first time was from mid-April to mid-June of 1974. During this period, she spent five weeks in the liberated zones (three and half in the south front and ten days in the East. The rest of her time she visited Boke and Conakry (Republic of Guinée). Independence was officially proclaimed after she left Guinea-Bissau. She returned in 1976 to a totally liberated country, and for two and half months she traveled throughout the country. Ibid., 15–17, 88.

134 Urdang, *Fighting Two Colonialisms*, 81. *Rapport sur le role politique-social-economique de la femme en Guinee-Bissau et aux Iles du Cap Vert*, Conacri, PAIGC, 1970, 1971, 1972). Fundacao Amilcar Cabral, Praia (Cabo Verde). Gomes, "The State of Art of Gender in Guinea-Bissau," 168–89; 168; PAIGC, *Programa do PAIGC-Programa Maior*, Conacry, 1965, Fundação Amilcar Cabral, Praia (Cabo verde), 2; Galvão Ines., Laranjeiro Catarina. "Gender Struggle in Guinea-Bissau: Women's Participation On and Off the Liberation Record," 98–107.

135 Diana Lima Handem, *Nature et Fonctionnement du Pouvoir chez les Balanta Brassa*, Bissau, Guinea-Bissau: Instituto Nacional de Estudos e Pesquisa, 1986.

136 For more on Amilcar Cabral as charismatic leader, see PAIGC, "Memorandum addressed to Portuguese Government by PAIGC." n.p., November 1960, 5 [Portuguese]. PAIGC, "Declaration proposant la realization immediate de

mesures concretes pour la liquidation pacificque de la domination coloniale en 'Guinée Portugais' et aux Îles du Cap Vert." Conakry, Octobre 13, 1961. 1 (French); PAIGC, "Note Ouverte au Gouvernement Portugais." Conakry, October 13, 1961. Signed by Amilcar Cabral, Secretary General of PAIGC, 2, PAIGC, "Guinée Portugais," 2. See also PAIGC, Maria Pulce Almada, "Sur la Situation des Peuples des Iles du Cap Vert. Declaration de PAIGC, presentée au Comité Special de L'OUA pour les territoires administers par le Portugal" June 1962. [n/p] 28 (French); PAIGC, "Nouveaux Crimes des Colonialistes Portugais," Conakry, March 24, 1962, Signed, secretary General of PAIGC, 1 (French), See also Chabal, "National Liberation in Portuguese Guinea," 81; Amilcar Cabral, *Revolution in Guinea*, 31; Davidson, *The Liberation of Guiné*, 28–32; Idahosa, "Going to the People," 29–58; de Andrade, *Amilcar Cabral, Essai de Biographie Politique*, 70–2; McCulloch, *In the Twilight of Revolution*, 49–56; Young, "Patterns of Social Conflict," 24; Ana-Maria Cabral, "Amilcar Cabral," 2; Amilcar Cabral, "The Agricultural Census in Guiné," 15; Amilcar Cabral, "Approaching the Utilization of the Soil in Black Africa," 13–14; Amilcar Cabral, "The Development of the Struggle," 100; Amilcar Cabral, "Towards the Final Victory," 240; Davidson, *Liberation of Guiné*, 77. Van Der Drift, "Democracy Warfare in Guinea Bissau," 229–30; Henriksen, "People's War in Angola, Mozambique, and Guinea-Bissau," 377–99.

137 On August 3, 1959, the PAIGC, after three years of organizing and gaining support from the people and workers of Guinea Bissau, instigated a dockworkers strike for better salaries at the Pijiguiti Docks of the Port of Bissau. The political police (P.I.D.E.) suppressed the strike; they opened fire on the striking workers and killed over 59 people, while blaming the PAIGC. In September of 1959, Cabral and several PAIGC members met in Bissau and decided that nonviolent protest would not bring change; they concluded that the only hope for achieving independence was through relocating in Conakry (Republic of Guinea) and instigating an armed struggle. For more on the 1959 Massacre, see PAIGC "Declaration by Amilcar Cabral, Secretary General, to Guinean Press Agency on August 3, 1965, on the Anniversary of the Massacre of Pigiguiti, and day of Solidarity with the Peuple of Portuguese colonies. Conakry, August 3, 1965, 1 [English]; Chaliand, *Lutte Armée en Afrique,* 114; Luís Cabral, *Crónica da Libertação*; Colin, "La Pensée et la Pratique Sociale et Politique Amilcar Cabral sur les Chemins de L'Histoire," 99; Houser, "Assessing Africa's Liberation Struggle," 22; Chabal, "National Liberation in Portuguese Guinea," 80–5; Luis Cabral, "Da Formaçao do Partido a Proclamaçao do Estado;" PAIGC, "Dans la

Zone Liberee: Le Peuple Edifie une Vie Nouvelle," dit le Camarade Secretaire General du PAIGC a l'Occasion du 8e Anniversaire du Massacre de Pijiguiti," in *Horoya*, Conakry (Guinee), August 3, 1967, 2–3; PAIGC, "Massacre De Pindjiguiti" by Amilcar Cabral, 1–6 [Portuguese].

138 Gjerstad and Sarrazin, *Sowing the First Harvest*, 35–7.

139 Amilcar Cabral made a statement on this subject in Conakry in June 1962 to the United Nations Special Committee on Territories under Portuguese administration. PAIGC, "Statues and Program." Conakry, 1960, 1–16 [English]. PAIGC, "Memorandum addressed to Portuguese Government by PAIGC." n.p., November 1960, 5 (Portuguese). See also, PAIGC, "Declaration proposant la realization immediate de mesures concretes pour la liquidation pacifique de la domination coloniale en 'Guinée Portugais' et aux Îles du Cap Vert." Conakry, Octobre 13, 1961, 1 [French]; PAIGC, "Note Ouverte au Gouvernement Portugais." Conakry, October 13, 1961. Signed by Amilcar Cabral, Secretary General of PAIGC, 2. See Handyside, *Revolution in Guinea*, 32. In the same discourse, Cabral mentions the arrests of Rafael Barbosa in 1961 by the PIDE. Barbosa was the PAIGC Chairman who for eighteen months lived in hiding in Bissau. After eight years of imprisonment without trial, he was released in August 1969.

140 See Amilcar Cabral's discourse at the third Conference of the African Peoples held in Cairo (Egypt), March 25–31, 1961. Handyside, *Revolution in Guinea*. 22.

141 See Amilcar Cabral's declaration to the OSPAAAL general Secretariat in December 1968. Handyside, *Revolution in Guinea*, 118.

142 PAIGC. "Portugal Denuncia: Cabe Ao Senegal toda a Responsabilidade; Dis Incidentes Ocurridos na Fronteira com a Guiné Portuguesa," *Diário Manhà*, Lisbon (Portugal), 18/03/1965; PAIGC. "Novos Ataques; Lançados Do Senegal Contra a Guiné Portuguesa," *Diario Popular*, Lisbon (Portugal), 27 Decembre 1969; PAIGC. "Le Sénégal fait Etat d'un Incident Frontalier avec La Guinée Portugaise," *Le Monde*, Paris (France), 16 Mars 1967; PAIGC. "La Plainte Sénégalaise contre le Portugal devant le Conseil de Sécurité" dans *Dakar Matin*, Dakar (Senegal), 18–19 Mai 1965.

143 Peterson and Runyan, *Global Gender Issues*, 1.

144 Francisca Pereira joined the PAIGC in 1959. From 1959 to 1961 she was the only woman member of the executive bureau. She represented the women of Guinea Bissau at the Women Pan African Organization.

145 PAIGC, "Le Senegal Fait Etat d'un incident Frontalier avec la Guinée Portugaise," in *Le Monde*, Paris (France), March 16, 1967; See also PAIGC, "Cabe Ao

Senegal; Toda a Responsabilidade; Dos Incidentes Ocorridos na Fronteira com Guine Portuguesa," in *Diario Da Manha,* March 18, 1965; PAIGC, "La Plainte Sénégalaise Contre le Portugal Devant le Conseil de Sécurité," in *Dakar Matin,* Dakar (Senegal), May 18, 1963[French]; PAIGC, "Novos Ataques Lançados do Senegal Contra a Guiné Portuguesa," in *Diario Popular,* December, 27, 1969, 17 [Portuguese].

146 Francisca Pereira, interviewed in French, August 9, 2008.
147 Teresa Nquamé, interviewed in Crioulo, July 28, 2010. Joanita Da Silva Rosa, interviewed in Crioulo, July 15 and 30, 2010.
148 Joanita da Silva Rosa, interviewed in Crioulo, July 15 and 30, 2010.
149 Angela Sofia Benoliel Coutinho, *Les Dirigeants du PAIGC, "Parti Africain Pour l'indépendance de la Guine et des Iles du Cap Vert" des origines a la Scission,* Paris, Université de Paris 1—Pantheon—Sorbonne UFR d' Histoire 2005, 26–7; Aristides Pereira, *O meu Testemunho uma Luta um Partido dois Paises,* Lisboa editorial Notícias, 2003, 85–7.

Chapter 1

1 Philip Havik, *Silences and Soundbytes,* 186–99.
2 Ibid.
3 Idahosa, "Going to the People," 46. See also Chaliand, *Armed Struggle in Africa,* 63–7.
4 Interview, Carmen Pereira in Crioulo, August 21, 2008.
5 Forrest, *Lineages of State Fragility,* 27.
6 Ibid. See also Brooks, *Landlords and Strangers,* 135–6.
7 Forrest, *Lineages of State Fragility,* 28; and Urdang, *Fighting Two Colonialisms,* 65–7.
8 Green, "Introduction," 1–3. See also Havik, "Guinea Bissau Rural Economy and Society," 55–60; Green, *The Rise of the Trans-Atlantic Slave Trade in Western Africa,* 31–94.
9 *Lineages of State Fragility,* 33.
10 Green, *The Rise of the Trans-Atlantic Slave Trade in Western Africa,* 47–8.
11 Havik, *Silences and Soundbytes,* 95.
12 Hawthorne, *Planting Rice and Harvesting Slaves,* 34.
13 Havik, *Silences and Soundbytes,* 93; De Oliveira, Havik, and Schiefer, "Armazenamento Tradicional na Guine-Bissau," 399–402.

14 Havik, *Silences and Soundbytes*, 95–9. Also see Funk, "Land Tenure, Agriculture and Gender in Guinea Bissau," 33–58; Da Mota, *Guiné Portuguesa,* 130–3; Roche, *Histoire Générale de la Casamance,* 103–4; Pélissier, *Naissance de la Guiné.*

15 Havik, "Les Noirs et Les Blancs de L'Ethnographie Coloniale," 62–3.

16 Hubbell, "A View of the Slave Trade from the Margin," 36.

17 Ibid., 36–7; Havik, *Silences and Soundbytes*, 123; Martin Klein, "Ethnic Pluralism and Homogeneity in the Western Sudan," 113–19.

18 Hawthorne, *Planting Rice and Harvesting Slaves,* 125.

19 Ibid., 120.

20 Da Mota, *Some Aspects of Portuguese Colonisation and Sea Trade in West Africa,* 15; Carney, *Black Rice,* 30. See also Lundy, "Challenging Adulthood," 584–606.

21 Havik, "Women and Trade in the Guinea Bissau Region," 88–9.

22 Hawthorne, *Planting Rice and Harvesting Slaves,* 34.

23 Ibid., 127.

24 Havik, "Women and Trade in the Guinea-Bissau Region," 94.

25 Ibid., 108.

26 For how and why foreign merchants married local [African] women, see Candido, *An African Slaving Port and the Atlantic World,* 93–4.

27 Havik, *Silences and Soundbytes,* 199. See also Santana, *Bruxas e Curandeiros na Lisboa Joanina,* 48; Walker, "Free Blacks and the Inquisition in Early Modern Portugal."

28 Havik, *Silences and Soundbytes,* 199.

29 Ibid. See also De Lespinay, "La Disparution de la Langue Baynunk"; Roche, *Histoire Générale de la Casamance,* 103–4; Barry, "Economic Anthropology of Precolonial Senegambia," 47; Searing, *West African and Atlantic Commerce,* 114; White, *Sierra Leone's Settler Women Traders.*

30 Havik, *Silences and Soundbytes,* 253.

31 Ibid., 253–4.

32 Ibid., 254.

33 Ibid., 310. See also Mouser, "Women Slavers in Guinea Conakry," 329; Zack-Williams, "Crisis Structural Adjustment and Creative Survival in Sierra Leone," 53–63; Havik, "Women and Trade in Guinea-Bissau Region," 88–120.

34 Havik, *Silences and Soundbytes,* 311; Havik, "Female Entrepreneurship in a Changing Environment," 205–25; Cardoso, "Conflictos Interetnicos-Dissolucao e Reconstrucao de Unidades Políticas nos rios da Guine e Cabo Verde," 51–2.

35 Havik, *Silences and Soundbytes,* 311.

36 Ibid., 331–44; White, *Sierra Leone's Settler Women Traders*, 103–11.
37 Stolen and Vaa, *Gender and Change in Developing Countries*, 1–2; and Kershaw, "The Changing Role of Men and Women in the Kikuyu Family by Socioeconomic Strata," 173–94.
38 Baerends, "Changing Kinship, Family and Gender Relations in Sub-Saharan Africa," 47.
39 Idahosa, "Going to the People," 39. See also Cabral, "The Agricultural Census in Guiné," 5–9; Chaliand, *Armed Struggle in Africa*, 6; Chabal, *Amilcar Cabral*, 18–19; Rudebeck, "Conditions of People's Development in Post-Colonial Africa."
40 Chabal, "National Liberation in Portuguese Guinea," 76.
41 Cabral, "Brief Analysis of the Social Structure in Guinea," 33.
42 Chabal, "National Liberation in Portuguese Guinea," 77; Valentim Alexandre, *Origens do Colonialismo Portugues Moderno*, Lisboa, Sa da Costa, 1979, 61; Rene Pelissier, *História da Guine, 1, Vol.* Lisboa, Estampa, 1997, 23–115; Cardoso, "A Ideologia e a Practica da Colonização Portuguesa na Guine e o seu Impacto na estructura Social," 41.
43 Havik, "Women and Trade in the Guinea Bissau Region," 110.
44 Funk, "Land Tenure, Agriculture, and Gender in Guinea-Bissau," 38.
45 Hay, "Women as Owners, Occupants and Managers of Property in Colonial Western Kenya," 110–23; and Okeyo, "Daughters of the Lakes and Rivers," 186–213.
46 Parpart and Staudt, eds., *Women and the State in Africa*, 8.
47 Van Onselen, *Chibaro; Mine Labour in Southern Rhodesia*, 181.
48 Caplan, "Cognatic Descent, Islamic Law and Women's Property on the East African Coast," 23–43.
49 Parpart, "Sexuality and Power on the Zambian Copperbelt," 117–22.
50 Saho, *Contours of Change*, 27, 32–41; Chanock, "Making Customary Law," 53–67; Schmidt, "Patriarchy, Capitalism and the Colonial State in Zimbabwe," 732–56; Parpart, "Sexuality and Power on the Zambian Copperbelt," 115; Schmidt, *Peasants, Traders, and Wives*, 71–98.
51 Cabral, "Brief Analysis of the Social Structure in Guinea," 33.
52 McNaughton, *The Mande Blacksmiths*.
53 Havik, *Silences and Soundbytes,* 121; Cissoko, "La Royauté Mansaya Chez les Mandingues de L'Ouest d'Apres leurs Traditions Orales," 333; Mané, "Contribution a L'Histoire du Kaabu," 111; Niane, *Histoire des Mandingues de L'Ouest*, 87.
54 Havik, *Silences and Soundbytes*, 123.

55 Ibid., 125.
56 Ibid.; Mané, "Contribution a L'Histoire du Kaabu," 89–159; Niane, *Histoire des Mandingues de L'Ouest*; Pélissier, *Naissance de la Guiné*, 307–15; Pereira, *La Guinée Portuguese*, 24.
57 Havik, *Silences and Soundbytes*, 125.
58 Havik, *Silences and Soundbytes*, 126; Bowman, *Ominous Transition*, 32–49; Niane, *Histoire des Mandingues de L'Ouest*, 125–38 and 149–54.
59 Havik, *Silences and Soundbytes*, 128; Pélissier, *Naissance de la Guiné*, 211–31; Bowman, *Ominous Transition*, 73–101.
60 Idahosa, "Going to the People," 46. See also Cabral, *Our People Move Mountains*, 86; and Urdang, *Fighting Two Colonialisms*, 85–92, and 123–5; PAIGC. "A Guinée O Plano; Intercalar de Fomento," *Diário Manhà*, Lisbon (Portugal), 14/03/1965.
61 Gomes, "Amilcar Cabral and Guinean Women in the Fight for Emancipation," 283.
62 PAIGC, *Program do PAIGC-Programa Maior*, 2; Gjerstad, "Carmen Pereira: Women Revolution," 61–6.
63 Gomes, "Amilcar Cabral and Guinean Women in the Fight for Emancipation," 283.
64 Gomes, "A Importância das Forças Armadas Revolucionárias do Povo (FARP)," 121–39.
65 PAIGC/UDEMU, *UDEMU, União Democràtica das Mulheres da Guine e Cabo Verde*, 1; Laranjeiro, "Arma Diplomatica e Ficçao," 51–2.
66 Gomes, "Amilcar Cabral and Guinean Women in the Fight for Emancipation," 287–8; Gjerstad, "Carmen Pereira," 66.
67 Lundy, Fernandes Jr., and Lartey, "The Integrity of Women in Re-Making a Nation," 59, 64. For more on the Bijagos archipelago women, see Bordonaro, "Modernity as Marginality," 117–37; Gallois Duquette, "Women, Power and Initiation in the Bissagos Islands," 31–5; Lundy, "Resistance Is Fruitful," 1–9.
68 Lundy, Fernandes Jr., and Lartey, "The Integrity of Women in Re-Making a Nation," 72.
69 Wright, "Technology, Marriage, and Women's Work," 71–85; and White, "A Colonial State and an African Petty Bourgeoisie," 167–94.
70 Denzer, "Towards a Study of the History of West African Women's Participation in Nationalist Politics," 65–85; and Geiger, "Women in Nationalist Struggle," 1–26.
71 Geiger, "Tanganyikan Nationalism as 'Women's Work,'" 465–578.

72 *Loi Organique des Provinces Portugaises d'Outre Mer.*
73 Mendy and Lobban Jr., *Historical Dictionary of the Republic of Guinea-Bissau*, 39.
74 Carmen Pereira, interviewed in Crioulo, August 21, 2008.
75 Schmidt, "'Emancipate Your Husbands!'" 283–5.
76 Luiz de Sena and Lambert, *L' Education en République de Guinée Bissau*, 79.
77 Rudebeck, *Study of Political Mobilization*, 36.
78 *World Survey on Education II, Primary Education*, 885.
79 Carmen and Francisca were not related, and neither of them was related to Aristides Pereira. For more about Carmen and Francisca Pereira, see Kohl, *A Creole Nation*, 148–52.
80 PAIGC, "Report on the Politico-Socio-Economic Role of Women in Guinea and the Cabo Verde Islands," 52.
81 For more on the dock workers' massacres, see Dhada, *Warriors at Work*, 4–6.
82 PAIGC, "Les Peuples de la Guinee (Bissao) et des Iles du Cap vert sur La Voie de la Liberté," 3.
83 Urdang, *Fighting in Two Colonialisms*, 15.
84 Ibid.
85 *Journal de l'Afrique de L'Ouest Française*, April 1, 1939.
86 Morgenthau, *Political Parties in French Speaking West Africa*, 40. Vice President Senegal 00029. Correspondance au President du Conseil a/s du Conseil des femmes de l'Afrique Occidentale tenue á Conakry, au Colloque sur l'éducation des adultes á Dakar et au Congres International des Femmes á Yaoundé et Rapport sur la Participation de la femme sur la vie Publique (1962).
87 Sissoko, "Profession de Foi."
88 *Climats* Newspaper (Grand Bassam, Ivory Coast: January 19, 1950).
89 *La Liberté* (Conakry, French Guinea, December 11, 1956).
90 Morgenthau, *Political Parties in French Speaking West Africa*, 106, 240.
91 Francisca Pereira, interviewed in French, August 9, 2008.
92 PAIGC. "Guiné-Bissau"; PAIGC. "Conférence de Presse du F. L. I. N. G. à l'occasion du Sixième Anniversaire de la Lutte Armée du Peuple de Guinée Bissao," dans *Dakar Matin*, Dakar (Senegal), 5 Août 1964.
93 PAIGC, "'Dans la Zone Libérée le Peuple Edifie une Vie Nouvelle' dit le Camarade Cabral, Secretaire Général á l'occasion du 8e Anniversaire du Massacre de Pijiguiti," in *Horoya*, Conakry (Guinée-Conakry), 1–3, August 3, 1967 [French].
94 PAIGC, *The Republic of Guinea-Bissau: Triumph over Colonialism*, by Jennifer Davis, Research Director, 3–4. See also PAIGC, "Symposium

International sur le Theme: Amilcar Cabral et la Lutte de Liberation Nationale et Sociale en Afrique," Organise par JAAC, UIE et AASU, Contribution de L'UDEMU (União Démocratique des Femmes) representee par la Camarada Francisca Pereira, Membre du Comité Central du PAIGC et Secretaire Générale de l'UDEMU, Bissau, March 26–7, 1983, 1–3.

95 Chaliand, *Armed Struggle in Africa*, 21; Juliao Soares Sousa, *Amilcar Cabral e a Luta pela Independencia da Guine e Cabo Verde, 1924–1973*, Coimbra Universidade de Coimbra faculdade de Letras, 2007; Luis Cabral, *Crônica da Libertacao*, Lisboa, *Edicoaes O Journal*, 1984, pp. 42–3.

96 Urdang, *Fighting in Two Colonialisms*, 125–6.

97 PAIGC, *The Republic of Guinea-Bissau: Triumph over Colonialism*, by Jennifer Davis, Research Director, 13–14.

98 See Brandon, Raul Mendes Fernandes Jr., and Kezia Lartey. "The Integrity of Women in Re-Making a Nation: The Case of Guinea-Bissau," 59–76.

99 Ines and Laranjeiro Catarina. "Gender Struggle in Guinea-Bissau," 85–110.

Chapter 2

1 Roque, "Mulheres, Nação e Lutas no Cinema anti/Pós-Colonial da Guiné-Bissau/Women, Nation and Struggles in Anti/Postcolonial Cinema in Guinea-Bissau," 278–9.

2 PAIGC, [Press Release: "The Liberation of the Boé Region", [Conakry?] June 3, 1965, 1.1 [French]; PAIGC, [Communique] Conakry, May 27, 1965. [French] and PAIGC, "Libertacao. Orgao do PAIGC", [n0. 57.August 3, 1965]. Tomas, *Amilcar Cabral: The Life of a Reluctant Nationalist*, 144–8.

3 Fantam Kawsara, interviewed in Pular, July 16, 2010.

4 Ibid.

5 Carmen Pereira, interviewed in Crioulo, August 21, 2008.

6 Fatoumata Diallo, interviewed in Pular, July 27, 2009.

7 Ibid.

8 Fatoumata Diallo, interviewed in Pular, July 27, 2009.

9 Urdang, *Fighting in Two Colonialisms*, 207–8. See also Gomes, "A Mulher Guineense Como Sujeito e Objecto do Debate Histórico Contemporâneo," 71–95.

10 Ibid., 215.

11 Sandé NHaga, interviewed in Crioulo, August 28, 2010.

12 Urdang, *Fighting in Two Colonialisms*, 223–4. NATO involvement see PAIGC, "Alguns dados sobre das Potencias da OTAN aos Colonialistas Portugueses," 1–18 [Portuguese]; PAIGC, "L'ONU Condamne le Portugal pour l'usage de Produits Chimiques et de Défoliants contre les Peuples Africains," *El Moudjahid*, Algiers (Algeria), April 15, 1971.

13 Eva Gomes, interviewed in Crioulo, August 13, 2008.

14 Eva Gomes, interviewed in Crioulo, August 13, 2008.

15 This is a question I asked of all my interviewees. It was suggested by my readings of Urdang's works on Guinea Bissau.

16 PAIGC, *O Militante*, "Páginas da História; 1 Congresso Do PAIGC; Conferência Geral de Quadros do Partido no interior do país; A Criação das FARP Foram um Passo decisivo para o Progresso da Nossa Luta" in *O Militante*, Bissau, *janeiro* de 1980, 16–18; Gomes, "A importância das Forças Armadas Revolucionárias do Povo (F.A.R.P.) na luta pela libertação da Guiné-Bissau," 121–39.

17 Cornwall, *Bush Rebels; Personal Account of Black Revolt in Africa*, 50.

18 Davidson, *Liberation of Guiné*, 78–80.

19 This decision was articulated in the village of Djagali in 1966 in front of 3,000 people. Several PAIGC military and political cadres, including Titina Silla, a woman fighter and political commissar in the Northern front accompanied Cabral. Chaliand, *Armed Struggle in Africa*, 93.

20 I am referring to Luis Cabral's argument during his conversation with Carmen Pereira. Carmen narrated the conversation to me in the presence of Juliao Mané.

21 Francisca Pereira, interviewed in French, August 9, 2008 and July 12, 2010.

22 Urdang, *Fighting in Two Colonialisms*, 226.

23 Gaitano Barboza, interviewed in Crioulo, and Mario Cissokho, interviewed in French, August 8, 2008. See also PAIGC, "Portuguese Guinea Insurgent Claims," 3; PAIGC, "Guinée Portugais," 2. See also PAIGC, Maria Pulce Almada, "Sur la Situation des Peuples des Iles du Cap Vert. Declaration de PAIGC, presentée au Comité Special de L'OUA pour les territoires administers par le Portugal"; PAIGC, "Nouveaux Crimes des Colonialistes Portugais," Conakry, March 24, 1962, Signed, secretary General of PAIGC, 1 [French].

24 PAIGC. "La Lutte de la Femme Africaine est Inséparable de la lutte Révolutionaire des Masses," *El Moudjahid*, 3 Avril 1967.

25 Urdang, *Fighting in Two Colonialisms*, 228.

26 Ibid.

27 Carmen Pereira, interviewed in Crioulo, August 21, 2008.

28 Urdang, *Fighting in Two Colonialisms*, 232.

29 Stéphanie Urdang interviewed Teodora Gomes in 1974. Urdang, *Fighting in Two Colonialisms*, 229.
30 Jose Pedro Castanheira, *Qui a Fait Tuer Amilcar Cabral?* 30–1. See also Galvão Ines., Laranjeiro Catarina. "Gender Struggle in Guinea-Bissau: Women's Participation On and Off the Liberation Record," 91.
31 On Amilcar Cabral's assassination, see Vladimirovich, *Combatant Pour La Cause du Peuple*, 19–24; Castanheira, *Qui a Fait Tuer Amilcar Cabral?* 58–80.
32 Urdang, *Fighting in Two Colonialisms*, 194.
33 Ibid. See also Lobban, "Strategic and Foreign Policy Objectives," 99.
34 Carmen Pereira, interviewed in Crioulo, 21 August 2008. PAIGC, "Portugal: Procès d'un Militaire Cubain Fait Prisonnier en Guinée Portugaise."
35 Ibid.
36 This section about Carmen Pereira is based on my personal interviews with her. I also acknowledge the works of Basil Davidson, "No Fist Is Big Enough to Hide the Sky"; Cornwall, *The Bush Rebels*, 190–5; Sarrazin, "Carmen Pereira: Woman Revolutionary," 60–5; and Urdang, *Fighting in Two Colonialisms*, 200–4.
37 Francisca Pereira, interviewed in French, 9 and 16 August 2008 and 12 July 2010. See also *Ceres*, "There Was No Room for Sex Discrimination during the Struggle."
38 Stéphanie Urdang interviewed Jacinta da Souza in 1974. See Urdang, *Fighting in Two Colonialisms*, 181.
39 See also Chaliand, who recalls how the Portuguese bombed the village of Djagali. Amilcar Cabral, Titina Silla, Chico Mendez, Osvaldo Vieira, Antonio Bana, and Innocentio and Gerard Chaliand spent the night in this village and had been awakened up by the roar of the Portuguese planes. They dressed quickly and got out. Later they were informed of the Portuguese bombings. "Two members of the [PAIGC] fighting forces arrived around 8:30. The Portuguese had bombed the village of Djagali and the number of dead and wounded was not yet known. Titina left immediately to supervise the treatment of the wounded." Chaliand, *Armed Struggle in Africa*, 98.
40 Chaliand, "The PAIGC without Cabral," 91.
41 Chaliand, *Armed Struggle in Africa*, 92.
42 Eva Gomes, interviewed in Crioulo, August 13, 2008.
43 PAIGC, "Páginas da História," 16.
44 PAIGC. "Notre Lutte en Guinee," [Interview of Amilcar Cabral], *Revolution Africaine*, no. 29, August 17, 1963, 4–5 [French]; PAIGC; Amilcar cabral, "800,000 hommes en Guerre," *Revolution Africaine*, no. 7, March 16, 1963,

8–9 [French] and PAIGC, "About the Development of Our Struggle, 1964," [Statement of the General secretary in a Press Conference], Conakry, 1964, 1–6 [English].
45 Davidson, *The Liberation of Guiné*, 45.
46 Sito Sadio (who was seventy-five at the time of my interview), interviewed in Crioulo, July 17, 2010.
47 Ndalla Mané, interviewed in Crioulo, July 2010.
48 Sito Sadio, interviewed in Crioulo, July 17, 2010.
49 The interview was published in *Tricontinal* no. 12. See also Handyside, *Revolution in Guinea,* 159–61.
50 Eva Gomes, interviewed in Crioulo, 13 August 2008. Tomas, *Amilcar Cabral: The Life of a Reluctant Nationalist*, 121–5.
51 Cabral, Luís. *Crónica da Libertação.* Lisboa: O Jornal, 1984.
52 Bacar Cassama, interviewed in Crioulo, 14 August 2008. See also Chaliand's interview with Antonio Bana in *Armed Struggle in Africa*, 72–6.
53 Tetreault, "Women and Revolution," 19.
54 Galvão Ines., Laranjeiro Catarina. "Gender Struggle in Guinea-Bissau: Women's Participation On and Off the Liberation Record." 87–8.

Chapter 3

1   Cock, "Keeping the Fires Burning," 65.
2   Decew, "The Combat Exclusion and the Role of Women in the Military," 56.
3   Lyons, *Guns and Guerilla Girls,* 21.
4   Peterson and Runyan, *Global Gender Issues*, 1.
5   Cooke, "Wo-man, Retelling the War Myth," 177.
6   Ridd, "Powers of the Powerless," 1 and 2.
7   Peterson and Runyan, *Global Gender Issues*, 1.
8   Jayawardena, *Feminism and Nationalism in the Third World,* 8.
9   Ranajit Guha, "The Small Voice of History," 1 and 7.
10 Giblin, *History of the Excluded,* 5.
11 Carmen Pereira, interviewed in English by Aliou Ly and translated into Bissau Guinean Creole by Juliao Lopez Mané, Bissau, on August 21, 2008; Francisca Pereira, interviewed in French and translated into English by Aliou Ly, Bissau, on August 9–16, 2008; and Eva Gomez, interviewed in English by Aliou Ly and translated into Bissau Guinean Creole by Juliao Lopez Mané, Bissau, on August 13, 2008.

12 James L. Giblin. *History of the Excluded*, 103–4.
13 Carmen Pereira interviewed in English by Aliou Ly and translated into Bissau Guinean Creole by Juliao Lopez Mané, Bissau, on August 21, 2008; Francisca Pereira interviewed in French and translated into English by Aliou Ly, Bissau, on August 9–16, 2008; and Eva Gomez interviewed in English by Aliou Ly and translated into Bissau Guinean Creole by Juliao Lopez Mané, Bissau, on August 13, 2008.
14 Bacar Cassama, interviewed in English by Aliou Ly and translated into Bissau Guinean Creole by Juliao Lopez Mané, Bissau, on August 14, 2008; and Mario Augusto Ramalho Cissokho interviewed and translated into English by Aliou Ly, Bissau, on August 8, 2008.
15 Peterson and Runyan, *Global Gender Issues*, 1.
16 Cooke, "Wo-man, Retelling the War Myth," 177.
17 Peterson and Runyan, *Global Gender Issues*, 1.
18 For information about women and wars in Zimbabwe and Namibia see Cleaver and Wallace, *Namibia: Women and War*; Lyons, *Guns and Guerilla Girls*; Staunton, *Mothers of the Revolutions*.
19 Sano Seydi, interviewed in Pular and translated into English by Aliou Ly, Gabu, on June 28, 2010.
20 Barnaté Sanha interviewed in English by Aliou Ly and translated into Bissau Guinean Creole by Juliao Pereira, Bissau, on July 28 and August 23, 2010.
21 Ibid. See also Galvão Ines., Laranjeiro Catarina. "Gender Struggle in Guinea-Bissau: Women's Participation On and Off the Liberation Record," 86.
22 Teresa NQuamé interviewed in English by Aliou Ly and translated into Bissau Guinean Creole by Juliao Pereira, Bissau, on July 28, 2010.
23 Juditi Gomes interviewed in English by Aliou Ly and translated into Bissau Guinean Creole by Bruno da Costa, Bissau, on July 28, 2010; Quinta Da Costa interviewed in English by Aliou Ly and translated into Bissau Guinean Creole by Bruno Da Costa, Bissau, on August 12, 2010.
24 For more on the relationship between interviewer and interviewees see Lawrence and Lehman, "Oral History as Motivating Factor among Adult Learners," 10.
25 Binetou Nankin Seydi, interviewed in French August 25, 2008.
26 Joanita Da Silva Rosa, interviewed in English and translated in Crioulo, July 15 and 30, 2010.
27 Even in my interviews with Carmen Pereira, Francisca Pereira, Teodora Gomes, Satou Camara, and Joanita da Silva Rosa, I had to ask specifically about women's roles. If I did not, they would have said nothing about women's participation.

28 Na Ndjati interviewed in English by Aliou Ly and translated into Bissau Guinean Creole by Juliao Pereira, Boé, on August 2, 2010.
29 Eva Gomes interviewed in English by Aliou Ly and translated into Bissau Guinean Creole by Juliao Lopez Mané, Bissau, on August 13, 2008.
30 Carmen Pereira interviewed on August 21, 2008.
31 Eva Gomes interviewed on August 13, 2008. See also Chaliand, *Armed Struggle in Africa* and Urdang, *Fighting in Two Colonialisms*. Francisca Pereira interviewed in French and translated into English by Aliou Ly, Bissau, on July 12, 2010.
32 Francisca on July 12, 2010.
33 Lyons, *Guns and Guerilla Girls*, 23.
34 Havik, *Silences and Soundbytes*, 18–19; Stoeltje, "Asante Queen Mothers," 41–71.
35 Havik, *Silences and Soundbites*, 19; See more on this topic in Bay, *Wives of the Leopard*; Olajubu, *Women in the Yoruba Sphere*; Agsiere, *Women in Igbo Life and Thought*.
36 Havik, *Silences and Soundbites*, 19. See also Potash, *Widows in African Societies*; Mann, *Marriage, Status and Social Change among Educated Elite in Lagos*; Robertson and Klein, *Women and Slavery in Africa*; Hafkin and Bay, *Women in Africa*; Hay, "Queens, Prostitutes and Peasants," 431–47.
37 Havik, *Silences and Soundbites*, 20.
38 Fanon, *A Dying Colonialism*, 23.
39 Ibid., 105.
40 Sano Seydi interviewed in Pular June 28, 2010.

Chapter 4

1 Chaliand, *Armed Struggle in Africa*, 93.
2 Teresa NQuamé, interviewed in Crioulo, July 28, 2010. Joanita Da Silva Rosa, interviewed in Crioulo, July 15 and 30, 2010.
3 Carmen Pereira, interviewed in Crioulo, August 21, 2008 and July 18, 2010.
4 See Chaliand, *Armed Struggle in Africa*; and Urdang, *Fighting in Two Colonialisms*.
5 Teresa NQuamé, interviewed in Crioulo, July 28, 2010 and Dialan Diamba, interviewed in Pular, July 1, 2010.
6 Fatu Turé, interviewed in Crioulo, July 27, 2010.
7 Juditi Gomes, interviewed in Crioulo, July 28, 2010.

8   Scott, *Gender and the Politics of History*, 15–21.
9   Ibid., 18.
10 Fatu Turé, interviewed in Crioulo, July 27, 2010.
11 Sandé NHaga, interviewed in Crioulo, August 28, 2010.
12 Barnaté Sanha, interviewed in Crioulo, August 23, 2010.
13 Hutna was recruited in 1968 by Marciano Lima. He is from the Quitafiné region in the south front. Hutna Yala interviewed in Crioulo, August 16, 2010.
14 Barnaté Sanha, interviewed in Crioulo, July 28 and August 23, 2010.
15 Sano Seydi interviewed in Pular, June 28, 2010.
16 Juditi Gomes, interviewed in Crioulo, July 28, 2010.
17 Fatu Turé, interviewed in Crioulo, July 27, 2010.
18 Ibid.
19 Ndalla Mané, interviewed Crioulo, August 20, 2010.
20 See the story of Sunjata Keita by Niane in *Soundjata ou L'Epopée Mandingue*, 1–30.
21 Niane, *Soundjata ou L'Epopée Mandingue*, 5.
22 See also Hale, *Scribes, Griot, and Novelist*: Narratives Interpreters of the Songhai Empire; Innes, *Sunjata; Three Mandinka Versions*.
23 Forrest, *Lineages of State Fragility*, 42.
24 Einarsdottir, *Tired of Weeping*, 31.
25 Teresa NQuamé, interviewed in Crioulo, July 28, 2010.
26 Bordonaro, "'Culture Stops Development,'" 69–89.
27 Teresa NQuamé, interviewed Crioulo, July 28, 2010, and Joanita da Silva Rosa, interviewed Crioulo, July 15 and 30, 2010.
28 Joanita Da Silva Rosa, interviewed in Crioulo, July 15 and 30, 2010.
29 Urdang, *Fighting in Two Colonialisms*, 269.
30 See Chaliand, *Armed Struggle in Africa*, 45. Francisca Pereira said during one of my interviews with her that the village committee was composed of five members and at least three of them must be women, while Eva Gomes said that of the five members, two were supposed to be women. Francisca Pereira, interviewed in French, August 9 and 16, 2008; and Eva Gomes, interviewed Crioulo, August 13, 2008.
31 An interview with Chaliand, "The PAIGC without Cabral: An Assessment," 91.
32 Eva Gomes interviewed Crioulo, August 13, 2008.
33 Fanta Sané, interviewed in Wolof, July 27, 2010.
34 Fatoumata Diallo, interviewed in Pular, September 1, 2009.
35 Segunda Sambu interviewed in Crioulo, August 2, 2010.

36 Ibid.
37 For more on UDEMU see Kohl, *A Creole Nation*, 148–54; Chilcote, *Emerging Nationalism in Portuguese Africa Documents*, 341–6; Andreini and Lambert, *La Guinee Bissau d'Amilcar Cabral a al Reconstruction Nationale*, 45; Galli and Jones, *Guinea-Bissau, Politics, Economics, and Society*, 84–6, 93–4.
38 Urdang, *Fighting in Two Colonialisms*, 283–384.
39 Ibid., 314.
40 This quote is from Francisca Pereira. In 1978, throughout Guinea Bissau, 800 women were registered as members of the women's organization, UDEMU. See Sheldon, *Historical Dictionary of Women in Sub-Saharan Africa*, 251.
41 Francisca Pereira interviewed in French, July 12, 2010.
42 Carmen Pereira, interviewed in Crioulo, August 21, 2008 and July 18, 2010.
43 Francisca Pereira, interviewed in French, July 12, 2010, and Carmen Pereira, interviewed in Crioulo, August 21, 2008 and July 18, 2010.
44 Eva Gomes, interviewed in Crioulo, August 13, 2008.
45 Segunda Sambu, interviewed in Crioulo, August 2, 2010.
46 NDo Mané, interviewed in Crioulo, August 2, 2010.
47 Juditi Gomes, interviewed in Crioulo, July 28, 2010.
48 Dialan was the wife of Umaro Dia. She is a Mandinka woman living in Gabu. During the war, she worked as nurse in the East front under the command of Domingo Ramos. Dialan Diamba, interviewed in Crioulo, July 1, 2010.
49 Joanita Da Silva Rosa, interviewed in Crioulo, July 15 and 30, 2010.
50 Ibid.

Chapter 5

1 According to the preamble of the internal statutes of the PAIGC schools, *Regulamento das escolas do Partido*.
2 Rudebeck, *Guinea Bissau; A Study of Political Mmobilization*, 206.
3 Cabral, *Sobre Alguns Problemas Práticos da nossa Vida e da nossa Luta*, 4.
4 Mario Augusto Ramalho Cissokho, interviewed in French, August 8, 2008.
5 Hughes, "Armed Conflict, International Linkages and Women's Parliamentary Representation in Developing Nations," 174.
6 Urdang, *Fighting in Two Colonialisms*, 267.
7 *O Militante*, Bissau, December 1977, no. 5: 19.
8 Forrest, *Guinea Bissau*, 127.

9   Bacar Cassama, interviewed in Crioulo, August 14, 2008.
10 This is how Udé Camara and NDo Mané viewed the relationship between the Bissau Guinean government and the Bissau Guinean women. I am the one who summarized their views. Udé Camara and NDo Mané, interviewed in Crioulo, August 2, 2010.
11 Galli and Jones, *Guinea-Bissau: Politics, Economics and Society*, 78.
12 Kohl, "Ethnicity and the Political System Post 1998," 166. See also Tomas, *Amilcar Cabral: The Life of a Reluctant Nationalist*, 5.
13 Kohl, *A Creole Nation*, 78.
14 Havik, *Silences and Soundbites*, 88, and 353–4 and "Kriol without Creoles," 52 and 60; Forrest, *Guinea-Bissau*, 38; Mendy, *Colonialismo Portugues em Africa*, 307; and Kohl, *A Creole Nation*, 50–1.
15 Kohl, *A Creole Nation*, 51. See also Forrest, *Guinea—Bissau*, 21; Philip Havik, *Silences and Soundbites*, 354.
16 Kohl, "Limitations and Ambiguities of Colonialism in Guinea-Bissau," 170, 180–8.
17 Chabal, "National Liberation in Portuguese Guinea," 76.
18 Wicks, "Manifestations of nationhood in the Writings of Amilcar Cabral," 50. On the absence of ethnic and cultural homogeneity in newly independent African countries, see Lonsdale, "Ethnicite, Morale, et Tribalisme Politique," 100–1; Mamdani, *Citizen and Subject*, 135; Hill, "Beyond the Other?" 147–8; Young, "Nation, Ethnicity and Citizenship: Dilemmas," 241–64; Kersting, "New Nationalism and Xenophobia in Africa," 7.
19 Bacar Cassama, interviewed in Crioulo, August 14, 2008.
20 Joanita Da Silva Rosa, interviewed in Crioulo, 15 and July 30, 2010. See also Chapter 4.
21 *La République de Guinée Bissau en Chiffres*, February 1974, table 4, p. 8.
22 Cabral, *Sobre Alguns Problemas Practicos da nossa Vida e da nossa Luta*, 11–12.
23 Ibid., 13.
24 Quinta Da Costa, interviewed in Crioulo, August 12, 2010.
25 Teresa NQuamé, interviewed in Crioulo, July 28, 2010.
26 Fodé Cassama was a very well-known freedom fighter according to Joao Pereira, one of my interpreters in Guinea Bissau. I interviewed Fodé in his house in Bairro Luanda at night, a house without electricity, as are most houses in Bissau. He joined the PAIGC in 1962 and went through military and political training in East Germany and the Soviet Union before being sent to the southern front to join Nino Vieira's forces, and later to the eastern front to join Osvaldo Vieira.

Now he is a seventy-five-year-old man, and all his activities, since he retired in 1995, revolve around the mosque and his house.

27 The Portuguese called native Bissau Guinean autochthones or indigenous. The appellation responded to the Portuguese desire to distinguish the *assimilados* or Bissau Guineans with Cabo-Verdean descent. Fodé Cassama, interviewed in Crioulo, August 28, 2010. See also Kohl, *A Creole Nation,* 61–6, 91–2; Mendy, *Colonialismo Portugues em Africa,* 309–12; de Matos, *As cores do Imperio,* 63.

28 Embalo, "From Cabral's Liberation War to Power Struggle and Ideological Erosion," 74.

29 da Cunha, *Missao de Estudo dos Movimentos Associativos em Africa,* 67; Kohl, *A Creole Nation,* 36; Dhada, "The Liberation War in Guinea-Bissau Reconsidered," 586–9; Embalo, "From Cabral's Liberation War to Power Struggle and Ideological Erosion," 75.

30 Kohl, *A Creole Nation,* 38.

31 Embalo, "From Cabral's Liberation War to Power Struggle and Ideological Erosion," 79–80.

32 Ibid, 38–44. On Amilcar Cabral's assassination see PAIGC, "Sur le Lâche Assassinat du Fondateur et Premier Dirigeant de Notre Parti, Amilcar Cabral." Message du Comité Exécutif de la Lutte a Notre Peuple et á nos Combatants," 10. On the potential tensions or not between Bissau Guinea Cabo Verdeans and autochthons see Chabal, *Amilcar Cabral, Revolutionary Leadership and People's War,* 134–45; Keese, "The Role of Cabo Verdeans in War Mobilization and War prevention in Portugal's African Empire," 510–11; Amado, *Guerra Colonial e Guerra de Libertacao Nacional,* 322–37; Pereira, *O meu Testemunho Uma Luta, um Partido, dois Paises,* 226–7; Dhada, *Warriors at Work,* 34, 46–7, and 95.

33 Embalo, "From Cabral's Liberation War to Power Struggle and Ideological Erosion," 74. Tomas, *Amilcar Cabral: The Life of a Reluctant Nationalist,* 187–98.

34 See also Havik, "Kriol without Creoles," 64; Forrest, *Guinea Bissau,* 22.

35 Tomas, *Amilcar Cabral: The Life of a Reluctant Nationalist,* 200–1.

36 *Centro de Informação e Documentação Amílcar Cabral, Bissau,* 1980, 6.

37 PAIGC. Amílcar Cabral, Sobre a Criação da Assembleia Nacional Popular da Guiné; Resultados das Eleições gerais realizadas nas Regiões Libertadas, em 1972, 8 de janeiro de 1973.

38 Galli and Jones, *Guinea-Bissau: Politics, Economics and Society,* 70. See figure 5.1.

39 Ibid. See figure 5.4.

40 Lobban and Mendy, *Historical Dictionary of the Republic of Guinea-Bissau,* 9.

41 Gaitano Barboza, interviewed in Crioulo, August 8, 2008.

42 Osvaldo Vieira and Man Fodé recruited Mamady Kamara as a PAIGC member in 1961. He went to jail for three months after being accused of sabotage by the Portuguese police in August 1962. His older brother, who was also captured with him, was imprisoned for three years. When the war started in 1963, Mamady was involved in direct combat operations. In 1965, he was sent to the eastern front under the command of Domingo Ramos and Malan Keita. In 1966, he replaced Malan Keita as an army instructor. That year, under the command of Domingo Ramos, they faced a Portuguese attack in Medina Boé, in which Domingo Ramos was wounded (he later died at the village of Diaribé in southern Guinea Bissau). After Domingo was wounded, Mamady and several other fighters from Domingo's group were transferred to Barro Seydi's group by the PAIGC commanding officers. Again, in 1971, he received another transfer order from his commanding officers and went to the northern front, where he stayed until the end of the war. Mamady Kamara, interviewed in Pular, August 23, 2010.
43 Ibid. For more on the decline of the PAIGC, see Embalo, "From Cabral's Liberation movement to Power Struggle and Ideological Erosion," 72–88.
44 Barnaté Sanha, interviewed in Crioulo, July 28 and August 23, 2010.
45 Since July 2008, I have had several conversations with these three women, who all have been very influential in the political activities of their country. See Chapters 1–4.
46 Quinta Da Costa, interviewed in Crioulo, August 12, 2010.
47 Joanita Da Silva Rosa, interviewed in Crioulo, July 15 and 30, 2010.
48 Carmen Pereira, interviewed in Crioulo, August 23, 2008.
49 Einarsdottir, *Tired of Weeping*, 31.
50 Ibid., 27.
51 The data is from the 1990 Bissau Guinean Ministry for Rural Development and Agriculture Report.
52 Einarsdottir, *Tired of Weeping*, 179.
53 Ibid., 31–5.
54 This was an informal group discussion in French, in Bairro Luanda, in the backyard of my host Armando Abelha on the afternoon of July 30, 2010. I was with Mr. and Mrs. Abelha, Famara Mballo, Abdoulaye Baldé and his wife Cira Buaro, Felicidad Mané, Juliao Mané, and Laidy Costa. The translation is mine.
55 This is Faniara Mballo during our informal discussion, July 30, 2010.
56 This was Felicidad Mané's assertion during our informal discussion, July 30, 2010.

57 Laidy was just coming back from Brazil, where she is registered as a university student. She is in her third year in Business Administration. This quote is from our informal discussion, July 30, 2010.
58 Cira Diallo, interviewed in Pular and translated into English by Aliou Ly, Bissau, on July 12, 2009.
59 This quote is from Ndella Dialan's speech during our informal discussion, July 30, 2010.
60 Adama Sy is one of my guides and interpreters.
61 Rosalind Shaw, *Memories from the Slave Trade*, 60–1, and Steady, "Polygyny and the Household Economy in the Fishing Village in Sierra Leone," 211–29.
62 Lifton, *Social Soundness and WID Analysis for USAID Legal Reform Project Paper*.
63 Einarsdottir, *Tired of Weeping*, 45.
64 Ibid.
65 Ibid., 48.
66 Quintara Sanha Naneira, interviewed in French, July 26, 2010.
67 Anna Maria Naneira interviewed in French, June 29, 2010.
68 Ibid.
69 Dalanda Biaye, interviewed in Crioulo, September 5, 2010.
70 Ibid.
71 Maria Gomez is a member of the *Juventude Africana Amilcar Cabral*, the PAIGC youth organization. She is thirty years old, from the region of Tombali.
72 Urdang, "The Role of Women in the Revolution in Guinea-Bissau," 120.
73 Urdang, *Fighting Two Colonialisms*, 267.
74 Forrest, *Guinea Bissau*, 127.
75 Funk, "Land Tenure, Agriculture and Gender in Guinea-Bissau," 38.
76 Ibid., 54–6.
77 Francisca Pereira, General Secretary Discourse at the First Congress of the UDEMU. Figueiredo and Gomes, "Para Alem Dos Feminismos," 910 (909–27).
78 Forrest, *Guinea Bissau*, 127.
79 Ibid., 53. For more on the 1980 Military coup in Guiné-Bissau, see Embalo, "From Cabral's Liberation War to Power Struggle and Ideological Erosion," 79–81.
80 Comissão Nacional das Mulheres da Guiné-CNMG, *Io Congresso das Mulheres—Congresso da Organização para o Enquadramento da Mulher no Desenvolvimento*, Bissau, 3 a 7 de novembro de 1982, 25; Alternag, *Estudo/Inquérito. A participação da mulher nas esferas de decisão*, estudo realizado sob a orientação das consultoras Maria Cecília Ramos da Fonseca e Maria da Conceição Moura, Bissau, agosto de 1996, CIDAC, Lisboa, cota-GW-M I-8, 45.

81 Dianké Mballo, interviewed in Pular, July 20, 2010; Barros, M., Semedo, O. (Orgs), 2012, *Manual de capacitação das mulheres em matéria de participação política com base no género*, Bissau, UNIOGBIS-Gabinete Integrado das Nações Unidas para a Consolidação da Paz na Guiné-Bissau, 84; CNMG, Io Congresso das Mulheres—a mulher e a reconstrução nacional, Bissau, 3 a 7 de Novembro de 1982, CIDAC, Lisboa, cota-GW-M I–2 dossier.; Comissão Nacional das Mulheres da Guiné-CNMG, *Io Congresso das Mulheres*, Caderno no 1 "Mulher antes da luta," Bissau, 3–7 Novembro de 1982, Abril 1982, Lisboa, Centro de Informação e Desenvolvimento Amílcar Cabral-CIDAC, cota GW-M I–2 dossier; *Plataforma política das mulheres da Guiné-Bissau (PPM-GB)-Plano Estratégico Operacional 2013–2016 (Educar, participar e transformar)*, Bissau Agosto de 2013.
82 Fatu Turé, interviewed in Crioulo, July 27, 2010. Ly, "Revisiting the Guinea-Bissau liberation War," 361–77, 364.

Conclusion

1 Ferreira, "Amilcar Cabral," 55–64; Temudo, "From 'People's Struggle' to 'This War of Today,'" 245–63.
2 *The Life of a Reluctant Nationalist*, 99–117.
3 Ferreira, Patricia Magalhaes, "Guinea-Bissau: Between Conflict and Democracy," 48.
4 PAIGC. *Amilcar Cabral's handwritten discourse for the Proclamation of the Beginning of the Insurrection on August 3, 1961,* Conakry (Guinée-Conakry); PAIGC. "En Guinée Portugaise; Le Leader Nationaliste Amilcar Cabral Décide d'Intensifier La Lutte," *Le Monde*, 11 Juin, 1966; PAIGC. "Les Peuples de la Guinée Bissao et des iles du cap Vert sur la Voie de la Liberté," dans *El Mwomendjahid*, Algiers, 3 Août 1967; PAIGC. "Portuguese Guinea Insurgent Claims," in *The Times* (London), April 10, 1965.
5 Mendy, "Guinea Bissau," 25.
6 Kohl, *A Creole Nation*, 3.
7 Mendy, "Guinea Bissau," 25.
8 Imbali, *Os Efeitos Socio-Economicos do Programa de Ajustamento Estructural na Guiné-Bissau*; Monteiro, O, *Efeitos Socio-Economicos do Programa de Ajustamento Estructural na Guiné-Bissau*.

9   Quinta Da Costa, interviewed in English by Aliou Ly and translated into Bissau Guinean Creole by one of my translators, Bruno Da Costa, August 12, 2010; PAIGC, *Programa do PAIGC-Programa Maior*, Conacry, 1965, Fundação Amilcar Cabral, Praia (Cabo Verde), 2.
10 Martins, *Testemunho de um Combatente*, 90–8; Pereira, *O meu Testemunho Uma Luta, um Partido, dois Paises, Versao Documentada*, 407–552; Jose Pedro Castanheira, *Em Quem Mandou Matar Amílcar Cabral*, 103, 442–3; Cabral, *Crónica da Libertação*, 42–3; Coutinho, *Les Dirigeants du PAIGC, "Parti Africain Pour l'indépendance de la Guine et des Iles du Cap Vert" des origines a la Scission*, 39.
11 Tomas, *Amílcar Cabral: The Life of a Reluctant Nationalist*, 117–18; See Lopes, *Cabo Verde Os Bastidores da Independencia*, 133–4.
12 For more on ethnopolitics in Guinea Bissau, see Kohl, *A Creole Nation*, 34–5; Termudo, "From 'People's Struggle' to 'This War of Today,'" 260; Ostheimer, "The Structural Crisis in Guinea-Bissau's Political System," 46; Ferreira, "Guinea-Bissau," 48. Tomas, *Amílcar Cabral*, 5.

Selected Bibliography

Adelman, David A. "Profile Amilcar Cabral." *African Report* (May 1970).
Adie, W. A. C. "China, Russia and the Third World." *China Quarterly*, no. 11 (1962): 200–13.
Ageron, Charles Robert, and Cecile Thiebault, eds. *La Guerre d' Algerie: Au Miroir des Decolonisations Francaises: En L'Honneur de Charles-Robert Ageron: Actes du Colloque International (Paris, Sorbonne, 23, 24, 25 Novembre 2000)*. Saint Denis: Société Française d'Histoire d' Outre Mer, 2000.
Agsiere, J. T. *Women in Igbo Life and Thought*. London: Routledge, 2000.
Ahlman, Jeffrey S. "The Algerian Question in Nkrumah's Ghana." In *Algerians without Border, The Making of a Global Frontier Society*, edited by Allan Christelow. Gainesville: University Press of Florida, 2012.
Ait-Mous, Fadma. "The Moroccan Nationalist Movement: From Local to National Networks." *Journal of North African Studies* 18, no. 5 (2013): 732–52.
Alexandre, Valentim. *Origens do Colonialismo Portugues Moderno*. Lisboa: Sa da Costa, 1979.
Allison, Roy. *The Soviet Union and the Strategy of Non-Alignment in the Third World*. Cambridge: Cambridge University Press, 1988.
Allman, Jean, Susan Geiger, and Nakanyike Musisi. "Women in African Colonial Histories: An Introduction." In *Women in Colonial Histories*, edited by Jean Allman, Susan Geiger, and Nakanyike Musisi. Bloomington: Indiana University Press, 2002.
Alternag. *Estudo/Inquérito. A participação da mulher nas esferas de decisão*, estudo realizado sob a orientação das consultoras Maria Cecília Ramos da Fonseca e Maria da Conceição Moura, Bissau, agosto de 1996, CIDAC, Lisboa, cota-GW-M I-8, 45 p.
Amado, Leopoldo. *Guerra Colonial e Guerra de Libertacao Nacional 1950–1974: O Caso da Guiné-Bissau*. Lisbon: Instituto Portugues de Apoio ao Desenvolvimento, 2011.
Andelman, David A. "Profile: Amilcar Cabral." *Africa Report* 15, no. 5 (May 1970): 18–19.
Anderson, Benedict. *Imaged Communities: Reflections on the Origin and Spread of Nationalism*. London: Verso, 1999.

Andrade, Elisa Silva, *Les Iles du Cap Vert de la Decouverte a l'indépendance Nationale 1460–1975*. Paris: Harmattan, 1996.

Andreini, Jean Claude, and Marie Claude Lambert, *La Guinée Bissau d'Amilcar Cabral a al Reconstruction Nationale*. Paris: Harmattan, 1978.

Andrew, Christopher, and Vasili Mitrokhin. *The World Was Going Our Way: The KGB and the Battle for the Third World*. New York: Basic Books, 2005.

Angolan National Seminar. *Toward Angolan Independence, Report of a Seminar Organized by WAY in Leopoldville in April 1963*, 4–31. Brussels: World Assembly of Youth 31, 1964.

Askew, Kelly M. *Performing the Nation: Swahili Music and Cultural Politics in Tanzania*. Chicago: Chicago University Press, 2002.

Baerends, Els A. "Changing Kinship, Family and Gender Relations in Sub-Saharan Africa." In *Negotiation and Social Space, A Gendered Analysis of Changing Kin and Security Networks in South Asia and Sub-Saharan Africa*, edited by Carla Risseeuw and Kamala Ganesh. London: Altamira Press, 1998.

Barboza, Gaitano. Interviewed in English and translated in Crioulo, August 8, 2008.

Barrig, Maruja. "Latin American Feminisms: Gains Losses and Hard Times." *NACLA Report on the Americas* 34 (March–April 2001).

Barros, M., Semedo, O. (Orgs). *Manual de capacitação das mulheres em matéria de participação política com base no género*, 84. Bissau: UNIOGBIS-Gabinete Integrado das Nações Unidas para a Consolidação da Paz na Guiné-Bissau, 2012.

Barry, Boubacar. "Economic Anthropology of Precolonial Senegambia from 15th through the 19th Centuries." In *Uprooted of the Western Sahel*, edited by L.G. Colvin. New York: Praeger, 1981.

Bastian, M. L. "Vultures of the Marketplace: Southeastern Nigerian Women and Discourses of the Ogu Umanwaaniy (Women's War) of 1929." In *Women in African Colonial Histories*, edited by J. Allman, S. Geiger, and N. Musisi. Bloomington: Indiana University Press, 2002.

Baxter, Peter, *Bush War Rhodesia, 1966–1980*. West Midlands, England: Helion, 2014.

Bay, Edna G. *Wives of the Leopard: Gender, Politics and Culture in the Kingdom of Dahomey*. Charlottesville: University of Virginia Press, 1998.

Bereketeab, Redie. "Introduction." In *National Liberation Movements as Government in Africa*, edited by Redie Bereketeab, 3–16. New York: Routledge, 2018.

Berman, Bruce. "Ethnicity, Patronage and the African State: The Politics of Uncivil Nationalism." *African Affairs* 97 (1998): 305–41.

Biaye, Dalanda. Interviewed in English and translated In Crioulo, September 5, 2010.

Blacky, Robert. "Fanon and Cabral: A Contrast in Theories of Revolution for Africa." *Journal of Modern African Studies* 12, no. 2 (June 1974): 191–210.

Bockel, Alain. "Amilcar Cabral: Marxist Africain." *Ethiopiques* 5 (Dakar) (Janvier 1976): 35–9.

Bordonaro, Lorenzo I. "'Culture Stops Development': Bijagós Youth and the Appropriation of Developmentalist Discourse in Guinea-Bissau." *African Studies Review Special Issue; Guinea-Bissau Today* 52, no. 2 (September 2009).

Bordonaro, Lorenzo I. "Modernity as Marginality: The Making of the Experience of Peripherality in the Bijagos Islands (Guinea-Bissau)." *Cadernos de Estudos Africanos* 18, no. 19 (2010): 117–37.

Bowman, Joye. *Ominous Transition: Expansion in the Senegambia and Guinea (1857–1919)*. Avebery: Aldershot, 1997.

Brooks, George. *Landlords and Strangers; Ecology, Society, and Trade in Western Africa, 1000–1630*. Boulder, Colorado: Westview Press, 1993.

Bull, Benjamin Pinto. *O Crioulo da Guiné-Bissau, Filosofica e Sabedoria*. Lisbon, Bissau: Instituto de Cultural e Lingua Portuguese, Instituto Nacional de Estudos e Pesquisa, 1989.

Bush, Barbara. "Feminizing Empire? British Women Activist Networks in Defending and Challenging Empire from 1918 to Decolonization." *Women's History Review* 25 (2016): 499–519.

Bush, Barbara. "Motherhood, Morality, and Social Order: Gender and Development Discourse and Practice in Late Colonial Africa." In *Developing Africa: Concepts and Practices in 20th Century Colonialism*, edited by Joseph M. Hodge, Gerald Hold, and Martina Kopf. Manchester: Manchester University Press, 2010.

Bush, Barbara. "Nationalism, Development and Welfare Colonialism: Gender and the Dynamics of Decolonization." In *The Oxford Handbook of the Ends of Empire*, edited by Martin Thomas and Andrew Thompson. Oxford: Oxford University Press, 2018.

Byfield, Judith A. "Taxation, and the Colonial State: Egba Women's Tax Revolt." *Meridians, Race, Transnationalism* 3, no. 2 (2003): 250–77.

Byrne, Jeffrey James. *Mecca of Revolution; Algeria Decolonization, and the Third World Order*. Oxford: Oxford University Press, 2016.

Cabral, Amílcar. "The Agricultural Census in Guiné; Final Comments (1953 estimate)." In *Unity and Struggle: Speeches and Writings of Amilcar Cabral, Texts Selected by the PAIGC*, Translated by Michael Wolfer series: NYU Monthly Review Press Classic, 3 (1979): 15.

Cabral, Amílcar. *Alguns Principios do Partido*. Lisbon: Seara Nova, 1974.

Cabral, Amílcar "Approaching the Utilization of the Soil in Black Africa." *Ufahamu* III, no. 3 (1973): 13–21.

Cabral, Amílcar. "Recenseamento Agrícola da Guiné: Estimativa em 1953." *Boletin Cultural da Guine Portuguesa (BCGP)* 11, no. 43 (July 1956): 229–43.

Cabral, Amílcar. "Brief Analysis of the Social Structure in Guinea." In *Revolution in Guinea*. New York: Monthly Review Press, 2003.

Cabral, Amílcar. "The Development of the Struggle." In *Revolution* In Guinea, London: Stage 1, Translated by Richard Handyside, Written in 1968, First Published 1969, 91–102.

Cabral, Amílcar. "Friends and Allies." *African Agenda; A Voice of Afro-American Opinion* 2, no. 3 (March 1973).

Cabral, Amílcar. "National Liberation and Culture (1969 Estimate)." *Unity and Struggle: Speeches and Writings of Amilcar Cabral, Texts Selected by the PAIGC* Translated by Michael Wolfer Series: NYU Monthly Review Press Classic, 3 1979: 138–154.

Cabral, Amílcar. *Our People Are Our Mountains*. (Speech given in London, 1971). London: Committee for the Freedom of Mozambique, Angola and Guine, 1972.

Cabral, Amílcar. *Palavras de Ordem Gerais do Camarada Amílcar Cabral aos Responsáveis do Partido*. Conakry: Partido Africano da Independencia da Guine e Cabo Verde. Direcçao Regional do PAIGC de S. Vicente, 1969.

Cabral, Amílcar. "Recenseamento Agricola da Guiné," 50.

Cabral, Amílcar. *Return to the Source: Selected Speeches of Amílcar Cabral*. New York: Monthly Review press, 1973.

Cabral, Amílcar. *Revolution in Guinea*. London: Stage 1, 1969.

Cabral, Amílcar. *Revolution in Guinea: An African People's Struggle*. London: Stage 1, 1970).

Cabral, Amílcar. *Revolution in Guinea; Selected Texts by Amilcar Cabral*, Translated and edited by Richard Handyside. New York: Monthly Review Press, 1969.

Cabral, Amílcar. *Sobre Alguns Problemas Práticos da nossa Vida e da nossa Luta*. Transcription of tape-recording from the meeting of the *Conselho Superior da Luta*, August 9–16, 1971, Conakry.

Cabral, Amílcar. "Towards the Final Victory." In *Cabral*. First Published in 1969. Amilcar Cabral, Revolution in Guinea, Stage 1. London, 1974. Translated by Richard Hanyside.

Cabral, Amílcar. *Unidade e Luta: A Arma da Teoria*. Lisbon: Seara Nova, 1976.

Cabral, Amílcar. *Unity and Struggle; Speeches and Writings of Amilcar Cabral*. New York: Monthly Review Press, 1979.

Cabral, Amílcar. "The Weapon of Theory." In *Revolution in Guinea*. New York: Monthly Review Press, 1969.

Cabral, Ana-Maria. "Amilcar Cabral." In *Speech Given at the Inauguration of the Foundation Amilcar Cabral*, 2. Praia: Cabo Verde, 1995, Posted at http://www.si.edu/folklife/policy/issues.htm.

Cabral, Juvenal. *Memorias e Reflexões*. Praia: Instituto da Biblioteca Nacional, 2002.

Cabral, Luís. *Crónica da Libertação*. Lisboa: O Jornal, 1984.
Cabral, Luís. "Da Formação do Partido a Proclamaçao do Estado." *No Pintcha* II, no. 228 (19 September 1976).
Camara, Pauletta. Interviewed in French, June 22, 2009.
Camara, Udé. Group interviewed in English and translated in Crioulo, August 2, 2010.
Candido, Mariana P. *An African Slaving Port and the Atlantic World: Benguela and Its Hinterland*. Cambridge: Cambridge University Press, 2013.
Caplan, Patricia. "Cognatic Descent, Islamic Law and Women's Property on the East African Coast." In *Women and Property-Women as Property*, edited by Renee Hirschon. London: Croonm Helm, 1984.
Cardoso, Carlos. "A Formação da Elite Política na Guiné-Bissau." *Centro de Estudos Africanos Occasional Paper 5* (2002).
Cardoso, Carlos. "Conflictos Interetnicos-Dissolucao e Reconstrucao de Unidades Políticas nos rios da Guine e Cabo Verde." Soronda, *Revista de Estudos Guineenses* 7, no. 7 (janeiro de 1989): 51–2.
Cardoso, Carlos. "A Ideologia e a Practica da Colonização Portuguesa na Guine e o seu Impacto na estructura Social." *Soronda-Revista de Estudos Guineenses* 14, no. 14 (julho de 1992): 41.
Carney, Judith. *Black Rice: The African Origin of Rice Cultivation in the Americas*. Cambridge, MA: Harvard University Press, 2001.
Carreira, Antonio. *Migracaoes nas Ilhas de Cabo Verde*. Praia: Institto Cabo-Verdiano do Livro, 1983.
Carreira, Antonio. *The People of Cabo Verde Islands: Exploitation and Emigration*, Edited and Translated by Fyfe. London: C. Hurst, 1982.
Castanheira, Jose Pedro. *Quem Mandou Matar Amílcar Cabral?* Lisboa: Rainho & Neves, Lda, 1995.
Castanheira, Jose Pedro. *Qui a Fait Tuer Amilcar Cabral?* Paris: L'Harmattan, 2003.
Castro, Fidel. *Cuba and Angola; Fighting for Africa's Freedom and Our Own*. New York: Pathfinder, 2013.
Ceres. "There Was No Room for Sex Discrimination during the Struggle." *Ceres* 8, no. 2 (March–April 1975).
Chabal, Patrick. "The African Crisis: Context and Interpretation." In *Postcolonial Identities in Africa*, edited by R.P. Werbner, and T.O. Ranger, 29–54. London: Zed Books, 1996.
Chabal, Patrick. *Amilcar Cabral: Revolutionary Leadership and People's War*. Cambridge: Cambridge University Press, 1983.
Chabal, Patrick. "Litterature et Liberation Nationale: Le Cas d'Amilcar Cabral." In *Les Litteratures Africaines de langue Portuguese: A La Recherche de L'Identite*

Individuelle et Nationale, edited by Actes du Colloque International de Paris, 28 Novembre–01 Decembre 1984. Paris: Fondation Caloustem Gulbenkian/Centre Culturel Portugais, 1985.

Chabal, Patrick. "National Liberation in Portuguese Guinea, 1956–1974." *African Affairs* 80, no. 318 (January 1981).

Chabal, Patrick. "Revolutionary Democracy in Africa: The Case of Guinea Bissau." In *Political Domination in Africa, Reflections on the Limits of Power*, edited by Patrick Chabal. Cambridge: Cambridge University Press, 1986.

Chabal, Patrick. "The Social and Political Thought of Amilcar Cabral; A Reassessment." *Journal of Modern African History* 19, no. 1 (March 1981).

Chabuca, Domingo Parafino. *Self Determination in International Relations: A Study of Mozambican Struggle for Independence*. Dar Es Salam: Centre for Foreign Relations, 1981.

Chaliand, Gérard. *Armed Struggle in Africa: With the Guerillas in "Portuguese Guinea."* New York: Monthly Review Press, 1969.

Chaliand, Gérard. *Guinée Portugaise et Cap Vert: En Lutte pour Leur Independence*. Paris: François Maspero, 1964.

Chaliand, Gérard. *Lutte Armée en Afrique*. Paris: François Maspero, 1967.

Chaliand, Gérard. "The PAIGC without Cabral: An Assessment." *Ufahamu* 3, no. 3 (Winter 1973).

Chaliand, Gérard. *Revolution in the Third World*. New York: Viking, 1977.

Chanock, Martin. "Making Customary Law: Men, Women and Courts in Colonial Rhodesia." In *African Women and the Law: Historical Perspectives*, edited by Jean Hay, and Marcia Wright. Boston: Boston University Press, Papers on Africa VII, 1982.

Chilcote, Ronald. *Amilcar Cabral's Revolutionary Theory and Practice; A Critical Guide*. Boulder, Colorado: Lynne Rienner, 1991.

Chilcote, Ronald. *Emerging Nationalism in Portuguese Africa*. Stanford: Stanford University Press, 1972.

Chilcote, Ronald. "The Political Thought of Amilcar Cabral." *Journal of Modern African Studies* 6, no. 3 (1968): 373–88.

Chingono, M. "Women, War and Peace in Mozambique: The Case of Manica Province." *African Journal of Peace Resolution* 15, no. 1 (2015): 107–30.

Christelow, Allan. *Algerians without Border: The Making of a Global Frontier Society*. Gainesville: University Press of Florida, 2012.

Cissoko, S. M. "La Royauté Mansaya Chez les Mandingues de L'Ouest d'Apres leurs Traditions Orales." *BIFAN*, serie B, 2. XXXI (1969): 325–36.

Cissokho, Mario Augusto Ramalho. Interviewed in French, August 8, 2008.

Cleaver, Tessa, and Marion Wallace. *Namibian Women in War*. London: Zed Books, 1990.

Climats Newspaper. Grand Bassam, Ivory Coast, January 19, 1950.
Cock, Jacklyn. *Colonels and Cadres: War and Gender in South Africa*. Oxford: Oxford University Press, 1991.
Cock, Jacklyn. "Keeping the Fires Burning: Militarization and the Politics of Gender in South Africa." *Review of African Political Economy* 45, no. 46 (1989).
Colburn, Forrest D. *The Vogue of Revolution in Poor Countries*. Princeton: Princeton University Press, 1994.
Colin, Roland. "La Pensée et la Pratique Sociale et Politique Amilcar Cabral sur les Chemins de L'Histoire." *Presence Africaine, Nouvelle Serie*, no. 185/186 (1er et 2eme semestre 2012): 95–105.
Comissão Nacional das Mulheres da Guiné-CNMG, *1o Congresso das Mulheres*, Caderno no 1 "Mulher antes da luta," Bissau, 3–7 novembro de 1982, abril 1982, Lisboa, Centro de Informação e Desenvolvimento Amílcar Cabral-CIDAC, cota GW-M I-2 dossier.
Comissão Nacional das Mulheres da Guiné-CNMG, *Io Congresso das Mulheres—Congresso da Organização para o Enquadramento da Mulher no Desenvolvimento*, 25. Bissau, 3 a 7 de novembro de, 1982.
Cooke, Miriam. "Wo-man, Retelling the War Myth." In *Gendering War Talk*, edited by Miriam Cooke, and Angela Woollacott. New Jersey: Princeton University Press, 1993.
Cooper, Frederick. *Africa since 1940: The Past of the Present*. London: Cambridge University Press, 2000.
Cornwall, Barbara. *The Bush Rebels; A Personal Account of Black Revolt in Africa*. New York: Holt, Rinehart, and Winston, 1972.
Costa, Laidy as participant of an informal group discussion in French, July 30, 2010.
Coutinho, Angela Sofia Benoliel, *Les Dirigeants du PAIGC, "Parti Africain Pour l'indépendance de la Guine et des Iles du Cap Vert" des origines a la Scission*. Paris: Université de Paris 1—Pantheon—Sorbonne UFR d' Histoire, 2005.
Couto, Hildo Honorio. *O Crioulo Português da Guiné-Bissau*. Hamburg: Helmut Buske Verlag, 1994.
Couto, Hildo Honorio. "Política e Planeamento Linguisto na Guiné-Bissau." *Brasileira de Estudos Crioulos e Similares* 1 (1990).
Da Costa, Quinta. Interviewed in English and translated in Crioulo, August 12, 2010.
Da Silva Rosa, Joanita. Interviewed in English and translated In Crioulo, July 15 and 30, 2010.
Da Cunha, J. M. Silva. *Missao de Estudo dos Movimentos Associativos em Africa: Relatorio da Campanha de 1958 (Guiné)*. Lisbon: Junta de Investigacoes do Ultramar, 1959.
Da Mota, A. Teixeira. *Guiné Portuguesa*, vol. 1. Lisbon: AGU, 1954.

Da Mota, A. Teixeira. *Some Aspects of Portuguese Colonisation and Sea Trade in West Africa in the Fifteenth and Sixteenth Centuries*. Bloomington: Indiana University Press, 1978.

Da Mota, A. Teixeira, Basil Davidson, and B. Munslow. "The Crisis of the Nation-State in Africa." *Review of African Political Economy* 49 (1990): 11.

Davidson, Basil. *No Fist Is Big Enough to Hide the Sky: The Liberation of Guinea-Bissau and Cabo Verde*. London: Zed Press, 1969.

Davidson, Basil. *The Liberation of Guiné: Aspect of an African Revolution*. Harmondsworth: Penguin, 1969.

Davidson, Basil, and B. Munslow. "The Crisis of the Nation-State in Africa." *Review of African Political Economy* 49 (1990).

De Andrade, Mario. *A Geraçào de Cabral*. Palestra Proferida na Escola-Pilot de Conacri (em 8/2/ 1973).

De Andrade, Mario. *Amilcar Cabral, Essai de Biographie Politique*. Paris-Verne: François Maspero, 1980.

De Andrade, Mario. "Amilcar Cabral: Profil d'un Revolutionaire Africain." *Présence Africaine* 2, no. 86 (1973).

De Andrade, Mario. *Amilcar Cabral Essai de Biographie Politique* (Petite Collection Maspero) (French Edition). Paris: F. Maspero (January 1, 1980).

De Andrade, Mario. *La Poesie Africaine d'Expression Portuguese, Evolution et Tendances Actuelles*. Honfleur: Pierre Jean Oswald, 1969.

De Braganca, Aquiano, and Immanuel Maurice Wallerstein. *The African Liberation Reader; Vol. 1: The Anatomy of Colonialism*. London: Zed Press, 1982.

De Braganca, Aquiano, and Immanuel Maurice Wallerstein. *The African Liberation Reader; Vol. 2: The National Liberation Movements*. London: Zed Press, 1982.

De Braganca, Aquiano, and Immanuel Maurice Wallerstein. *The African Liberation Reader; Vol. 3: The Strategy of Liberation*. London: Zed Press, 1982.

De Lespinay, Charles. "La Disparution de la Langue Baynunk." In *Cahiers du CRA*. Paris (1987): 23–9.

De Matos, Patricia Ferraz. *As cores do Imperio: Representações raciais no Imperio colonial Portugues*. Lisbon: Imprensa de Ciencias Sociais, 2006.

De Olivia, O. B., Philip Havik, and U. Schiefer. *Armazenamento Tradicional na Guiné-Bissau*. Bissau: Munter, 1993.

De Sena, Luis, and Marie Laure Lambert. *L' Education en République de Guinée Bissau: Situation et perspectives*. Paris: IRFED, 1977.

Decew, Judith Wagner. "The Combat Exclusion and the Role of Women in the Military." *Hypathia* 10, no. 3 (Winter 1995).

Decker, Alicia C. "Women and National Liberation in Africa." *The International Encyclopedia of Revolution and Protest, 1500 to the Present* 7 (2009): 3545–50.

DeFronzo, James. *Revolutions and Revolutionary Movements*. Boulder, Colorado: Westview Press, 2011.

Denzer, LaRay. "Towards a Study of the History of West African Women's Participation in Nationalist Politics; The Early Phase, 1935–1950." *Africana Research Bulletin* 6, no. 4 (1976).

Dhada, Mustafah. "The Liberation War in Guinea-Bissau Reconsidered." *Journal of Military History* 62, no. 3 (July 1, 1998): 571–93.

Dhada, Mustafah. *Warriors at Work; How Guinea Was Really Set Free*. Niwot, Colorado: University Press of Colorado, 1993.

Dialan, Ndella. as participant of an informal group discussion in French, July 30, 2010.

Diallo, Cira. Interviewed in Pular, July 12, 2009.

Diallo, Fatoumata. Interviewed in Pular, July 27 and September 1, 2009.

Diamba, Dialan. Interviewed in Pular, July 1, 2010.

Dinerman, Alice. *Revolution, Counter-Revolution and Revisionism in Postcolonial Africa: The Case of Mozambique, 1975–1994*. London: Routledge/Taylor and Francis Group, 2006.

Duncan, Raymond, ed. *Soviet Policy in the Third World*. New York: Pergamon Press, 1980.

Easterly, E. "Design and Reform of Institutions in LDCS and Transition Economies: Institution – Top Down or Bottom Up?" *American Economic Review* 98, no. 20 (2008).

Einarsdottir, Jonina. *Tired of Weeping; Mother Love, Child Death, and Poverty in Guinea-Bissau*. Madison: University of Wisconsin Press, 2004.

Elkins, Caroline M. *Imperial Reckoning: The Untold Story of Britain's Gulag in Kenya*. New York: Henry Holt, 2005.

Embalo, Brigit. "From Cabral's Liberation Movement to Power Struggle and Ideological Erosion: The Decline of PAIGC in Guinea Bissau." In *National Liberation Movements as Government in Africa*, edited by Redie Bereketeab, 72–88. New York: Routledge, 2018.

Embalo, Filomena. "O Crioulo da Guiné-Bissau: Lingua Nacional e Factor de Identidade Nacional." *Papia Brasileira de Estudos Crioulos e Similares* 18 (2008): 101–7.

Eriksen, Thomas Hylland. "Creolization in Anthropological Theory in Mauritius." In *Creolization: History, Ethnography, Theory*, edited by Charles Stewart. Walnut Creek, California: Left Coast Press, 2007.

Fadia, Aliu. Interviewed in French, June 10, 2010.

Fanon, Frantz. *A Dying Colonialism*. New York: Grove Press, 1994.

Fanon, Frantz. "Algeria Unveiled." In *A Dying Colonialism*, translated by H. Chevalier. New York: Grove Press, 1965.

Ferreira, Eduardo De Sousa. "Amilcar Cabral: Theory of Revolution and Background to His Assassination." *UFAHAMU: Journal of African Studies* 3, no. 3 (1973): 49–68.

Ferreira, Patricia Magalhaes. "Guinea-Bissau: Between Conflict and Democracy." *African Security Review* 13 (2004): 45–56.

Figueiredo, Ângela, and Patrícia Godinho Gomes; "Para Alem Dos Feminismos: Uma Experiencia Compaparada Entre Guiné-Bissau e Brazil." *Estudos Feministas, Flotianopolis* 24, no. 3 (398—setembro-dezembro 2016): 910 (909–927).

Filho, Wilson Trajano. "A Construção e o Fim dos Projetos Crioulos: Os Casos de Cabo Verde e da Guiné-Bissau." In *"Lusofia" em Africa: História, Democracia e Integração Africana*, edited by Teresa Cruz e Silva, Manuel G. Mendes de Araújo, and Carlos Cardoso. Dakar: CODESRIA, 2005.

Filho, Wilson Trajano. "Rumores: Uma Narrativa da Nação." *Serie Anthropologia* 143 (1993).

Filho, Wilson Trajano. "Some Problems with the Creole Project for the Nation: The Case of Guinea-Bissau." Paper Presented at the Powerful Presence of the Past: Historical Dimensions of Integration and Conflict in the Upper Guinea Coast Conference, *Max Planck Institute for Social Anthropology*. Hall (Saale), October 19–21, 2006.

Fontanellaz, Adrien, and Tom Cooper. *War of Intervention in Angola: Volume 2. Angolan and Cuban Forces*. Silihull, West Midlands: Helion & Company, 2019.

Formes, Malia B. "Beyond Complicity versus Resistance: Recent Work on Gender in European Imperialism." *Journal of Social History* 3 (1995): 629–41.

Forrest, Joshua B. *Lineages of State Fragility; Rural Civil Society in Guinea-Bissau*. Athens: Ohio University Press, 2003.

Forrest, Joshua B. *Guinea Bissau, Power, Conflict and Renewal in a West African Nation*. Boulder, Colorado: Westview Press, 1992.

Forrest, Joshua B. "Guinea Bissau since Independence; a Decade of Power Struggles." *The Journal of Modern African Studies* 25, no. 1 (1987): 95–116.

FRELIMO Central Committee. *A History of FRELIMO*. Harare: Longman Zimbabwe, 1982.

FRELIMO Central Committee. *Lusaka Agreement*. Lorenco Marques: Imprensa Nacional de Mozambique, 1975.

FRELIMO Central Committee. *The Mozambican Woman in the Revolution*. Richmond, B. C.: Liberation Support Movement, 1972.

FRELIMO Central Committee. *7 April 1972: 2nd Anniversary of the Death of Comrade Josina Machel, Mozambique Women Fighter*. Toronto: TCLPOAC, 1972.

Friedman, Jeremy Scott. "Reviving Evolutions: The Sino-Soviet Split, the Third World and the Fate of the Left." PhD Dissertation, Princeton University, 2011.
Funk, Ursula. "Land Tenure, Agriculture, and Gender in Guinea-Bissau." In *Agriculture, Women and Land; the African Experience*, edited by Jean Davison. Boulder, Colorado: Westview Press, 1988.
Galli, Rosemary E., and Jocelyn Jones. *Guinea-Bissau; Politics, Economics and Society*. Boulder, Colorado: Lynne Rienner, 1987.
Gallois Duquette, Danielle. "Women, Power and Initiation in the Bissagos Islands." *African Arts* 12, no. 3 (1979): 31–5.
Galvez, William. *Che in Africa; Che Guevara's Congo Diary in Africa*. Melbourne: Ocean Press, 1999.
Cassama, Bacar. Interviewed in English and translated in Crioulo, August 14, 2008.
Gassama, Fodé. Interviewed in Crioulo, August 28, 2010.
Gassama, Diabira. Interviewed in English and translated in Crioulo, July 27, 2010.
Geiger, Susan. "Tanganyikan Nationalism as 'Women's Work': Life Histories, Collective Biography and Changing Historiography." *Journal of African History* 37, no. 3 (1996).
Geiger, Susan. "Women in Nationalist Struggle: TANU Activists in Dar Es Salam." *International Journal of African Historical Studies* 20, no. 1 (1987).
Geisler, Gisela. *Women and the Remaking of Politics in Southern Africa: Negotiating Autonomy, Incorporation and Representation*. Nordiska Afrikainstitutet, 2004.
Gellner, Ernest. *Nations and Nationalism*. Oxford: Blackwell, 1998.
George, Edward. *The Cuban Intervention in Angola, 1965–1991: From Che Guevara to Cuito Cuanavale*. London: Routledge, 2012.
Giblin, James L. *A History of the Excluded; Making Family a Refuge from State in Twentieth Century Tanzania*. Oxford, Dar Es Salam and Athens: James Currey, Mkuki na Nyota and Ohio University Press, 2005.
Gibson, Nigel C. "Some Reflections on Amilcar Cabral's Legacy." In *Claim No Easy Victories: The Legacy of Amilcar Cabral*, edited by Firoze Manji, and Bill, Fletcher. Jr. Dakar: CODESRIA, 2013.
Gibson, Richard. *African Liberation Movements; Contemporary Struggles against White Minority Rule*. London: Oxford University Press, 1972.
Gjerstad, Ole, and Chantal Sarrazin. *Sowing the First Harvest: National Reconstruction in Guinea-Bissau*. Oakland, California: LSM Information Center, 1978.
Gleijeses, Piero. *Havana, Washington and Africa, 1959–1976*. Chapel Hill: University of North Carolina Press, 2002.

Gomes, Crispina. "The Women of Guinea-Bissau and Cabo Verde in the Struggle for National Independence." In *The Life, Thought, and Legacy of Cabo Verde's Freedom Fighter Amilcar Cabral (1924–1973); Essays on His Liberation Philosophy*, edited by John Fobanjong and Thomas Ranuga. Lewiston, Queenston, Lampeter: The Edwin Mellen Press, 2006.

Gomes, Eva. Interviewed in English and translated in Crioulo, August 13, 2008.

Gomes, Juditi. Interviewed in English and translated in Crioulo, July 28, 2010.

Gomes, Patricia Godinho. "Amilcar Cabral and Guinean Women in the Fight for Emancipation." In *Claim No Easy Victories: The Legacy of Amilcar Cabral*, edited by Firoze Manji, and Bill, Fletcher Jr. Dakar: CODESRIA, 2013.

Gomes, Patricia Godinho. "The State of Art of Gender in Guinea-Bissau: A Preliminary Approach." *Oustros Tempos* 12, no. 19 (2015): 168–89.

Gomes, Patricia Godinho. "A Importancia das Forças Armadas Revolutionárias do Povo (FARP) na Luta pela Libertação da Guiné-Bissau." *Poiésis* 3, no. 6 (2010): 121–39.

Gomes, Patricia Godinho. "Mindjeris di Guiné, ka bô m'pina, Ka bô burgunhu 1: narrativas de mulheres na/sobre a luta de libertação na Guiné-Bissau (trajetórias, construções e percursos emancipatórios)." *AbeAfrica: Revista Brasileira de Estudos Africanos* 6, no. 6 (Octubro de 2021): 81–106.

Gomes, Patricia Godinho. "A Mulher Guineense Como Sujeito e Objecto do Debate Histórico Cotemporaneo: Excerto da História de Vida de Teodora Inacia Gomes." *Africa Development* XLI, no. 3 (2016): 71–95.

Green, Toby. *The Rise of the Trans-Atlantic Slave Trade in Western Africa, 1300–1589*. Cambridge: Cambridge University Press, 2012.

Green, Toby, and Chabal Patrick. "Introduction." In *Guinea-Bissau; Micro-State to Narco-State*, edited by Patrick Chabal, and Toby Green. London: Hurst Publishers, 2016.

Greene, Sandra. *Gender, Ethnicity and Social Change on the Upper Slave Coast, A History of the Anlo-Ewe*. London: James Currey, 1996.

Guevara, Ernesto "Che." *The African Dream: The Diaries of the Revolutionary War in the Congo*. New York: Grove Press, 2000.

Guha, Ranajit. *History at the Limit of World History*. New York: Columbia University Press, 2002.

Guha, Ranajit. "The Small Voice of History." In *Subaltern Studies*, vol. 9 edited by Shahid Amin and Dipesh Chakrabarty. Delhi: Oxford University Press, 1997.

Guimaraes, Fernando Andresen. *The Origins of the Angolan Civil War: Foreign Intervention and Domestic Political Conflict*. New York: Macmillan, 1998.

Hafkin, Nancy, and Edna Bay. *Women in Africa: Studies in Social and Economic Change*. Stanford: Stanford University Press, 1976.

Hale, Thomas. *Scribes, Griot, and Novelist: Narratives Interpreters of the Songhai Empire*. Gainesville: University of Florida Press, 1990.

Handem, Diana Lima. *Nature and Fonctionnement Chez les Balanta Brassa*. Bissau: INEP, 1986.

Handyside, Richard (translated and edited). *Revolution in Guinea; Selected Texts by Amilcar Cabral*. New York: Monthly Review Press, 1969.

Hansen, Karen Tranberg, ed. *African Encounters with Domesticity*. New Brunswick, New Jersey: Rutgers, The State University, 1992.

Hatem, Mervant. "Toward the Development of Post-Islamist and Post-Nationalist Feminist Discourses in the Middle East." In *Arab Women*, edited by Judith E. Tucker. Bloomington: Indiana University Press, 1993.

Havik, Philip J. "Female Entrepreneurship in a Changing Environment: Gender Kinship and Trade in the Guinea Bissau Region." In *Negotiation and Social Space: A Gendered Analysis of Changing Kin and Security Networks in South Asia and Sub-Saharan Africa*, edited by Carla Risseeuw et al. New Delhi: Sage, 1998.

Havik, Philip J. "Guinea Bissau Rural Economy and Society: A Reassessment of Colonial and Post-Colonial Dynamics." In *Guineas Bissau, Micro-State to Narco State*, edited by Toby Green, and Patrick Chabal. London: Hurst Publishers, 2016.

Havik, Philip J. "Kriol without Creoles: Afro-Atlantic Connections in the Guinea Bissau Region (16th to 20th Centuries)." In *Cultures of the Lusophone Black Atlantic, Studies of the Americas*, edited by Nancy Priscilla Naro, Roger Sansi-Roca and Dave H. Treece. New York: Palgrave Macmillan, 2007.

Havik, Philip J. "Les Noirs et Les Blancs de L'Ethnographie Coloniale: Discours sur le Genre en Guinee Portugaise (1915-1935). *Lusotopie* XII, no. 1-2 (2005): 54-76.

Havik, Philip J. "Mundasson I Kambansa: Espaço Social e Movimentos Políticos na Guiné Bissau (1910-1944)." *Reviusta Internacional de Estudos Africanos* 18-22 (1995-1999): 120-30.

Havik, Philip J. *Silences and Soundbytes: The Gendered Dynamics of Trade and Brokerage in the Pre-Colonial Guinea-Bissau Region*. Leiden: Lit Verlag Munter, 2004.

Havik, Philip J. "Traders, Planters and Go-Betweens: The Kriston in Portuguese Guinea." *Portuguese Studies Review* 19 (2011): 197-226.

Havik, Philip J. "Women and Trade in the Guinea Bissau Region: The Role of African and Luso-African Women in Trade Networks from the Early 16th to the Mid 19th Century." *Studia* 52 (1994): 88-120.

Hawthorne, Walter. *Planting Rice and Harvesting Slaves; Transformations along the Guinea-Bissau Coast, 1400-1900*. Portsmouth, New Hampshire: Heinemann, 2003.

Hay, Margaret Jean. "Queens, Prostitutes and Peasants: Historical Perspectives on African Women, 1971–1986." *Canadian Journal of African Studies* XXII, no. 3 (1988): 431–47.

Hay, Margaret Jean. "Women as Owners, Occupants and Managers of Property in Colonial Western Kenya." In *African Women and the Law: Historical Perspectives*, edited by Hay and Wright. Boston: Boston University Papers on Africa, no. 7, 1982.

Henriksen, Thomas H. "People's War in Angola, Mozambique, and Guinea-Bissau." *The Journal of Modern African History* 14, no. 3 (1976).

Herbst, J. "Responding to State Failure in Africa." *International Security* 21, no. 3 (1999–1997): 120–1.

Hill, Jonathan. "Beyond the Other? A Postcolonial Critique of the Failed State Thesis." *African Identities* 3 (2005): 139–54.

Hobsbawm, Eric. *Nations and Nationalism since 1780; Programme, Myth, Reality*. Cambridge: Cambridge University Press, 1999.

Houser, George M. "Assessing Africa's Liberation Struggle." *Africa Today* 34, no. 4, *Africa's Liberation Struggle: Retrospect and Prospect (4th Quarter 1987)*: 17–32.

Hubbard, Maryinez L. "Culture and History in a Revolutionary Context: Approach to Amilcar Cabral." *UFAHAMU, Journal of African Studies* 3, no. 3 (1972): 69–86.

Hubbell. "A View of the Slave Trade from the Margin: Sououdougou in the Late Nineteenth Century Slave Trade of the Niger Bend." *Journal of African History* 42, no. 1 (2000).

Hughes, Melanie M., "Armed Conflict, International Linkages and Women's Parliamentary Representation in Developing Nations." *Social Problems* 56, no. 1 (February 2009).

Hutchison, Alan. *China's Africa Revolution*. Boulder; Colorado: Westview Press, 1976.

Iandolo, Alessandro. "Imbalance of Power: The Soviet Union and the Congo Crisis, 1960–1961." *Journal of Cold War Studies* 12, no. 2 (2014) 32–55.

Iandolo, Alessandro. "The Rise and Fall of the Soviet Model of Development in West Africa, 1957–64." *Journal of Cold War History* 12, no. 4 (2012): 683–704.

Idahosa, Pablo Luke. "Going to the People: Amilcar Cabral's Materialist Theory and Practice of Culture and Ethnicity." *Lusotopia* 2 (2002): 29–58.

Imbali, Faustino. *Os Efeitos Socio-Economicos do Programa de Ajustamento Estructural na Guiné-Bissau*. Bissau: Edicoes INEP, 1993.

Ines, Galvão, Laranjeiro Catarina. "Gender Struggle in Guinea-Bissau: Women's Participation On and Off the Liberation Record." In *Resistance and Colonialism. Cambridge Imperial and Post-Colonial Studies Series*, edited by N. Domingos, M. Jerónimo, and R. Roque, 85–123. Cham: Palgrave Macmillan, 2019.

Ingles, Paulo. "The MPLA Government and Its Post-Liberation Record in Angola." In *National Liberation Movements as Government in Africa*, edited by Redie Bereketeab. New York: Routledge, 2018.

Innes, Gordon. *Sunjata: Three Mandinka Versions*. London: University of London, 1974.

Jackson, Steven F. "China's Third World Foreign Policy: The Case of Angola and Mozambique, 1961-93." *China Quarterly*, no. 142 (1995): 388-422.

Jacobs, Bart. "Upper Guinea Creole: Historical and Linguistic Evidence in Favor of Santiago Origin." *Journal of Pidgin and Creole Languages* 25, no. 2 (2010): 289-343.

James, W. Martin III. *A Political History of the Civil War in Angola, 1974-1990*. New Brunswick (USA) and London (UK): Routledge, 1992.

Jayawardena, Kumari. *Feminism and Nationalism in the Third World*. London: Zed Books, 1986.

Jespersen, S. B. *In Search of Recognition; a Study of War Veterans in Guinea Bissau*. Copenhagen: Institute of Anthropology, University of Copenhagen, 2002.

Journal de l'Afrique de L'Ouest Française. Paris, France, April 1, 1939.

Kamara, Mamady. Interviewed in Pular, August 23, 2010.

Kanogo, Tabitha. "Kikuyu Women and the Politics of Protest: Mau-Mau." In *Images of Women in Peace and War*, edited by S. MacDonald, P. Holden, and S. Ardener. London: Macmillan, 1987.

Kanogo, Tabitha. *Squatters and the Roots of Mau-Mau*. London, Nairobi, and Athens: James Currey, Heinemann and Ohio State University, 1987.

Katsakioris, Constantin. "L'Union Sovietique et les Intellectuels Africains: Internationalisme, Pan Africanisme et Negritude pendant les Annees de la Decolonisation, 1954-1964." *Cahier du Monde Russe*, no. 1 (2006): 15-32.

Kawsara, Fantam. Interviewed in Pular, July 16, 2010.

Keese, Alexander. "The Role of Cabo Verdeans in War Mobilization and War Prevention in Portugal's African Empire, 1955-1965." *International Journal of African Historical Studies* 40 (2007): 497-511.

Kennedy, James. "Religion, Nation and European Representation of the Past." In *The Contested Nation: Ethnicity, Class, Religion and Gender in National Histories*, edited by Stefan Berger, and Chris Lorenz. Basingstoke: Palgrave Macmillan, 2008.

Kershaw, Greet. "The Changing Role of Men and Women in the Kikuyu Family by Socioeconomic Strata." *Rural Africana* 29 (1975).

Kersting, Norbert. "New Nationalism and Xenophobia in Africa: New Inclination?" *Africa Spectrum* 44 (2009): 7-18.

Klein, Martin. "Ethnic Pluralism and Homogeneity in the Western Sudan: Saaloum, Segu, Wassulu." *Mande Studies* 1 (1999).

Klinghoffer, Arthur Jay. *The Angolan War: A Study in Soviet Policy in the Third World*. Boulder, Colorado: Westview Press, 1980.

Knauss, Peter R. *The Persistence of Patriarchy: Class, Gender and Ideology in 20th Century Algeria*. New York: Praeger Publishers, 1987.

Knorr, Jaqueline. "Contemporary Creoleness; or the World in Pidginization?" *Current Anthropology* 51 92010: 731–59.

Knorr, Jaqueline. "Towards Conceptualizing Creolization and Creoleness." *Max Planck Institute for Social Anthropology Working Papers* 100 1 (2008): 4–5 and 13–14.

Knutsen, Torbjorn L. *A History of International Relations*. Manchester: Manchester University Press, 1997.

Kohl, Christoph. *A Creole Nation: National Integration in Guinea-Bissau*. Oxford: Berghahn, Books, 2018.

Kohl, Christoph. "Ethnicity and the Political System Post 1998." In *Guinea-Bissau: Macro State to Narco State*, edited by Toby Green, and Patrick Chabal. London: Hurst Publishers, 2016.

Kohl, Christoph. "Limitations and Ambiguities of Colonialism in Guinea-Bissau. Examining the Creole and Civilized Space in Colonial Society." *History in Africa* 43 (2016): 169–203.

Kohl, Christoph. "National Integration in Guinea Bissau since Independence." *Cadernos de Estudos Africanos* 20 (2010): 86–109.

Kohl, Christoph, and Anita Schroven. "Suffering for the Nation: Bottom-Up and Top-Down Conceptualization of the Nation in Guinea-Bissau." *Max Planck Institute for Social Anthropology Working Papers* 152 (2014).

Krautsova, T. I. "Amilcar Kabral." *Narody Azii i Africa* (Moscow) 3 (1973).

Kriger, Norma J. *Guerilla Veterans in Post War Zimbabwe: Symbolic and Violent Politics, 1980–1987*. Cambridge: Cambridge University Press, 1992.

Kriger, Norma J. *Zimbabwe's Guerilla War: Peasant Voices*. Cambridge: Cambridge University Press, 1992.

Kristof, Nicholas D. *Half the Sky; Turning Oppression into Opportunity for Women Worldwide*. New York: Vintage Books, 2010.

S. Lamine and all. *La Liberté*. Conakry: French Guinea, December 11, 1956.

La République de Guinée Bissau en Chiffres, February 1974, table 4, p. 8.

Laranjeiro, Catarina. "Arma Diplomatica e Ficçao: as Mulheres no films da Luta de Libertação da Guine-Bissau/Diplomatic Weapon and Fiction: Women in Guinea-Bissau's Liberation Struggle Films." *Revista de Communicaçao e linguagens/Journal of Communication and Languages*, no. 54 (2021): 47–64.

Larkin, Bruce D. *China and Africa, 1949–1970: The Foreign Policy of the People's Republic of China*. Berkeley: University of California Press, 1971.

Lawrence, Janet H., and Esther Lehman, "Oral History as Motivating Factor among Adult Learners." Paper presented at the *American Educational Research Association Annual Meeting* (San Francisco, California, April 8–12, 1979). East Lansing: Michigan State University, 1979.

Lazreg, Marnia. *The Eloquence of Silence: Algerian Women in Question*. New York: Routledge, 1994.

Lefaucheux, Marie-Helene. "Le Role de la Femme dans le Development des Pays Tropicaux et Subtropicaux; Aspects Social et Culturel." In INCIDI, *Women's Roles in the Development of Tropical and Sub-Tropical Countries*. Brussels: INCIDI, 1959.

Lenin, V.I. *Materialism and Empirio-Criticism*, English edition. Moscow: FLPH, 1952.

Lerner, Gerda. *The Creation of Feminist Consciousness: From the Middle Ages to the Eighteen Century*. Oxford: Oxford University Press, 1994.

Levine, Philippa. *Gender and Empire*. Oxford: Oxford University Press, 2007.

Liberation in Southern Africa; The Organization of Angolan Women. Chicago: CCLAMG, 1974.

Liberation Support Movement. *The Mozambican Woman in the Revolution*. Richmond, B. C.: LSM Information Center, 1974.

Lifton, Carey. *Social Soundness and WID Analysis for USAID Legal Reform Project Paper*. Bissau: USAID, 1991.

Lippert, Anne. "Algerian Women's Access to Power: 1962–1985." In *Studies in Power and Class in Africa*, edited by Irving Leonard Markovitz, 209–32. Oxford: Oxford University Press, 1987.

Lobban, Richard A. "Strategic and Foreign Policy Objectives." In *Claim No Easy Victories: The Legacy of Amilcar Cabral*, edited by Firoze Manji and Bill, Fletcher Jr. Dakar: CODESRIA, 2013.

Lobban, Richard A., and P. K. Mendy. *Historical Dictionary of the Republic of Guinea-Bissau, African Historical Dictionaries N. 22*, Third edition. London: The Scarecrow Press, 1997.

Loi Organique des Provinces Portugaises d'Outre Mer, Law no. 5/72, Lisbon, June 1972 (Official French Translation) and *Statut Politico-Administratif de la Province de Guiné*, decree no. 45 372, Article 37.

Lonsdale, John M. "Ethnicite, Morale, et Tribalisme Politique." *Politique Africaine* 61 (1996): 98–115.

Lopes, Carlos. *Guinea-Bissau: From Liberation Struggle to Independent Statehood*. Boulder, Colorado: Westview Press, 1987.

Lopes, Carlos. *Kaabunké: Espaço, Território e Poder na Guiné-Bissau—Gâmbia e Casamance Pré-coloniais*. Lisbon: CNCDP, 1999.

Lopes, Carlos. *Para Uma Leitura Sociologica da Guiné-Bissau*. Lisbon: Editorial Economia e Socialismo, Instituto Nacional de Estudos e Pesquisa, 1988.

Lopes, Jose Vicente. *Cabo Verde: Os Bastidores da Independencia*, Second edition. Praia: Spleen Edicoes, 2002.

Luke, Timothy W. "Cabral's Marxism: An African Strategy for Socialism Development." *Studies in Comparative Communism: An International Interdisciplinary Journal* 14, no. 4 (Winter 1980): 307–30.

Lundy, Brandon. "Challenging Adulthood: Changing Initiation Rites among the Balanta of Guinea Bissau." *African Studies* 77, no. 4 (2018): 584–606.

Lundy, Brandon. "Resistance Is Fruitful: Bijagos of Guinea-Bissau." *Peace and Conflict Management Working Paper*, no. 1 (2015): 1–9.

Lundy, Brandon, Raul Mendes Fernandes Jr., and Kezia Lartey. "The Integrity of Women in Re-Making a Nation: The Case of Guinea-Bissau." *Journal of Global Initiatives* 11, no. 1 (2016): 59–76.

Ly, Aliou: "Revisiting the Guinea-Bissau Liberation War; PAIGC, UDEMU and the Question of Women's Emancipation." *Portuguese Journal of Social Sciences* 14, no. 3: 361–377, 364.

Lyon, Hudson M. "Marxism and Ethno-nationalism in Guinea Bissau, 1956–1976." *Ethnic and Racial Studies* 3, no. 2 (1980): 156–68.

Lyons, Tanya. *Guns and Guerilla Girls: Women in the Zimbabwean Liberation Struggle*. Trenton, New Jersey: Africa World Press, 2004.

Machel, Josina. "The Role of Women in the Revolution." *Mozambican Revolution* 41 (1969).

Maddox, Gregory, and Timothy K. Welliver. *Colonialism and Nationalism in Africa; A Four Volume Anthology of Scholarly Articles: African Nationalism and Independence, Vol. 3*. New York: Garland Publishing, 1993.

Maddox, Gregory, and Timothy K. Welliver. *Colonialism and Nationalism in Africa; A Four Volume Anthology of Scholarly Articles: African Nationalism and Revolution, Vol. 4*. New York: Garland Publishing, 1993.

Mahamba, Irene Ropa Rinopfuka. *Woman and Struggle*. Harare: Mambo Press, 1986.

Malley, Robert. *The Call from Algeria; Third Worldism, Revolution, and the Turn to Islam*. Berkeley: University of California Press, 1996.

Maloba, W. O. *African Women in Revolution*. New York: Africa World Press Inc., 2007.

Maloba, W. O. *Mau-Mau and Kenya: An Analysis of a Peasant Revolt*. Bloomington: Indiana University Press, 1998.

Mamdani, Mahmood. *Citizen and Subject: Contemporary Africa and the Legacy of Late Colonialism*. Princeton: Princeton University Press, 1996.

Mané, Felicidad. As participant of an informal group discussion in French, July 30, 2010.

Mané, Mamadou. "Contribution á L'Histoire du Kaabu, des Origines au XIX Siècle." *Bulletin de L'IFAN* Dakar, 1978, Tome 40 Serie B. 1, 87–159.

Mané, Ndalla. Interviewed in English and translated in Crioulo, July 17, 2010.

Mané, Ndo. Interviewed in English and translated in Crioulo, August 2, 2010.

Mann, Kristin. *Marriage, Status and Social Change among Educated Elite in Lagos.* Cambridge: Cambridge University Press, 1985.

Mao Tse-Tung. *Four Essays on Philosophy.* Beijing: Foreign Languages Press, 1968.

Marcum, John A. *The Angolan Revolution, Vol.1: The Anatomy of an Explosion, 1950–1962.* Cambridge, MA: MIT Press, 1969.

Marcum, John A. *The Angolan Revolution, Vol. 2: Exile Politics and Guerilla Warfare, 1962–1976.* Cambridge, MA: MIT Press, 1978.

Marcum, John A. *Conceiving Mozambique.* Santa Cruz, California: Palgrave Macmillan, 2018.

Marcum, John A. "Sekou Touré & Guinea." *Africa Today* 6, no. 5 (1959): 5–8.

Mark, Peter. "The Evolution of 'Portuguese' Identity: Luso Africans on the Upper Guinean Coast from the Sixteenth to the Nineteenth Century." *Journal of African History* 40 (1999): 173–91.

Mark, Peter. *"Portuguese" Style and Luso-African Identity; Precolonial Senegambia, 16th–19th Centuries.* Bloomington: Indiana University Press, 2002.

Markakis, John. "Liberation Movements and the 'Democratic Deficit.'" In *National Liberation Movements as Government in Africa*, edited by Redie Bereketeab, 33–41. New York: Routledge, 2018.

Marshall, Francine. "Cuba's Relation with Africa: The End of an Era." In *Cuba's Ties to a Changing World*, edited by Donna Rich Kaplowitz. Boulder, Colorado: Lynne Rienner, 1993.

Martin-Marquez, Susan. *Disorientations: Spanish Colonialism in Africa and the Performance of Identity.* New Haven: Yale University Press, 2008.

Martins, Pedro. *Testemunho de um Combatente.* Praia-Mindelo: Instituto Camoes Centro Cultural Portugues, 1990.

Marx, Karl. "Theses on Feuerbach." In *Selected Works* By Karl Marx and Frederick Engels, English edition, Volume II. Moscow: FLPH, 1958.

Matera, Marc, Misty Bastian, and Susan Kingsley Kent. *The Women's War of 1929: Gender and Violence in Colonial Nigeria.* London: Palgrave Macmillan, 2012.

Mazov, Sergei. *A Distant Front in the Cold War: The USSR in West Africa and Congo, 1956–1964.* Stanford: Stanford University Press, 2010.

Mballo, Dianké. Interviewed in Pular, July 20, 2010.

Mballo, Famara. As participant of an informal group discussion in French, July 30, 2010.

McCall, Daniel. "Introduction." In *Writing African History*, edited by John Edward Philips. New York: University of Rochester Press, 2006.

McCollester, Charles. "The Political Thought of Amilcar Cabral." *Monthly Review* 24, no. 10 (March 1973).

McCulloch, Jock. "Amilcar Cabral, a Theory of Imperialism." *The Journal of Modern African Studies* 19, no. 3 (September 1981): 503-11.

McCulloch, Jock. *In the Twilight of Revolution: The Political Theory of Amilcar Cabral*. Oxfordshire (UK): Routledge and Kegan Paul, 1983.

McNaughton, Patrick R. *The Mande Blacksmiths: Knowledge, Power and Art in West Africa*. Bloomington: Indiana University Press, 1993.

Mendy, Peter Karibe. *Amilcar Cabral; Nationalist and Pan-Africanist Revolutionary*. Athens: Ohio University Press, 2019.

Mendy, Peter Karibe. "Amilcar Cabral and the Liberation of Guinea-Bissau: Context, Challenges and Lessons for Effective African Leadership." In *Africa's Contemporary Challenges: The Legacy of Amilcar Cabral*, edited by Carlos Lopes. London: Routledge, 2010.

Mendy, Peter Karibe. "Amilcar Cabral and the Liberation of Guinea-Bissau: Context, Challenges and Lessons for Effective African Leadership." *African Identities* 4, no. 1 (2006): 7-21.

Mendy, Peter Karibe. *Colonialismo Portugues em Africa: Tradiçao de Resistencia na Guiné-Bissau (1879-1959)*. Lisbon: Instituto Nacional de Estudos e Pesquisa, 1994.

Mendy, Peter Karibe. "Guinea Bissau: State Decay and Factional Struggles 1973-1998." *Sapem* (May 1999).

Mendy, Peter Karibe. "Portugal's Civilizing Mission in Colonial Guinea Bissau: Rhetoric or Reality?" *International Journal of African Historical Studies* 36, no. 1 (2003): 35-53.

Mesa-Lago, Carmelo, and June S. Belkin, eds. *Cuba and Africa*. Pittsburg: Center for Latin American Studies University of Pittsburgh, 1982.

Midgley, Clare. "Introduction: Gender and Imperialism, Mapping the Connections." In *Gender and Imperialism*, edited by Clare Midgley, 1-18. Manchester: Manchester University Press, 1998.

Migani, Guia. "Sekou Touré et la Contestation de l'Ordre Colonial en Afrique Sub Saharienne, 1958-1963." *Monde(s)* 2, no. 2012: 257-73.

Mikell, G., ed. *African Feminism: The Politics of Survival in Sub-Saharan Africa*. Philadelphia: University of Pennsylvania Press, 1997.

Millar, Lanie. *Forms of Disappointment: Cuban and Angolan Narrative after the Cold War*. Albany: State University of New York Press, 2019.

Milton, K. "Ecologies: Anthropology, Culture and the Environment." *International Social Science Journal* (Oxford) XLIX, no. 4 (1997).

Mitchell, Juliet. *La Condizione Della Donna*. Torino: Einaudi, 1972.

Mondaini, Marco, Colin Darch, and Aquino de Colin. *Independence and Revolution in Portuguese—Speaking Africa: Selected Articles and Interviews, 1980–1986*. Cabo Town: HSRC Press, 2019.

Monteiro, Isaac. *O, Efeitos Socio-Economicos do Programa de Ajustamento Estructural na Guiné-Bissau: Análise dos Efeitos Socio-Economicos*. Bissau: Edicoes INEP, 1996.

Moore, David B. "Democracy, Violence and Identity in the Zimbabwean War of National Liberation: Reflexions from the Realms of Dissent." *Canadian Journal of African Studies* 29 (1995).

Moorman, Marissa, and Kathleen Sheldon. "Gender in the Lusophone World: History, Identity and Nation." *Lusotopia* 1, no. 2 (2005): 35–41.

Morgado, Michel S. "Amilcar Cabral's Theory of Cultural Revolution." *Black Images* 3, no. 2 (Summer 1974): 3–16.

Morgenthau, Ruth Schachter. *Political Parties in French Speaking West Africa*. Oxford: Clarendon Press, 1964.

Morison, David. *The USSR and Africa*. Oxford: Oxford University Press, 1964.

Moser, G. "The Poet Amilcar Cabral." *African Literature* (Bloomington) 9 (1978).

Mouser, Bruce L. "Women Slavers in Guinea Conakry." In *Women and Slavery in Africa*, edited by Claire Robertson and Martin Klein. Madison: University of Wisconsin Press, 1983.

Mugabe, Robert, and Nomi Pasiharigutwi Nhiwatiwa. *Women's Liberation in the Zimbabwean Revolution: Materials from the ZANU Women's Seminar, Maputo, Mozambique, May 1979*. San Francisco: John Brown Book Club, 1979.

Mugbane, Bernard. "Amilcar Cabral: Evolution and Revolutionary Thought." *Ufahamu* 2 (Fall 1971): 71–87.

Munslow, Barry. *FRELIMO and the Mozambican Revolution*. Manchester: University, Faculty of Economic and Social Studies, 1980.

Muthoni, Liki Mani. *Passbook Number F47927: Women and Mau-Mau in Kenya*. London: Macmillan, 1985.

Nafafe, Jose Lingna. "Challenges of the African Voice: Autonomy, Commerce and Resistance in Precolonial Western Africa." In *Brokers of Change: Atlantic Commerce and Cultures in Precolonial Western Africa*, edited by Toby Green. Oxford/British Academy: Oxford University Press, 2012.

Nafafe, Jose Lingna. *Colonial Encounters: Issues of Culture, Hybridity and Creolization; Portuguese Mercantile Settlers in West Africa*. Frankfurt am Main: Peter Lang/Oxford, 2007.

Nafafe, Jose Lingna. "Lançados' Culture and Identity: Prelude to Creole Societies on the Rivers of Guinea and Cabo Verde." In *Creole Societies in the Portuguese*

Colonial Empire, edited by M. D. Newitt, and Philip Havik. Cambridge: Scholars Publishing, 2015.

Naneira, Anna Maria. Interviewed in French, June 29, 2010.

Naneira, Victor. Interviewed in English and translated in Crioulo, August 15, 2009.

Nassum, Manuel. "Política Linguistic Pós-Colonial: Ruptura ou Continuidade?" *Soronda* 17 (1994): 45–78.

Ndjati, Na. Interviewed in English and translated in Crioulo, August 2, 2010.

NHaga, Sandé. Interviewed in English and translated in Crioulo, August 28, 2010.

Niane, Djibril Tamsir. *Histoire des Mandingues de L'Ouest*. Paris: Karthala/ARSAN, 1989.

Niane, Djibril Tamsir. *Soundjata ou L'Epopée Mandingue*. Paris: Présence Africaine, 1960.

Nquamé, Teresa. Interviewed in English and translated in Crioulo, July 28, 2010.

Nuvunga, Adriano. "From Former Liberation Movement to Four Decades in Government: The Maintenance of the FRELIMO State." In *National Liberation Movements as Government in Africa*, edited by Redie Bereketeab, 57–71. New York: Routledge, 2018.

Nyang, Sulayman Sheih. "The Political Thought of Amilcar Cabral." *Odu* 13 (1976): 3–20.

Nzenza, Sekai. *Zimbabwean Woman: My Own Story*. London: Karia Press, 1986.

Nzomo, M. "Kenyan Women in Politics and Public Decision Making." In *African Feminism: The Politics of Survival in Sub-Saharan Africa*, edited by G. Mikell. Philadelphia: University of Pennsylvania Press, 1997.

O'Gorman, Eleanor. *The Front Line Runs through Every Woman: Women and Local Resistance in the Zimbabwean Liberation War*. Woodbridge: James Currey, 2011.

O Militante. Bissau, Decembre 1977, no. 5, p. 19.

Ogbomo, Enaiwu W. *When Men and Women Mattered: A History of Gender Relations Among the Owan of Nigeria*. Rochester: University of Rochester Press, 1997.

Okeyo, Achola Pala. "Daughters of the Lakes and Rivers: Colonization and the Land Rights of Luo Women." In *Women and Colonization: Anthropological Perspectives*, edited by M. Etienne, and E. Leacock. New York: Praeger, 1980.

Olajubu, Oyeronke. *Women in the Yoruba Sphere*. New York: State University of New York, 2003.

Ostheimer, Andrea. "The Structural Crisis in Guinea-Bissau's Political System." *African Security Review* 10 (2010): 45–57.

PAICV. *Continuar Cabral: Simposio Internacional Amilcar Cabral, Cabo Verde, 17 a 20 de janeiro de 1983*. Cabo Verde: Edição Grafedito/Prelo-Estampa, 1984.

PAIGC. *Amilcar Cabral's Letter to Kwame Nkrumah (handwritten rough draft by himself)* no date.

Selected Bibliography

PAIGC. "Massacre De Pindjiguiti" by Amilcar Cabral, [Portuguese].

PAIGC. *The Republic of Guinea-Bissau: Triumph over Colonialism*, by Jennifer Davis, Research Director, 1976, Africa Fund.

PAIGC. *UDEMU, União Democràtica das Mulheres da Guine e Cabo Verde*, Union Démocratique des Femmes de la Guinée Portugaise et des Iles du Cap Vert. UDEMU: Status. [French]

PAIGC. *Ministério da Marinha a Comando Da Defesa Maritima da Guiné ao Estado Maior da Armada*. Bissau: Partido Africano da Independencia da Guine e Cabo Verde. Direcçao Regional do PAIGC de S. Vicente, 18 de agosto de, 1959.

PAIGC. "Amilcar Cabral and Aristides Pereira. Rapport sur la Lutte de Liberation des Peuples de la Guinée Portugaise et des Iles du Cap Vert" [n. p.], 1960.

PAIGC. "Memorandum addressed to Portuguese Government by PAIGC," n.p., November 1960. [Portuguese]

PAIGC. "Statues and Program." Conakry, 1960. [English]

PAIGC. "Statutes and Program," Conakry, 1960. [French]

PAIGC. *Amilcar Cabral's Handwritten Discourse for the Conference of the Revolutionary Movements of Guinea Bissau and Cabo Verde*, Dakar (Senegal) 12–14 Juillet 1961.

PAIGC. "Declaration proposant la realization immediate de mesures concretes pour la liquidation pacificque de la domination coloniale en 'Guinée Portugais' et aux Îles du Cap Vert." Conakry, Octobre 13, 1961. [French]

PAIGC. "Guinée Portugais: Dernier d 'Heure"?' [Interview with Aristides Pereira, General Secretary of PAIGC," *Revolution Africaine*, no. 99, December 19, 1961.

PAIGC. "Note Ouverte au Gouvernement Portugais." Conakry, October 13, 1961. Signed by Amilcar Cabral, Secretary General of PAIGC.

PAIGC. "Nouveaux Crimes des Colonialistes Portugais," Conakry, March 24, 1962, Signed, secretary General of PAIGC. [French]

PAIGC. Le Peuple de Guinée "Portuguesa" devant l'Organisation des Nations Unies. [Declaration du Secretaire General du PAIGC, Ingenieur Amilcar Cabral.] Conakry, June 1962. [French]

PAIGC. "Sur la Situation des Peuples des Iles du Cap Vert. Declaration de PAIGC, presentée au Comité Special de L'OUA pour les territoires administers par le Portugal" June 1962. [French]

PAIGC. "800,000 hommes en Guerre." *Revolution Africaine*, no. 7 (March 16, 1963). [French]

PAIGC. *Amilcar Cabral's Handwritten Discourse for the Proclamation of the Beginning of the Insurrection on August 3, 1961*, Conakry (Guinée-Conakry): Partido Africano da Independencia da Guine e Cabo Verde. Direcçao Regional do PAIGC de S. Vicente, 1963.

PAIGC. "Le Crime de Colonialisme," *Revolution Africaine*, no. 17 (May 25, 1963).

PAIGC. "Notre Lutte en Guinee." [Interview of Amilcar Cabral], *Revolution Africaine*, no. 29, August 17, 1963. [French]

PAIGC. "La Plainte Sénégalaise Contre le Portugal Devant le Conseil de Sécurité," In *Dakar Matin*. Dakar (Senegal), May 18, 1963. [French]

PAIGC. "About the Development of Our Struggle, 1964," [Statement of the General secretary in a Press Conference], Conakry, 1964. [English]

PAIGC "Conférence de Presse du F. L. I. N. G-P. A. I. G. C,. à l'occasion du Sixième Anniversaire de la Lutte Armée du Peuple de Guinée Bissao." dans *Dakar Matin*, Dakar (Senegal), 5 Août 1964.

PAIGC. "Guiné-Bissau; A propos de l'Unification du F. L. I. N. G-P. A. I. G. C." *Afrique Nouvelle*, Semaine du 10 au 16 Juillet 1964.

PAIGC. "Alguns dados sobre das Potencias da OTAN aos Colonialistas Portugueses." Conakry, September 1965. [Portuguese]

PAIGC. "Cabe Ao Senegal; Toda a Responsabilidade; Dos Incidentes Ocorridos na Fronteira com Guine Portuguesa." *Diario Da Manhã*, March 18, 1965.

PAIGC. [Communique] Conakry, May 27, 1965. [French]

PAIGC. "Declaration by Amilcar Cabral, Secretary General, to Guinean Press Agency on August 3, 1965, on the Occasion of the Anniversary of the Massacre of Pindjiguiti, and day of Solidarity with the Peuple of Portuguese colonies." Conakry, August 3, 1965. [English]

PAIGC. "A Guinée O Plano; Intercalar de Fomento." In *Diário Manhà*. Lisbon (Portugal), March 14, 1965.

PAIGC. [Press Release: "The Liberation of the Boé Region], [Conakry?] June 3, 1965. [French].

PAIGC. "Libertacao. Orgao do PAIGC." [no. 57. August 3, 1965].

PAIGC. "A Nosse Luta pela Educacao das Masses e Pela Formacao de Quadros." Conakry, September 1965. [Portuguese]

PAIGC. "Notes on AC's [Second] Visit to London," April 5, 1965

PAIGC. *La Plainte Sénégalaise contre le Portugal devant le Conseil de Sécurité dans Dakar Matin*, Dakar (Senegal): Dakar-Matin, 18–19 Mai 1965.

PAIGC. "Portuguese Guinea Insurgent Claims." In *The Times*, London: Dakar-Matin, April 10, 1965.

PAIGC. *Program do PAIGC-Programa Maior*. Conacry: Fundação Amilcar Cabral, Praia (Cabo Verde), p. 2. 1965.

PAIGC. Amilcar Cabral, "Structure Social de la Guinee 'Portugaise." *Revolution Africaine*, no. 178 (June 24–July 1, 1966). [French]

PAIGC. "Les Fondements et les Objectifs de la Liberation Nationale en Rapport avec la Structure Sociale." [Extrait du Discours pronounce au Comité des

Peuples des Colonies Portuguese, par le Camarade Amilcar Cabral, Secretaire General du Parti, a la Premiere Conference des Peuples d'Afrique, d'Asie et Amerique Latine, La Havana, Janvier 3–14, 1966], Conakry, Departement de Secretariat, Information, Culture et Formation de Cadres Collection, "Discours et Interventions," [French]

PAIGC. "En Guinée Portugaise; Le Leader Nationaliste Amilcar Cabral Décide d'Intensifier La Lutte," *Le Monde,* 11 Juin, 1966.

PAIGC. "'Dans la Zone Libérée le Peuple Edifie une Vie Nouvelle' dit le Camarade Cabral, Secretaire Général á l'occasion du 8e Anniversaire du Massacre de Pijiguiti," In *Horoya,* 1–3. Conakry (Guinée-Conakry), August 3, 1967. [French]

PAIGC. "La Lutte de la Femme Africaine est Inséparable de la lutte Révolutionaire des Masses," *El Moudjahid,* 3 Avril 1967.

PAIGC. "Les Peuples de la Guinée Bissao et des iles du cap Vert sur la Voie de la Liberté," dans *El Mwomendjahid,* Algiers, 3 Août 1967.

PAIGC. "Les Peuples de la Guinée (Bissao) et des Iles du Cap Vert sur La Voie de la Liberté," *El Moudjahid*, March 8, 1967. [French]

PAIGC. "Le Senegal Fait Etat d'un incident Frontalier avec la Guinee Portugaise," In *Le Monde.* Paris (France): Societe Editrice du Monde, March 16, 1967.

PAIGC. "Les Crimes des Colonialistes Portugais Face a la Declaration Universelle des Droits de l'Homme." [Declaration du Secretaire General du Parti, Amilcar Cabral, devant la Commission des Droits de l'Homme, de l'O.N.U., Conakry, Commission d'Information et Propagande du Comite Central du PAIGC, 1968. [French]

PAIGC. [Interview with Amilcar Cabral. "Lutter jusqu'a l'indépendance complete." *Review de la Politique Internationale*, no. 434 (May 1968). [French]

PAIGC. "Novos Ataques Lançados do Senegal Contra a Guiné Portuguesa," *Diario Popular*, December 27, 1969. [Portuguese]

PAIGC. Amilcar Cabral. *Communiqué Final Sur L'Agression Portugaise du 22–23 Novembre 1970 contre La Republique de Guinée par le Secretaire general du PAIGC,* 18 Janvier 1971.

PAIGC. "L'ONU Condamne le Portugal pour l'usage de Produits Chimiques et de Défoliants contre les Peuples Africains," *El Moudjahid,* Algiers (Algeria), April 15, 1971.

PAIGC. "Portugal: Procès d'un Militaire Cubain Fait Prisonnier en Guinée Portugaise," *Le Monde,* April 27, 1971.

PAIGC. *Rapport sur le role politique-social-economique de la femme en Guinee-Bissau et aux Iles du Cap Vert.* Conacri: PAIGC, 1970, 1971, 1972). Fundacao Amilcar Cabral, Praia (Cabo Verde).

PAIGC. "Amilcar Cabral Demande L'Etat Independent de la Guiné-Bissau." [Propos recueillis par Aquino de Braganca.] *Afrique-Asie*, no. 18, November 27, 1972. [French]

PAIGC. Amilcar Cabral, "Nkrumah: un-Combatant de la Liberte," *Afrique Asie,* no. 11–12, August 12, 1972.

PAIGC. "Guinea (B) on Verge of Victory." [Interview with Amilcar Cabral.] *Guardian*. November 1, 1972. [English]

PAIGC. *Amílcar Cabral, Sobre a Criação da Assembleia Nacional Popular da Guiné; Resultados das Eleições gerais realizadas nas Regiões Libertadas, em 1972,* 8 de janeiro de 1973.

PAIGC. "Report on the Politico-Socio-Economic Role of Women in Guinea and the Cabo Verde Islands." Published in English in *Women in the Struggle for Liberation*. New York: World Student Christian Federation, 1973.

PAIGC. "Sur le Lâche Assassinat du Fondateur et Premier Dirigeant de Notre Parti, Amilcar Cabral. Message du Comité Exécutif de la Lutte a Notre Peuple et á nos Combatants." [Oslo, Conference Internationale d'Experts pour le Soutien des Victimes du Colonialisme et de apartheid en Afrique Australe, April 9–14, 1973, p. 10. [French]

PAIGC. "Páginas da História: I Congresso Do PAIGC: Conferencia Geral de Quadros do Partido no Interior do Pais: Em Cassacá Lançaram-se as Bases de uma Nova Organização Politica e Militar do Partido." In *O Militante*. Bissau: Guinea Bissau, Janeiro 1980.

PAIGC. "Symposium International sur le Theme: Amilcar Cabral et la Lutte de Liberation Nationale et Sociale en Afrique," Organise par JAAC, UIE et AASU, Contribution de L'UDEMU (União Démocratique des Femmes) representee par la Camarada Francisca Pereira, Membre du Comité Central du PAIGC et Secretaire Générale de l'UDEMU, Bissau, March 26–7, 1983.

PAIGC schools. *Regulamento das Escolas do Partido*. Conakry: PAIGC (September 19, 1966).

Parpart, Jane L., "Sexuality and Power on the Zambian Copperbelt." In *Patriarchy and Class, African Women in the Home and Workforce*, edited by Sharon B. Stichter, and Jane L. Parpart. Boulder, Colorado: Westview Press, African Modernization and Development Series, 1988.

Parpart, Jane L., and Kathleen A. Staudt, eds. *Women and the State in Africa*. Boulder, Colorado: Lynne Rienner, 1989.

Patrícia Gomes, "A importância das Forças Armadas Revolucionárias do Povo (F.A.R.P.) na luta pela libertação da Guiné-Bissau." *Poiésis*. 3, no. 6, 2010: 121–39.

Pélissier, René. *História da Guine, 1, Vol*. Lisboa: Estampa, 1997.

Pélissier, René. *Naissance de la Guiné: Portuguais et Africains en Sénégambia, 1841–1936*. Orgeval, France: Pélissier, 1989.
Pereira, Aristides. *O meu Testemunho Uma Luta, um Partido, dois Paises, Versao Documentada*. Lisbon: Editorial Notícias, 2003.
Pereira, Aristides. *Uma Luta, Um Partido, Dois Paises*, (Lisbon: Editorial Notícias, 2002).
Pereira, Carlos. *La Guinée Portuguese (Subsides pour son etude)*. Lisbon: A Editora Lda, 1914.
Pereira, Carmen. Interviewed in English and translated in Crioulo, August 21, 2008.
Pereira, Francisca. General Secretary Discourse at the First Congress of the UDEMU. *Ies Congresso Mulheres da Guiné-Bissau, Organização Para o Encquadramenrto da Mulher no Desenvolviemento, Memoria* (Edição do Department de Informação e Propaganda do Conselho Nacional da UDEMU).
Pereira, Francisca. Interviewed in French, August 9 and 16, 2008, and July 12, 2010.
Peterson, Charles F. *Dubois, Fanon, Cabral: The Margins of Elite Anti-Colonial Leadership*. Lanham: Lexington Books, 2007.
Peterson, V. Spike, and Anne Sisson Runyan. *Global Gender Issues*. Boulder, Colorado: Westview Press, 1993.
Pinto-Bull, Benjamin. *O Crioulo da Guiné-Bissau, Filosofica e Sabedoria*. Lisbon, Bissau: Instituto de Cultural e Lingua Portuguese, Instituto Nacional de Estudos e Pesquisa, 1989.
Plataforma política das mulheres da Guiné-Bissau (PPM-GB) -Plano Estratégico Operacional 2013–2016 (Educar, participar e transformar), Bissau Agosto de 2013.
Potash, Betty. *Widows in African Societies: Choices and Constraints*. Stanford: Stanford University Press, 1986.
Presley, Cora Ann. *Kikuyu Women, the Mau-Mau Rebellion, and Social Change in Kenya*. Boulder, Colorado: Westview Press, 1992.
Quawas, R. B. "'A Sea Captain in Her Own Right': Navigating the Feminist Thought of Huda Shaarawi." *Journal of International Women's Studies* 8, no. 1: 219–34.
Rabaka, Reiland. "Contours of Cabralism: Amilcar Cabral's Contributions to the Africana Tradition of Critical Theory." In *A Luta Continua: (Re) Introducing Amilcar Cabral to a New Generation of thinkers*, edited by P. Khalil Saucer. Trenton, New Jersey: Africa World Press, 2017.
Raeburn, Michael. *Black Fire: Accounts of the Guerilla War in Rhodesia*. London: Julian Friedmann, 1978.
Rahmato, Dessalegn. *Cabral and the Problem of the African Revolution*. Addis Ababa: Addis Ababa University, Institute of Development Research, January 1982.
Ranger, Terence. *Peasant Consciousness and Guerilla War in Zimbabwe: A Comparative Study*. Berkeley, California: University of California Press, 1985.

Ridd, Rosemary. "Powers of the Powerless." In *Caught Up in Conflict: Women's Responses to Political Strife*, edited by Rosemary Ridd and Helen Callaway. Oxford: Macmillan, 1986.

Robertson, Claire, and Martin Klein. *Women and Slavery in Africa*. Madison: University of Wisconsin Press, 1983.

Rocha, Edmundo. *Angola: Viriato da Cruz: O Homen e o Mito: Porto Amboim (Angola) 1928—Beijing (China) 1973*. Lisboa/Luanda: Prefacio/ Caxinde, 2008.

Roche, Christian. *Histoire Générale de la Casamance: Conquete et Resistance: 1850–1920*. Paris: Karthala, 1985.

Roessler, Philip G., and Harry Verhoeven. *Why Comrades Go to War: Liberation Politics and the Outbreak of Africa's Deadliest Conflict*. Oxford: Oxford University Press, 2016.

Roque, Silvia: "Mulheres, Nação e Lutas no Cinema anti/Pós-colonial da Guiné-Bissau/Women, Nation and Struggles in Anti/Postcolonial Cinema in Guinea-Bissau" in *Revista de Communicaçao e linguagens/ Journal of Communication and languages*, No. 54 (2021), p. 276–94.

Ruddick, Sara. *Material Thinking: Toward a Politics of Peace*. Boston: Beacon Press, 1989.

Rudebeck, Lars. "Conditions of People's Development in Post-Colonial Africa." In *Rethinking the Third World*, edited by Rosemary Galli. New York: Crane Rusack, 1992.

Rudebeck, Lars. *Guinea-Bissau: A Study of Political Mobilization*. Uppsala: Scandinavian Institute of African Studies, 1974.

Rudebeck, Lars. "Reading Cabral on Democracy." In *Africa's Contemporary Challenges: The Legacy of Amilcar Cabral*, edited by Carlos Lopes. London: Routledge, 2010.

Saadi, Noureddine. *La Femme et les Lois en Algerie*. Algiers: Bouchene, 1991.

Sadio, Sito. Interviewed in English and translated in Crioulo, July 17, 2010.

Sadomba, Zvakanyorwa Wilbert. *War Veterans in Zimbabwe's Revolution: Challenging Neo-Colonialism and Settler and National Capital*. Harare: Weaver Press, 2011.

Saho, Bala. *Contours of Change; Muslim Courts, Women, and Islamic Society in Colonial Bathurst, 1905–1965*. East Lansing: Michigan State University Press, 2018.

Salih, Mohamed M. A. "Varieties of African Liberation Movements." In *National Liberation Movements as Government in Africa*, edited by Redie Bereketeab, 17–32. New York; Routledge, 2018.

Salma, Maria Jose. "Provinces Portugaises d' Afrique." In *Women's Roles in the Development of Tropical and Sub-Tropical Countries*. Brussels: INCIDI, 1959.

Sambu, Segunda. Interviewed in English and translated in Crioulo, August 2, 2010.

Sané, Fanta. Interviewed in Wolof, July 27, 2010.

Sanha, Barnaté. Interviewed in English and translated in Crioulo, July 28 and August 23, 2010.
Sanha, Quintara. Interviewed in French, July 26, 2010.
Santana, Francisco. *Bruxas e Curandeiros na Lisboa Joanina*. Lisbon: Academia Portuguesa de História, 1997.
Sarrazin, Chantal. "Carmen Pereira: Woman Revolutionary." In *Sowing the First Harvest: National Reconstruction in Guinea-Bissau* by Chantal Sarrazin and Ole Gjerstad. Oakland: LSM Information Center, 1978.
Saucier, P. Khalil. "Returning to Cabral: An Introduction to Guerilla Intellectualism." In *A Luta Continua: (Re) Introducing Amilcar Cabral to a New Generation of Thinkers*, edited by P. Khalil Saucier. Trenton, New Jersey: Africa World Press, 2017.
Schmidt, Elizabeth. *Cold War and Decolonization in Guinea, 1946-1958*. Athens: Ohio University Press, 2007.
Schmidt, Elizabeth. "'Emancipate Your Husbands!' Women and Nationalism in Guinea, 1953-1958." In *Women in African Colonial Histories*, edited by Jean Allman, Susan Geiger and Nakanyike Musisi. Bloomington: Indiana University Press, 2002.
Schmidt, Elizabeth. *Foreign Intervention in Africa: From Cold War to the War on Terror*. Cambridge: Cambridge University Press, 2013.
Schmidt, Elizabeth. "Patriarchy, Capitalism and the Colonial State in Zimbabwe." *Signs* 16, no. 4, Special Issue: Women, Family, State and Economy in Africa (1991).
Schmidt, Elizabeth. *Peasants, Traders, and Wives: Shona Women in the History of Zimbabwe, 1870-1939*. Portsmouth: Heinemann, Baobab and James Currey, 1992.
Schwarz, Carlos. "An Agronomist Before His Time." In *Claim No Easy Victories: The Legacy of Amilcar Cabral*, edited by Firoze Manji and Bill, Fletcher Jr. Dakar: CODESRIA, 2013.
Scott, Catherine V. "Men in Our Country Behave Like Chiefs: Women and the Angolan Revolution." In *African Women in Revolution*, edited by W. O. Maloba. New York: Africa World Press, Inc., 2007.
Scott, James C. *Seeing Like a State: How Certain Schemes to Improve the Human Condition Have Failed*. New Haven, Connecticut: Yale University Press, 1998.
Scott, Joan Wallach. *Gender and the Politics of History*, Revised edition. New York: Columbia University Press, 1999.
Searing, James. *West African and Atlantic Commerce: the Senegal River Valley, 1700-1860*. Cambridge: Cambridge University Press, 2003.
Seferdjeli, Ryme. "French 'Reforms' and Muslim Women's Emancipation during the Algerian War." *Journal of North African Studies* 9, no. 4 (2004): 19-61.

Seibert, Gerhard. "Creolization and Creole Communities in the Portuguese Atlantic: Sao Tome, Cabo Verde, the Rivers of Guinea and Central Africa in Comparison." In *Brokers of Change: Atlantic Commerce and Cultures in Precolonial Western Africa*, edited by Toby Green. Oxford: Oxford University Press, 2012.

Seibert, Gerhard. "Creolization and Creole Communities in the Portuguese Atlantic: Sao Tome, Cabo Verde, the Rivers of Guinea and Central Africa in Comparison." In *Creole Societies in the Portuguese Colonial Empire*, edited by M.D. Newitt and Philip Havik, 29–51. Cambridge: Scholars Publishing, 2015.

Seydi, Binetou Nankin. Interviewed in French, June 20 and August 25, 2008.

Seydi, Sano. Interviewed in Pular, June 28, 2010.

Shanklin, E. "Anlu Remembered: The Kom Women's Rebellion of 1958–61." *Dialectical Anthropology* 15, no. 2–3 (1990): 159–81.

Shaw, Rosalind. *Memories from the Slave Trade, Ritual and the Historical Imagination in Sierra Leone*. Chicago: University of Chicago Press, 2002.

Sheldon, Kathleen E. *African Women: Early History to the 21st Century*. Bloomington: Indiana University Press, 2017.

Sheldon, Kathleen E. "Colonialism and Resistance: Protests and National Liberation Movements." In *Holding the World Together: African Women in Changing Perspective*, edited by Nwando Achebe and Claire Robertson, 81–103. Madison: University of Wisconsin Press, 2019.

Sheldon, Kathleen E. *Historical Dictionary of Women in Sub-Saharan Africa*. Lanham, Maryland: Scarecrow Press, 2005.

Sheldon, Kathleen E. "Women and Revolution in Mozambique, *A Luta Continua*." In *Women and Revolution in Africa, Asia, and the New World*, edited by M.A. Tetreault. Columbia: University of South Carolina Press, 1994.

Shumaher, A., and Maria and Elisabeth Vargas. "Lugar en El Gobierno: Alibi o Conquista?" *Debate Feminista* 15 (April 1997).

Silva, Antonio Duarte. *Independência da Guiné-Bissau e a Descolonizaçao Portuguesa: Estudo de História, Direito e Política*. Porto: Edições Afrontamento, 1997.

Silva, Antonio Duarte. *Invenção e Construção da Guiné-Bissau: Administração Colonial, Nacionalismo, Constitucionalismo*. Lisbon: Almedina, 2010.

Simbanegavi, Josephine. *Zimbabwean Women in the Liberation Struggle: ZANLA and its Legacy, 1972–1985*. Ph.D. Thesis, Faculty of Modern History, University of Oxford, 1997.

Simoque, Miguel Geraldo. *MaFuyana: Mother of the Zimbabwean Revolution*. Gweru, Zimbabwe: Vision Publications, 1998.

Sissoko, Fily Dabo. *Profession de Foi*. Bamako: French Soudan-Imprimerie, September 1945.

Soares, Maria Joao. "Contradições e Debilidades da Política Colonial Guineense: O Caso de Bissau." In *An Africa e a Instalação do Sistema Colonial (C. 1885-1930)*, edited by Maria Emilia Madeira Santos, 123-56. Lisbon: Instituto de Investigação Cientifica Tropical, 2000.

Solodovnikov, V. "The Theoretical Legacy of Amilcar Cabral." In *The Ideology of African Revolutionary Democracy*. Moscow: Social Sciences Today, 1984.

Sousa, Juliao Soares. *"Amilcar Cabral (1924-1973)" Vida e Morte de um Revolucionário*, 2nd edition. Lisbon: Vega, 2012.

Sousa, Juliao Soares. *Amilcar Cabral e a Luta pela Independencia da Guine e Cabo Verde, 1924-1973*, Coimbra: Coimbra Universidade de Coimbra faculdade de Letras, 2007.

Spikes, Daniel. *Angola and the Politics of Intervention: From Local Bush War to Chronic Crisis in Southern Africa*. Jefferson, North Carolina: McFarland, 1975.

Spivak, Gayatri Chakravarty. "Can the Subaltern Speak?" In *Marxism and the Interpretation of Culture*, edited by Cary Nelson and Lawrence Grossberg. Chicago: University of Illinois Press, 1988.

Staunton, Irene. *Mothers of the Revolutions: The War Experiences of Thirty Zimbabwean Women*. Bloomington: Indiana University Press, 1991. London: James Currey, 1990.

Steady, Filomina Chioma. "Polygyny and the Household Economy in the Fishing Village in Sierra Leone." In *Transforming of African Marriage*, edited by David Parkin, and David Nyamwaya, 211-29. Manchester: Manchester University Press for the International African Institute, 1987.

Stoeltje, Beverly. "Asante Queen Mothers, a Study in Female Authority." In *Queens, Queen Mothers, Priestesses and Power: Case Studies in African Gender*, edited by Kaplan, 41-71. New York: New York Academy of Sciences, 1997.

Stolen, Kristi Ann, and Mariken Vaa. *Gender and Change in Developing Countries*. Oslo: Norwegian University Press, 1991.

Stoler, Ann Laura. *Race and the Education of Desire: Foucault's History of Sexuality and the Colonial Order of Things*. Durham, North Carolina: Duke University Press, 1995.

Stott, Leda. *Women and the Armed Struggle for Independence in Zimbabwe (1964-1979)*. Edinburgh University, Centre of African Studies, Occasional papers, 25, 1990.

Stowasser, Barbara F. "Women's Issues in Modern Islamic Thought." In *Arab Women*, edited by Judith E. Tucker. Bloomington: Indiana University Press, 1996.

Stucki, Andreas. *Violence and Gender in Africa's Iberian Colonies: Feminizing the Portuguese and Spanish Empire, 1950s-1970s*. Cambridge: Palgrave Macmillan, 2019.

Sy, Adama. As participant of an informal group discussion in French, July 30, 2010.
Tamarkin, M. "Culture and Politics in Africa: Legitimizing Ethnicity, Rehabilitating the Post-Colonial State." *Nationalism and Ethnic Politics* (London) II, no. 3 (1996).
Temudo, Marina. "From the Margins of the State to the Presidential Palace: The Balanta Case in Guinea-Bissau." *African Studies Review* 52, no. 2 (2009): 47–67.
Temudo, Marina. "From 'People's Struggle' to 'This War of Today': Entanglements to Peace and Conflict in Guinea-Bissau." *Africa* 78, no. 2 (2008): 245–63.
Tetreault, Mary Ann, ed. *Women and Revolution in Africa, Asia and the New World*. Columbia: University of South Carolina Press, 1994.
Thompson, Dorothy. *Over Our Dead Bodies: Women against the Bomb*. London: Virago, 1983.
Tomas, Antonio. *Amilcar Cabral: The Life of a Reluctant Nationalist*. Oxford; Oxford university Press, 2021.
Tripp, Aili Mari. "Women and Politics in Africa." In *Holding the World Together: African Women in Changing Perspective*, edited by Nwando Achebe and Claire Robertson, 145–68. Madison: University of Wisconsin Press, 2019.
Turé, Fatu. Interviewed in English and translated in Crioulo, July 27, 2010.
Turshen, Meredith, and Clotilde Twagiramariya, eds. *What Women Do in Wartime: Gender and Conflict in Africa*. St. Martins: Zed Press, 1998.
UN, *The United Nations and the Advancement of Women, 1945–1996*. New York: Department of Public Information, United Nations, 1996.
UNESCO. *World Survey on Education II, Primary Education*. Paris; UNESCO, 1958.
Urdang, Stéphanie. *And Still, They Dance, Women, War and the Struggle for Change in Mozambique*. London: Earthscan Publications, 1989.
Urdang, Stéphanie. *Fighting in Two Colonialisms: Women in Guinea Bissau*. New York: Monthly Review Press, 1979.
Urdang, Stéphanie. "'Precondition for Victory': Women's Liberation in Mozambique and Guinea Bissau." *Journal of Opinion* 8, no. 1 (1978): 25–31.
Urdang, Stéphanie. "The Role of Women in the Revolution in Guinea-Bissau." In *The Black Women Cross-Culturally*, edited by Filomina Chioma Steady. Cambridge, MA: Schenkman Publishing, 1981.
Urdang, Stéphanie. "Towards a Successful Revolution: The Struggle in Guinea-Bissau." *Objective: Justice* 6, no. 1 (Spring 1975).
Van Allen, J. "Aba Riots, Or Igbo Women's War? Ideology, Stratification, and Invincibility of Women." In *Women in Africa: Studies in Social and Economic Change*, edited by N. J. Halfkin and E. G. Bay. Stanford: Stanford University Press, 1976.
Van Allen, J. "'Sitting on a Man': Colonialism and the Lost Political Institutions of Igbo Women." *Canadian Journal of African Studies* 6, no. 2 (1972): 165–81.

Van Der Drift, Roy. "Democracy Warfare in Guinea Bissau." *Lusotopia* no. 6 (1999): 225–40.

Van Onselen, Charles. *Chibaro; Mine Labour in Southern Rhodesia: 1900–1933*. Johannesburg: Pluto, 1972.

Vice President Senegal 00029. Correspondance au President du Conseil a/s du Conseil des femmes de l'Afrique Occidentale tenue á Conakry, au Colloque sur l'education des adultes á Dakar et au Congres International des Femmes á Yaoundé et Rapport sur la Participation de la femme sur la vie Publique (1962).

Vice President Senegal. 00144: Ministére des Affaires Etrangéres; Actualités Politiques et Informations diplomatiques concernant Guinée, Maroc et Vietnam: coupures de Presse et Correspondances (1958–1961).

Vice President Senegal. 00208: Ministére de l'Interieur: Affaires Politiques, Problémes Frontaliers entre Guinée Bissao, le Sénégal et la Guinée; Arrestation d'Agitateurs au frontier de la Casamance. Declaration du PAIGC relatives aux Iles du Cap Vert, Correspondences et Rapports (1962).

Vice President Senegal. 00203: Ministére de l'Interieur: Activités, et Incidents á Ziguinchor et á Ngoudiane Peye; complot anti-nationalist (1957–1962).

Villafana, Frank. *Cold War in the Congo: The Confrontation of Cuban Military Forces; 1960–1967*. New Brunswick (USA) and London (UK): Transaction Publishers, 2009.

Villagas, Harry "Pombo." *Cuba & Angola: The War for Freedom*. New York: Pathfinder, 2017.

Vines, Alex. *RENAMO, from Terrorism to Democracy in Mozambique?* York (United Kingdom), Amsterdam: Center for Southern African Studies, University of York, Eduardo Mondlalane Foundation, 1996.

Vitalis, Robert. "The Midnight Ride of Kwame Nkrumah and Other Fables of Bandung." *Humanity: An International Journal of Human Rights, Humanitarianism and Development* 4, no. 2 (2013): 261–88.

Vladimirovich, Anatolilii. *Combatant Pour La Cause du Peuple: Amilcar Cabral*. Moscou: Editions de l'Agence de Presse NOVOSTI, 1973.

Walker, Cherryl. *Women and Resistance in South Africa*. London: Onyx Press, 1982.

Walker, Timothy. "Free Blacks and the Inquisition in Early Modern Portugal: Race, as a Factor in Magical Crimes." *Bulletin of the Society of Spanish and Portuguese Historical Studies* XXV, no. 2 (2000): 44.

Weber, Eugen. *Peasants into Frenchmen: The Modernization of Rural France, 1870–1914*. Stanford: Stanford University Press, 1976.

Weigert, Stephen L. *Angola; A Modern Military History, 1961–2002*. New York: Palgrave Macmillan, 2011.

Welch, Gita Honwana, Francesca Dagnino, and Albie Sachs. *Transforming the Foundations of the Family Law in the Course of the Mozambican Revolution*. Maputo: Edicil, 1985.

White, E. Frances. *Sierra Leone's Settler Women Traders: Women on the Afro-European Frontier*. Ann Arbor: University of Michigan Press, 1987.

White, Luise. "A Colonial State and an African Petty Bourgeoisie: Prostitution, Property, and Class Struggle in Nairobi, 1936–1940." In *Struggle for the City: Migrant Labor, Capital and the State in Urban Africa*, edited by Frederick Cooper. Beverly Hills: Sage, 1983.

Wicks, Alexis. "Manifestations of Nationhood in the Writings of Amilcar Cabral." *African Identities* 4, no. 1 (2006): 45–70.

Wipper, A. "Kikuyu Women and the Harry Thuku Disturbances: Some Uniformities of Females Militancy." *Africa* 59, no. 3 (1989): 300–37.

Womack, Brantly. *The Foundation of Mao Zedong's Political Thought 1917–1935*. Honolulu: University Press of Hawaii, 1992.

Wright, Marcia. "Technology, Marriage, and Women's Work in the History of Maize-Growers in Mazabuka, Zambia: A Reconnaissance." *Journal of Southern African Studies* 10, no. 1 (1983).

Wylie, Raymond. *The Emergence of Maoism*. Stanford: Stanford University Press, 1980.

Yala, Hutna. Interviewed in English and translated in Crioulo, August 16, 2010.

Young, Crawford. "Nation, Ethnicity and Citizenship: Dilemmas of Democracy and Civil Order in Africa." In *Making Nations, Creating Strangers, States and Citizenship in Africa*, edited by Sara Dorman, Daniel Hammett, and Paul Nugent, 241–64. Leiden: Brill, 2007.

Young, Crawford. "Patterns of Social Conflict: State, Class and Ethnicity." *Daedalus* (Cambridge) CXI, no. 2 (1995): 24.

Zack-Williams, A. B. "Crisis Structural Adjustment and Creative Survival in Sierra Leone." *Africa Development* XVIII, no. 1 (1993): 53–63.

ZANU Women. *Liberation through Participation: Women in the Zimbabwean Revolution, Writings and Documents from ZANU and ZANU Women's League*. New York: National Campaign in Solidarity with ZANU Women's League, 1980.

Index

acephalous/decentralized communities 30, 34–6, 78
Africa/African 5, 11–13, 16, 31–2, 34–5, 99
   sub-Saharan 34
African Union Organization Conference, Khartoum 64
Afro-Atlantic 33
Algeria/Algerian 4–5, 13, 20, 131 n.14
   Algiers 4, 61, 78
   women's role in Algerian wars 78
Amilcar Cabral's African Youth (JAAC/ Juventude Africana Amilcar Cabral) 112
Amilcar Cabral University 22
anti-colonialism 16, 20, 51, 68, 78, 101. *See also* colonial/colonialism
anti-colonial organizations, women and 38–9
   1938–59 39–43
   PAIGC (1959–62) 43–8
archival documents/evidence of liberation wars 16, 22–6
armed struggles 4–5, 10–11, 13, 23, 43, 46, 55, 101, 118, 140 n.137
Assimilados/Civilizados 40–2, 98, 156 n.27
Association des Ressortissants de Bissau Guinée Bissau a Conakry (Bissau Guinean Immigrants in Conakry Association) 45
Atlantic trade/traders 31–4, 37. *See also* trade (women traders)
autochthons 100–3, 119–20, 156 n.27, 156 n.32

Balantas 11, 18, 21, 25–6, 28, 30–2, 35, 54, 70–2, 86, 101, 107, 109, 120
b'alante b'ndang (elders) 31–2
Bana, Antonio 9–11, 17
Barbosa, Rafael 141 n.139
Bijagos 26, 30, 32, 39, 42, 86, 107, 145 n.67
bi-nationalist 115, 119–20
Bockel, Alain 6–7

bombings, Portuguese 55, 60, 63–4, 70, 73, 149 n.39
Brazzaville Conference (1944) 44
brokers, women 32–3, 35

Cabo Verde/Cabo Verdeans 3, 8, 22–3, 31–2, 34, 42, 45, 95, 98, 100–3, 119–20
Cabral, Amilcar 1, 11–12, 28–9, 35, 38, 40–2, 45–8, 53, 56–7, 59–60, 62, 64–5, 68–9, 71–2, 74, 79–80, 84, 90, 96, 99–102, 112, 116–20, 131 n.17, 134 n.53, 141 n.139
   assassination/death of 98, 101, 115–16, 119
   and Marxism 3–10
   and pro-women 29, 47
   speech at Rome International Conference 8
Cabral, Luis 29, 46, 57–8, 98, 100–2, 112, 115, 117, 120, 148 n.20
Camara, Udé 97, 122, 155 n.10
Cape Verdeans 101
Carmen Pereira, Tia 1–2, 12, 29, 39–43, 48, 52–3, 56, 58–61, 68–9, 73–5, 81, 89, 91, 103, 111, 146 n.79, 148 n.20, 149 n.36
cash crop trade/economy 31, 33–6, 61, 65, 111
Cassacá Congress (1964) 23, 59, 62, 64, 81, 85, 88, 98–9
Cassama, Bacar 98–9
Cassama, Fodé 100, 155 n.26
Center for African Studies 3
Chabal, Patrick 3–4, 11
Chaliand, Gerard 7, 11, 17, 80, 149 n.39
   Armed Struggle in Africa; With the Guerillas in "Portuguese" Guinea 11, 18
   Tchico Té (Francisco Mendes) 88
Chilcote, Ronald, *Amilcar Cabral's Revolutionary Theory and Practice; A Critical Guide* 11–12

Christians 32, 40
Cissokho, Mario Augusto Ramalho 1, 19
colonial/colonialism 3, 6–7, 9, 11, 13, 15–16, 26, 29, 31, 40, 42, 46, 48–9, 58, 68, 78, 84, 101–2, 115–16. *See also* anti-colonialism
  assimilation 102
  colonial administration 13, 22, 26, 54, 58, 100–1
  and gender (oppression of women traders) 34–8
colonization 33
Conakry 4, 9, 24–6, 41, 43–5, 47, 53, 59–61, 79, 81, 116, 140 n.137, 141 n.139
Conselho Superior de Luta (CSL/Superior Council for the Fight) 61, 101
Crato, Fina 55, 62–3
cross-cultural trade 32–4

Da Costa, Quinta 70, 72, 103, 118, 123
Da Costa Ribero, Eusebio 103
Da Silva Rosa, Joanita 25, 87–9, 91, 99, 103, 121–2
Da Souza, Jacinta 61–2
Davidson, Basil 3, 17, 80, 149 n.36
  The Liberation of Guiné: Aspects of an African Revolution 10
de Andrade, Mario Pinto 3, 6
Debray, Regis 7
decolonization 16, 80
dialectical materialism 6
Diallo, Cira 106–7
Diallo, Fatoumata 52–3, 89
Djalo, Umaro 29, 41, 58–9, 101
domestic relationships 35–6

education/educational system 15–16, 41–2, 86, 96, 102–3, 110, 117
egalitarian 30, 38, 86
Einarsdottir, Jonina 104, 108–9
emancipation of women 12, 14, 16, 20–1, 26, 29–30, 38, 43–4, 47, 57–8, 68, 74, 79, 91, 93, 95, 97–8, 112, 114–15, 120
Escola Piloto (Pilot School) 9
ethnic/ethnicity 3, 26, 29–30, 32, 35, 38–40, 42, 104, 119–20. *See also specific groups*

Europe/European 4, 31, 35–6, 40–1
  European Enlightenment 41
exclusion of women 10, 17, 24, 67–9, 93, 98, 112, 118
Executive Committee of the Struggle/Conselho Executivo da Luta (CEL) 101

Fanon, Frantz 20, 78
feminism 67–8
feminization 16
First Republic, female participants in 100–4
Forças Armadas Locais (FAL/Local Armed Force) 59
Forças Armadas Revolucionárias do Povo (FARP/People's Revolutionary Army) 56, 59, 62, 105
forced/arranged marriages 21, 52, 55, 91–2, 104–8, 110, 114
forced labor 24, 53–4, 65, 92
Forrest, Joshua 97, 113
France/French 27, 33, 35, 42, 44–5, 78
Front for the Liberation of Mozambique (FRELIMO) 20, 56
Fula/Fulani 26, 29, 31, 35, 37–8, 53, 58, 86, 105, 107, 113
  Islamized 38

Geiger, Susan, Tanganyika case 40
gender 2–3, 13–14, 74
  and colonial administration 34–8
  equality 11–12, 16, 28, 36, 57, 78, 88, 95–7
  gendered liberated zones 88–9
  gender relations 12, 14, 17, 30, 33–5, 48, 90
  ignorance of women combatants in historical records 15–19
  inequality 55–7, 67, 96, 102, 111, 119–20
  understating the role of women combatants 68–73
  and war zone space 81–4
Giblin, James 68–9
Gibson, Nigel C. 7
Gomes, Carlos, Jr. 1, 74
Gomes, Eva 55, 61–2, 88, 91, 103, 113, 153 n.30

Gomes, Juditi 72, 82, 84
Gomes, Teodora 54, 59, 89, 111
Gomez, Maria 110, 158 n.71
guerillas/guerilla fighters 5, 7, 20–1, 25, 53–4, 56–7, 60, 62, 71, 73, 82
Guha, Ranajit 17, 68
Guinea Bissau 1–6, 12–14, 20–2, 30, 35, 37, 39–40, 55–6, 58, 71, 74, 78–80, 84, 100–3, 114–16, 119
  Assimilados/Civilizados in 40–2, 98, 156 n.27
  Biombo 104
  Bissau 1, 9, 23, 38, 46, 51, 53, 69, 102, 107
  Boé 23, 25
  Cacheu 23–4, 53, 109
  census in 9, 98
  Diola 86
  Djagali 148 n.18, 149 n.39
  education/education system in 15–16, 41–2, 86, 96, 102–3, 110, 117
  Farim 105
  interviews with war participants (male and female) 21–6
  massacre of dockworkers (*see* Pijiguiti Massacre, Bissau (1959))
  PAIGC and failure of gender equality 111–13
  polygyny (forced/arranged marriage practices) in 104–11 (*see also* forced/arranged marriages; polygyny)
  population 98
  pre-colonial (*see* pre-colonial period)
  societal structure of 85–8, 95–104
  women/gender issues in 11
  women's representation in National Assembly 96–7
Guturama (practiced by Kenyan women) 13

Havik, Philip 29, 38, 78
health care, women in 99
Henriksen, Thomas H. 130 n.5

Idahosa, Pablo Luke 3, 8
Igbo Women's War 13
imperialism 8
indigenous people 8, 30, 36, 40–2, 62, 98, 101–2, 156 n.27

International Conference on Women's Role in the Development of Tropical and Sub-Tropical Countries, Brussels (1958) 15
International Institute of Differing Civilizations (INCIDI) 15

Kamara, Mamady 84, 102, 157 n.42
Kawsara, Fantam 52
Keita, Malan 157 n.42
Kikuyu women 13
Kohl, Christoph 98

Lamine Gueye, Amadou 44, 47
"*Lar dos Combatentes*" (Home of the Fighters), Bonfi, Conakry 9
Leninist 8
liberated zones 3, 21, 28, 52, 59–63, 95–6, 139 n.133
  gendered 88–9
liberation movements 6, 24, 29, 44, 47, 52, 75, 79–80, 120
Luke, Timothy W. 7
Luso-African 31

male fighters 13, 24–5, 29, 51, 55, 61, 65, 83, 87, 89, 92–3, 95, 119, 124
  interviews with 11, 17–18
  women to serve the needs of 78
Mandinka 30, 35, 37–8, 85–6, 106–7, 110, 154 n.48
Mané, Felicidad 105–6
Mané, Juliao, Jr. 103–4
Mané, Juliao Lopes 1, 74
Mané, Ndalla 63, 85
Mané, NDo 92, 97, 122, 155 n.10
Mané, Samba Lamine 102
Manjacas 30, 35, 109
Marxism/Marxist 3–10, 16–17, 22, 49, 68, 79, 118, 130 n.5
Marxist-Leninist 7
Mballo, Dianké 113
Mballo, Famara 105
Mballo, Faniara 105
Mendes, Francisco 10, 88, 101
Mendes, Simon 104
merchants 31–2, 143 n.26

mobilization 3, 19–21, 27–8, 41, 44, 51–5, 59, 81, 97, 115, 118
political 3–4, 9, 44, 111
Movimento pela Libertação das Colónias Portuguesas (MLCP/Movement for the Liberation of the Portuguese Colonies) 45
Mozambique women 20

Na Ndjati 76, 79, 122
Na N'Kanka 11, 17–18
naras (women traders from Afro-Atlantic) 33
nationalism 2–6, 16–17, 22, 29, 40, 51–2, 67–8, 74, 79, 100, 114
nationalist movements 5–6, 29, 39–40, 44, 48, 51, 61, 68, 116
national liberation 2, 4–5, 7, 12, 14, 24, 29, 68, 75–6, 79–80, 118
National Popular Assembly (ANP) 101
National Union of Workers of Guinea-Bissau (UNTG/União Nacional dos Trabalhadores de Guine) 112
Native Statute of 1954 40
Neto, Agostino 3
NHaga, Sandé 54, 83
NQuamé, Teresa 25, 71–2, 87–8
nurses, female 11, 18, 60–2, 65, 89, 99, 117

official narrative/discourse 19, 21–2, 27, 68–9, 73–5, 78–81, 83, 87, 89–90, 93, 95, 118, 120

Pan African Women's Congress 61
Partido Africano da Independencia da Guine e Cabo Verde (PAIGC/ African Party for the Independence of Guinea and Cape Verde) 1, 3–9, 12, 17, 19–20, 26, 38, 40–1, 71–2, 88, 90, 95, 99–100, 105, 114, 116–19
and failure of gender equality 111–13
headquarters in Bissau 121
reasons for female participation 51–5
roles of women in (with exceptions) 11, 24–5, 41–7, 55–62, 64–5, 71–4, 81–2
social freedom for women 21
Parti Démocratique de Côte D'Ivoire-Rassemblement Démocratique Africain (PDCI/RDA/Ivory Coast Democratic Party section of the African Democratic Rassemblement) 44–5
patriarchy 29, 34, 38, 41, 55, 71
peasants/peasantry 7, 9–10, 47, 111, 119
Pereira, Aristides 46
Pereira, Francisca 24, 28, 42, 45, 51, 56–7, 60–1, 68–9, 73, 75, 87, 91, 103, 111, 114, 141 n.144, 146 n.79, 153 n.30, 154 n.40
Permanent Commission (CP) 97, 101
Pijiguiti Massacre, Bissau (1959) 23, 43, 45, 48, 53, 116, 140 n.137
commemoration of 125–6
Policia Internacional e de Defesa Do Estado (PIDE) 23, 43, 46, 53, 64, 116, 140 n.137, 141 n.139
political mobilization 3–5, 9, 25, 44, 111
polygyny 12, 21, 29, 35, 44, 52, 55, 83, 92, 104, 106, 108–11, 114
Portugal/Portuguese 5–6, 16, 18, 20, 22–4, 26, 28–9, 31, 34–5, 37, 40–1, 46, 51–2, 54, 60, 63–5, 83, 100, 102–4
Portuguese Colonial Act of 1930 40
Portuguese Guinea 1, 3–5, 7–8, 10–11, 14, 18, 35, 42–3, 80, 93
pre-colonial period 6, 26, 29–30, 37, 78
women in 30–5

Ramos, Domingo 157 n.42
resistance movements 40–1, 44
revolutionary movements 2, 5, 8, 118
Rudebeck, Lars 3, 42

Sambu, Cau 47, 85
Sambu, Segunda 90–2, 123
Sané, Fanta 89, 91
Sanha, Barnaté 71–2, 84, 102, 124
Sanha, Malan (Malam Bacai Sanha) 18–19, 25, 79, 138 n.117
Sanha, Quintara 109
Santos, Maria 90–1
sapadura 25, 72, 89
Sarrazin, Chantal 12
Section Française de l'Internationale Ouvriére (SFIO/French Socialist Party) 44
Sekou Touré, Ahmed 41, 47

self-paradox agenda 27, 65, 68–9, 73–7, 79, 93, 118, 120
Senegal 23–4, 42, 44, 47, 53, 86, 116
    Dakar 18, 43
    Ziguinchor 24, 53, 60–1
Senegambia region 33, 37
    Kaabu 38
sexism 40, 67
sexual harassment 27, 43, 49, 52–3, 55, 63–4
Seydi, Binetou 75, 113
Seydi, Sano 79
Sibili, Fatimata 58, 60
Sissoko, Fily Dabo 44
slave trade 31, 33
social associations 40
societal structures 30, 85–8, 95–104, 119
sociocultural 9, 14, 20, 26–7, 36, 38–9, 42, 45–6, 49, 58, 65, 68, 77, 90, 95–6, 115–17
socioeconomic agents, women as 35, 48, 61–2
Soviet Union 4, 59, 61–2, 155 n.26
Spain/Spanish 16
stateless society 26, 30
Stucki, Andreas 16
subalterns 3, 17, 25–6, 28, 34, 65, 80, 95

tabanças (villages) 31, 88
Titina Silla 11, 18, 25, 28, 59–61, 71–2, 81, 84–5, 87, 89, 113, 148 n.19, 149 n.39
trade (women traders) 31–3, 70, 111
    Atlantic trade/traders 31–4, 37
    Balanta women 32, 35
    cash crop trade/economy 31, 33–6, 61
    cross-cultural trade 32–4
    in Guinea Bissau 32, 35
    naras (women traders from Afro-Atlantic) 33
    oppression during colonial period 36–8
    slave trade 31, 33
Tuga (Portuguese colonialists/Portuguese colonial army) 54, 82, 113
tungama of Mandinga origin 37
Turé, Fatu 83, 85, 113

under-representation of women 68–73, 97–8, 102–3, 120

União Democrática das Mulheres da Guiné e Cabo Verde (UDEMU/Democratic Union of the Women of Guinea and Cabo Verde) 12, 21, 39, 47–8, 65, 90–1, 111–13
Upper Volta 42
Urdang, Stéphanie 2, 12, 20–1, 26, 43, 54, 57–8, 68, 80, 90–1, 93, 97, 115, 139 n.133
Fighting the Two Colonialisms 51

Vieira, Joao Bernardo "Nino" 19, 28, 59, 70, 100–2, 117, 120, 155 n.26
village council, women in 11–12, 21, 91

warfare and sufferings 63–4
war zone, gender and 81–4
weapon transporters, women as 13, 19, 49, 57–8, 64
women combatants 2–3, 49, 120
    in Algerian war 78
    and domestic tasks 27–8
    exclusion of 10, 17, 24, 67–9, 93, 98, 112, 118
    in First Republic 100–4
    ignored in historical records 15–19
    in liberation war with exceptions 10–15
    official discourses of (*see* official narrative/discourse)
    perspectives on war and manhood 84–93
    portrayal in official records 28
    reasons for participation in wars 27, 51–5
    roles of women in combats 11, 13, 18–19, 49, 55–62, 64–5, 70–1, 73–4, 81–3, 89–90, 93, 99, 117
    understating the roles of 68–73, 97–8, 102–3, 120
    valued the roles/participation in war 89–93
Women's Commission 97, 111

Yala, Hutna 84, 153 n.13

Zimbabwe African National Union (ZANU) 20